MW01528391

Liberal Government and Politics, 1905–15

Also by Ian Packer

LETTERS OF ARNOLD STEPHENSON ROWNTREE TO MARY KATHERINE
ROWNTREE, 1910–1918 (*editor*)

LLOYD GEORGE

LLOYD GEORGE, LIBERALISM AND THE LAND: the Land Issue and Party
Politics in England, 1906–1914

Liberal Government and Politics, 1905–15

Ian Packer

palgrave
macmillan

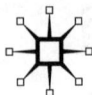

© Ian Packer 2006

All rights reserved. No reproduction, copy or transmission of this
publication may be made without written permission.

No paragraph of this publication may be reproduced, copied or transmitted
save with written permission or in accordance with the provisions of the
Copyright, Designs and Patents Act 1988, or under the terms of any licence
permitting limited copying issued by the Copyright Licensing Agency,
90 Tottenham Court Road, London W1T 4LP.

Any person who does any unauthorised act in relation to this publication
may be liable to criminal prosecution and civil claims for damages.

The author has asserted his right to be identified
as the author of this work in accordance with the Copyright,
Designs and Patents Act 1988.

First published 2006 by
PALGRAVE MACMILLAN
Houndmills, Basingstoke, Hampshire RG21 6XS and
175 Fifth Avenue, New York, N.Y. 10010
Companies and representatives throughout the world

PALGRAVE MACMILLAN is the global academic imprint of the Palgrave
Macmillan division of St. Martin's Press, LLC and of Palgrave Macmillan Ltd.
Macmillan® is a registered trademark in the United States, United Kingdom
and other countries. Palgrave is a registered trademark in the European
Union and other countries.

ISBN-13: 978–0–333–91798–5 hardback
ISBN-10: 0–333–91798–7 hardback

This book is printed on paper suitable for recycling and made from fully
managed and sustained forest sources.

A catalogue record for this book is available from the British Library.

Library of Congress Cataloging-in-Publication Data
Packer, Ian, 1962–
    Liberal government and politics, 1905–15 / Ian Packer.
        p.   cm.
    Includes bibliographical references and index.
    Contents: Government and party — Foreign, defence and
colonial policy — Liberals and the United Kingdom — Liberalism and
democracy — Nonconformist party? — The economy and finance —
Social reform and labour relations — Epilogue: a liberal war?.
    ISBN 0–333–91798–7 (cloth)
    1. Great Britain—Politics and government—1901–1910.
    2. Great Britain—Politics and government—1910–1936.
    3. Liberal Party (Great Britain)—History—20th century.
    4. Liberalism—Great Britain—History—20th century.   I. Title.
DA570.P33 2006
941.082′3—dc22   2005058537

10   9   8   7   6   5   4   3   2   1
15   14   13   12   11   10   09   08   07   06

Printed and bound in Great Britain by
Antony Rowe Ltd, Chippenham and Eastbourne

Contents

Acknowledgements

Queen's University, Belfast and the University of Lincoln have provided helpful and stimulating environments in which to write this book. I would like to thank all my colleagues in the history departments of these two institutions for their support and understanding while I have wrestled with the complexities of Edwardian politics. I owe a special debt of gratitude to Professor Jeremy Black for originally suggesting that I should write this book for Palgrave and to Professor Peter Jupp for all his encouragement and words of wisdom. I am also grateful to my students in Belfast and Lincoln for giving me the opportunity to think through and test out some of my ideas.

My parents were supportive as ever. Yet again, I could not have written this book without the encouragement and help of Lynda. This is for her.

I am grateful to the following institutions and individuals for access to and permission to quote from manuscript sources: the Bodleian Library, Oxford and J. Bonham Carter (Asquith papers), Hon. Mrs C. Gascoigne (Sir W. Harcourt papers); the British Library (Balfour, Burns, Campbell-Bannerman, Herbert Gladstone papers); Cheshire and Chester Archives; Churchill College Library, Cambridge; Gloucestershire Record Office (W. H. Dickinson papers); Hampshire Record Office (Portsmouth papers); the Clerk of the House of Lords Record Office; Lincolnshire Archives; the National Archives (Cabinet, Grey papers); the National Archives of Scotland; the Trustees of the National Library of Scotland (Elibank, Haldane, Muirhead, Rosebery papers); the National Library of Wales (E. W. Davies papers); Nuffield College Library, Lord Gainford and Professor Cameron Hazlehurst (Gainford papers); the Trustees of the Joseph Rowntree Foundation; University College of North Wales, Bangor, Library; University of Birmingham Library (Allard, Austen and Joseph Chamberlain papers); University of Glasgow Library (MacCallum Scott papers); University of Keele Library (Josiah Wedgwood papers); University of Manchester, John Rylands Library (C. P. Scott papers); University of Newcastle Library; West Sussex Record Office; West Yorkshire Archive Service.

Introduction

This book examines all the major fields of activity of the 1905–15 Liberal governments. Rather than looking again at the series of debates about whether this period witnessed the onset of the 'decline of Liberalism', it seeks to understand the governments' actions by analysing their relationship to definitions of Liberalism. In doing so it builds on a rich and innovative body of historiography. The Edwardian era has been a particularly fruitful site for historians seeking to investigate the relationship between ideology and politics. The key text in this field has undoubtedly been Peter Clarke's *Lancashire and the New Liberalism*. But Clarke followed this ground-breaking work with *Liberals and Social Democrats* and Stefan Collini and Michael Freeden also published distinguished analyses of Liberal politics and thought at about the same time.[1] Subsequently, E. H. H. Green and Matthew Fforde have produced contrasting views of the role of ideas in Edwardian Conservatism and Duncan Tanner and Frank Trentmann among others have given serious consideration to the ideology of the early Labour party.[2] All these works have argued that while British politics has often claimed to be non-ideological it is impossible to understand how political parties selected their goals and negotiated their approach to political issues without reference to a framework of ideas and a notion of what terms like 'Liberalism' and 'Conservatism' meant.

This does not imply that any Edwardian party had an agreed formal statement of its beliefs. But, as Green has argued, there was still 'a hinterland of rhetoric, values, and received ideas, which may be expressed in day-to-day political argument, speeches, correspondence, and legislative acts'.[3] Through an examination of these areas it is possible to determine what contemporaries understood the aims and parameters of their parties to be and how they sought to shape political argument in ways

1

that would accord with these ideas. This approach eschews the search for great ideologues before whom politicians had to bow down and instead looks at the assumptions that were implicit in the views and actions of politicians, journalists and MPs. In this sense, ideology was crucial to the functioning of politics.

However, the relationship between party and ideology was always fraught and complex. In all parties there were variant interpretations of the party's values and traditions. Moreover, ideologies were not hermetically sealed within parties. Much of the Liberal approach to politics was shared by many in the Labour party, except on some questions of industrial policy and social reform. Some Liberals, on the other hand, argued that Liberalism had to accommodate other ideologies which did not claim to be specifically Liberal, like those of national security or gender roles, in policy making. Ideology was not and could not be a rigid framework. Its boundaries were always being tested and redefined and its essence was revealed only within the process of argument and debate.

This process has been examined in Victorian Liberalism at cabinet level by Jonathan Parry and for popular Liberalism by Eugenio Biagini.[4] Both looked at a wide range of policy issues and concluded that Liberalism was not just a bundle of special interest groups or a disparate collection of people who found Conservatism unpalatable and so gathered under the Liberal banner. Instead, at both the elite and popular levels, Liberalism represented a distinctive and reasonably coherent way of looking at the political world. But these wide-ranging studies have not been replicated for the early twentieth-century. Instead, the formative works by historians like Clarke and Freeden have concentrated on the New Liberalism and the ways in which the party's ideology was adapted to accommodate social reform. This is understandable as these historians were responding to the prevailing orthodoxy of the 1960s and 1970s that Liberalism was doomed to decline by the inevitable rise of the Labour party to be the predominant party of the British left and the wider assumption that the key political development in twentieth-century Britain was the growth of collectivism.[5] But it means that the current understanding of Edwardian Liberalism tends to concentrate on just one aspect of party ideology, rather than seeing Liberal attitudes to social reform as one aspect of a wider complex of ideas and debates. General books about the achievements of the 1905–15 governments do not rebalance this equation because they tend to give little space to ideas as opposed to political tactics and legislative outcomes.[6]

This book seeks to readjust this perspective by examining a broad range of Liberal policies and ideas. By looking at what Liberal governments did and how Liberals argued about what they should be doing it aims to make explicit what Liberals understood their creed to mean and how ideology provided points of reference for the government's choices. As the first chapter explains, the focus is overwhelmingly on the activities of the Liberal leadership and parliamentary party, as the mass membership was largely confined to a supporting role and methods of ascertaining their opinions are unreliable. Early twentieth-century Liberalism was a 'modern' party in that initiative rested with the leadership group, who had the primary role in reconciling the party's actions with wider notions of Liberalism.

The book goes on to examine Liberal ideology and policy in the fields of foreign affairs, defence and colonial policy, attitudes to nationality and democracy, religion, policies towards the economy and the role of the state and finally, as an epilogue, the war conducted by the Liberal cabinet in August 1914 to May 1915. Contextualizing the significance of the New Liberalism allows the party's attitudes and debates to be cast in a new light. While Liberals disagreed about the role of social reform in their ideology, it was only one controversy within the party. In many ways tensions between those who shared and opposed a Liberal Imperialist outlook were far more significant. The Liberal Imperialist viewpoint had first been defined and organised during the Boer war. It insisted that Liberals should give general support to the Unionist government's war, if not necessarily to all the government's methods of waging it or its plans for a post-war settlement. After the end of the Boer war in 1902 this position seemed less controversial within Liberalism and the 1905–15 governments did not exhibit major disagreements about colonial policy. Some historians have been happy to consign the concept of Liberal Imperialism to irrelevance in determining the politics of the Edwardian Liberal government. Colin Matthew's study of the Liberal Imperialists pointedly stopped in 1905.[7]

But this is only one way of looking at the matter. Liberal Imperialism was only partly about the Boer war. This was merely a section of its adherents' aim to persuade the Liberal party to modify or abolish its commitment to a range of policies which they regarded as electorally disastrous and totally out of touch with contemporary world events. Liberal Imperialists wished their party's foreign policy and defence policy to accord with notions of the national interest which they largely held in common with their Conservative opponents. They were also sceptics about Irish home rule and consistently tried to downgrade and delay this policy – an attitude that helped lead many Liberal Impe-rialists to argue for reform rather than emasculation of the House of

Lords. In effect, Liberal Imperialism wished to reach an accommodation between Liberalism and powerful, though not specifically Liberal, ideas about the need to retain Britain's position as a leading world power. In some ways, Liberal Imperialism can be seen as a reformulation of the moderate or Whig position in the nineteenth-century Liberal party and its insistence on toning down what it perceived to be impractical or visionary Liberal enthusiasms. This programme produced far more strains within the party than arguments over social reform. But it never tore Liberalism apart because, at crucial moments, Liberal Imperialist policies could also be defended as variants of Liberalism rather than as attempts to discard it as irrelevant. Sir Edward Grey did not think of himself as conducting a 'Liberal' foreign policy, but his actions, including the declaration of war on Germany on 4 August 1914, could be presented as consistent with at least some versions of what a Liberal approach to external affairs should be.

Moreover, even core Liberal notions did not necessarily produce harmony. No Liberal would have disputed that their party stood for free trade, democracy and religious equality. All these causes produced visceral enthusiasm in the party ranks. But it was not always easy to translate them into detailed policies. Liberals argued about whether free trade meant minimal government interference in all aspects of the economy, about how to apply democracy to the reform of the House of Lords or women's role in national politics and what the implications of religious equality were for the place of religious instruction in schools. Argument and debate were the norm in Liberal politics. In this context disagreements about social reform do not appear as particularly strenuous or unusual. In fact the party negotiated its engagement with the New Liberalism with remarkable ease, compared to its arguments on a range of other topics – a process that it is examined in Chapters 6 and 7.

But if Liberals argued incessantly, they also retained a powerful sense of collective identity. This was partly based on their sense of the party's long history, which for many Liberals could be traced back to the struggles of the seventeenth century against absolutist Stuart monarchs. This gave Liberals a gallery of potential heroes and stirring events which they could identify with and use to legitimise their cause. The struggle against the House of Lords in 1909–11, for instance, was replete with references to the Lords' iniquities under Charles I and II.[8] But this perspective also confirmed Liberals in the fundamentals of their faith. This was often expressed as a belief in liberty or freedom. But in practice what this had usually meant was that the population should be able to conduct their lives without interference from the traditional authorities of the Monarchy, Lords and Church. This programme still had considerable relevance in Edwardian Britain, as debates over the role of the Lords in the constitution and the Church in education showed. But it had also developed in different ways. Part of it had become a tradition of generalised hostility to state interference, which could be very powerful, as in Liberal attitudes to free trade and, during the First World War, conscription.

But Liberals were obviously not opposed to most aspects of state action in the Edwardian era. This was because the other tradition that derived from the old cry of freedom was that of popular control of government. Once the people had seized the levers of power Liberals generally believed they would act in the best interests of all and so there was less need to be suspicious of the state. In the late nineteenth century Liberals were already calling for popular control of liquor licences, schools and the land, as well as fighting for Irish home rule. To Liberals their party was the people's party as much as it was the home of liberty. This crucial idea was the site of the Liberals' claim to be the truly patriotic party. What held these concepts together was an extended idea of the common enemies of the people and liberty. Liberals believed they were engaged in a constant battle against sinister and powerful 'interests' who were attempting to use government for their own ends. By the early twentieth century this label was applied not just to the Lords and the Church, but to landowners, brewers and even those businessmen who sought to use tariff reform to boost their profits.

To Liberals, all these unsavoury elements were combined in the Unionist party. If Liberalism represented the progressive emancipation of the people from the thrall of the 'interests', Toryism represented the organised attempt by the 'interests' to obstruct this journey. It was truly 'the other' against which Liberals defined themselves. Conservatives might claim they were the party who wished to defend Britain's leading role in the world, but to Liberals this was merely a crude jingoism with which to deceive the masses and create a militarised society dominated by the landowners who had always monopolised power in the army. Tory defence of the traditional constitution was seen as an attempt to preserve the privileges of the Lords and the Church over the people. Liberals just as vehemently attacked the Conservatives' claim to be the party that defended the existing distribution of property and the social hierarchy. To Liberals, not all property was worth defending, especially if it acted against the interests of the people as a whole, as with concentrations of landholding. Existing networks of social authority should not be allowed to exclude each individual reaching his full potential.

They certainly did not bestow any right to rule. More recent Tory policies, like tariff reform, were merely attempts to defend the 'interests' by other means.

But Liberal attitudes to Labour and Irish Nationalism were more complicated. Liberals believed it was the duty of all progressive forces to rally together and defeat Conservatism. The existence of other parties was superfluous. It also implied that the organised working class had interests opposed to that of the rest of society and that the Irish nation was in conflict with the other nations of the United Kingdom. Liberals could not accept these notions. But, on the other hand, Liberal governments did acknowledge the right of Labour MPs to represent the trade union point of view when legislation was considered and that the Nationalist leadership were the authentic voice of the Irish people. Moreover, for most Liberals their enemy was Conservatism and they did not usually define their identity in opposition to either Labour or Irish Nationalism. Points of conflict in policy and ultimate goals existed, but Liberalism could not construct itself as an anti-trade union or anti-Nationalist party. This meant that co-operation remained feasible throughout the Edwardian period and Liberals could assume, for most of the time, that they were the main force of the army of progress, flanked by two useful but troublesome allies.

This book delineates how Liberals tried to grapple with reconciling their varying senses of what their party stood for with the exceptionally difficult series of challenges the 1905–15 Liberal governments faced. In doing so it provides a way of understanding what Liberalism was and how Liberals understood the choices in front of them. Liberalism undoubtedly benefited from the flexibility that the New Liberalism provided. But this was only part of its identity throughout the Edwardian period. The traditions and goals of liberty and popular government remained central to the party and helped shape and merged into ideas about social reform. The 'old' Liberalism was far from dead or irrelevant in 1905–15. When the Liberal government finally ended in May 1915 after more than nine years in office it was not because its ideology had proved unable to withstand the challenges of early twentieth-century politics.

1
Government and Party

Leadership

Any enthusiastic Liberal, or indeed anyone with more than a passing interest in politics, could not escape knowing the identities of the party leadership. Their speeches filled the columns of the national and provincial newspapers, cartoons, drawings and photographs of them regularly appeared in the press and on posters and leaflets and their lives and actions even provided some of the material for music hall songs.[1] If none quite achieved the eminence of Gladstone, the 'Grand Old Man', then figures like Campbell-Bannerman, Asquith, Lloyd George, Grey, Morley, Churchill and John Burns could at least claim to be sub-deities on the Liberal Olympus.

But for all their celebrity, the actual workings of the relationships between the Liberal leaders remained something of a mystery, if only because the functioning of the Liberal leadership was so enmeshed with the arcane practices of the British parliamentary system from which the national party had gradually emerged in the nineteenth century. The Liberal MPs and Peers each, theoretically, elected a leader in their own House. But in both cases the leading figures in the party 'arranged' matters and then presented a single candidate to the MPs or Peers. There was never an actual election in this period, and the first Liberal leader in the Commons to win a contest among his fellow MPs was Jeremy Thorpe in 1967. The MPs could sometimes be presented with a surprising choice. Campbell-Bannerman was a secondary figure in the 1892–5 cabinet, but by 1899 he was one of only four ex-cabinet ministers still active in front-line politics in the Commons and, once Asquith had declined to put himself forward, the only one acceptable to his colleagues.[2] But once a leader was installed, the only mechanism for removing him was his own resignation and Campbell-Bannerman's determination allowed him to remain leader almost until his death in 1908. Only a coup organised by the rest of the leaders could have removed an incumbent, but this never occurred in this period and even Lloyd George was only able to engineer Asquith's downfall in 1916 by using his Conservative partners in a coalition government.

Matters were further complicated by the theory that only someone who had been appointed a Liberal prime minister by the monarch could claim to have overall authority over the party in both Commons and Lords. Ironically for a party that made much play of its devotion to democracy, the ultimate arbiter of the Liberal leadership was the unelected head of state rather than the Liberals themselves. Queen Victoria chose Lord Rosebery as prime minister and thus Liberal leader in 1894, rather than his rivals, Sir William Harcourt and Earl Spencer.[3] In 1903–5 there was some speculation that Edward VII would not invite Campbell-Bannerman, the leader of the Liberal MPs, to form a government, but would call instead on Spencer, the leader of the Liberal Peers.[4] But, as these examples show, in practice the monarch could only select someone who commanded the acquiescence of the Liberal leadership, even if this still left some freedom of manoeuvre. These convolutions only served to re-emphasise the separation of the leaders from their followers on the backbenches and in the country. Entry to this elite group was also governed by rules that were hard to pin down. Theoretically, the leader could bring anyone in parliament into the party's inner circle by reposing his confidence in them and choosing to consult them. They did not even have to be a Liberal – Lord Cromer was certainly a Unionist when Campbell-Bannerman offered him the Foreign Secretaryship in 1905 and Kitchener was not a member of any party when he was appointed Secretary of State for War under Asquith.[5] The outward sign of this trust was membership of the cabinet of twenty or so. This group, in constitutional theory, decided government and thus Liberal policy and membership was crucial even when the party was out of office, as the leader usually only felt obliged to consult 'ex-cabs'.[6]

But, in practice, a Liberal leader was far less of an autocrat, and more part of a leadership group, than the theoretical position suggested. A Liberal prime minister could not appoint just anyone to cabinet office, for instance. A minimum standard of ability to conduct departmental business, and to defend policies in parliament was essential, so the most straightforward route to the cabinet was through effective performance in a junior office, though the long period in the wilderness in 1895–1905 meant Campbell-Bannerman appointed six men without government experience to his cabinet. However, a first step on the ministerial ladder was usually gained on the recommendation of the whips office, rather than the prime minister, and was a reward for feats performed in the debating chamber of either House.[7] It might be a recognition of either assiduous loyalty or effective troublemaking. But the whips were also keen to balance the various sections and interest groups of the parliamentary party and important cabinet ministers often had protégées they wished to promote, so the process had something of the lottery about it. The one thing that was clear by 1905 was that only a man who was prepared to consider politics a full-time profession could hope for office. Indeed, Campbell-Bannerman required his cabinet ministers to relinquish their company directorships on taking up their posts.[8] This ruled out a significant percentage of MPs who had no wish, or could not afford to, take this route. Nevertheless, business was an important factor in the background of many members of the 1905–15 cabinets, perhaps not surprisingly as it remained the largest occupational category among Liberal MPs.[9] Campbell-Bannerman, Walter Runciman, Jack Pease, McKinnon Wood and Alfred Emmott all spent some time working in their family's firm and Samuel and Montagu relied on their relatives business to finance their career.[10] Both Asquith and Harcourt were married to the daughters of very wealthy businessmen and Grey and Fowler had been directors of major companies. On the other hand, landowners were over-represented, despite their minimal presence in Liberalism by the Edwardian era. They made up seven out of nineteen Cabinet members in 1905, a figure that had only declined to six in 1915. This was partly due to the need to maintain a ministerial presence in the House of Lords and partly to the early and well-connected start in politics of men like Loulou Harcourt and Sir Edward Grey. Apart from the token working class presence of John Burns, the rest of the cabinet were members of the professional middle class, mainly lawyers with a sprinkling of writers of various kinds, including Morley, Birrell and Masterman, who were all expert purveyors of the higher journalism.

Once in a junior post, a minister could only wait his chance for a cabinet job to become vacant. Occasional culls could be expected as the prime minister disposed of colleagues who had outlived their usefulness, but a chance of promotion to the cabinet elite was fairly rare. Indeed, eight of the nineteen cabinet ministers appointed in 1905 were still in office on the eve of the First World War. Campbell-Bannerman only made two new cabinet appointments in 1905–8 (McKenna and Harcourt) and Asquith twelve in peacetime, so vacancies averaged not much more than one per year until the First World War provoked a spate of changes. This continuity again reinforced the leadership's sense of identity and its separation from the rest of the party.

Moreover, though all cabinet ministers depended on the prime minister's patronage for their posts, remarkably few were protégées of the prime minister on whom he could rely at all times. In Campbell-Bannerman's reign this description would probably only fit John Sinclair, a close friend of the prime minister's (indeed he was rumoured to be his illegitimate son), but Sinclair held the minor office of Secretary for Scotland and never progressed any further.[11] Asquith claimed to have most confidence in Lord Crewe, also a secondary cabinet member.[12] Only Edwin Montagu owed his whole career to the prime minister and even he found his loyalties divided between his old patron and Lloyd George after he went to work for the Welshman at the Treasury in February 1914.[13] Reginald McKenna started his ministerial career under Asquith at the Treasury, but it was Campbell-Bannerman who promoted him to the cabinet and McKenna and Asquith had at least one major disagreement in 1911, which resulted in McKenna's enforced move from the Admiralty to the Home Office.[14] A large proportion of Asquith's cabinet appointees, like Lord Beauchamp and Charles Hobhouse, were minor figures who must have sensed they could easily be dropped from the cabinet by the prime minister, but this did not prevent them participating in major cabinet revolts, like that over naval expenditure in January 1914.[15]

In practice, whatever his powers of appointment, a Liberal prime minister was much more like the chairman of the particularly opinionated and obstreperous board of a company, than a dictator. Campbell-Bannerman was surrounded by men like Asquith, Lord Ripon and Morley, who had been at least his equals in the cabinets of 1892–5. In addition, because he had to form his cabinet in December 1905, before he had the authority of a victorious election campaign behind him, Campbell-Bannerman had to put party unity before personal preference. He felt obliged to re-appoint nearly all of the surviving cabinet of 1895 who were still active in politics. Moreover, he had to include not only figures like Asquith and Grey with whom he had quarrelled in the past, but their friend and ally, Haldane, whom Campbell-Bannerman actively despised.[16] Asquith, too, had to be aware that men like Grey and Lloyd George had a standing in the Liberal party, parliament and the country that made them far more than just subordinates. When Asquith had the chance to force Lloyd George's resignation over the Marconi affair in 1913, he conspicuously failed to take it.[17] Indeed, it is difficult to pinpoint a single instance in which

Asquith dismissed a fellow cabinet minister because he had disagreed with the prime minister or because Asquith feared him as a rival, unless Morley and Burns's resignation over the decision to go to war in 1914 are counted. Ministers left the cabinet because they were too old (Ripon, Wolverhampton, Carrington), mad (Tweedmouth) or tarnished by blunders (Sir Rufus Isaacs, Seely), but even major crises like that over military relations with France in 1911 produced a reshuffle rather than a bloodbath.[18] Edwardian Liberal cabinets were genuinely collegial institutions. This situation was reinforced by the absence of governmental mechanisms whereby the prime minister could drive through his wishes against the opinion of his cabinet. There was no prime ministerial staff beyond one or two private secretaries, a parliamentary private secretary (unpaid) and two or three typists.[19] The cabinet had no secretary and no fixed agenda, which meant ministers could raise any points they wished and debate them to exhaustion.

In this situation, contemporary fears about prime ministerial domination, voiced by commentators like Ostrogorski and Sidney Low were wide of the mark.[20] Too much emphasis has also been placed on the temperaments of Campbell-Bannerman and Asquith in refusing to 'drive' their cabinets and Liberalism in a particular direction. It is certainly true that Campbell-Bannerman was in poor health for much of his premiership, was greatly affected by his wife's death in 1906 and liked long Continental holidays, while Asquith had a fondness for bridge, champagne and the company of Society, as well as a lawyerly ability to see both sides of any argument.[21] But even if both had been driven by a personal vision to enact a detailed legislative programme, it is difficult to see how they could have done this without the sort of governmental revolution that it took the First World War to produce.

This did not mean, of course, that Liberal prime ministers had no authority beyond acting as chairmen of a committee. In any cabinet argument, the prime minister's backing was crucial for victory and might enable a departmental minister's proposals, or even those of a majority of the cabinet to be overturned. Campbell-Bannerman certainly got his way on key issues like the form of the 1906 Trades Disputes Act and proposed reform of the House of Lords, over the heads of a good many of his cabinet.[22] Asquith, too, was able to overcome majority opinion in the cabinet when it opposed many of the features of the 1909 budget and increased naval expenditure in 1908–9 and 1913–14.[23] But on none of these issues did the prime minister stand alone and this raises the issue of whether real authority in the cabinet lay with an 'inner ring' of ministers, rather than with the whole body. In one sense this was, of course, true. Not all ministers were of equal standing. This was partly a matter of which office they held. The Postmaster-General wielded less authority than the Chancellor of the Exchequer. But it also reflected seniority, energy and achievements when in office. On this basis, the key ministers in Asquith's cabinet were, arguably, Grey, Lloyd George, Churchill and Haldane, with McKenna a possible inclusion.[24] If all these men agreed with the prime minister then the rest of the cabinet would be hard put to resist them. But, equally, there is no evidence that these men represented a permanent grouping within the cabinet. On some issues they disagreed with each other, as when Lloyd George and Churchill were ranged against Grey, Haldane and McKenna over naval expenditure in 1908–9.[25] They did not confer together on any regular or institutional basis and friendships split them up into the pairing of Lloyd George with Churchill and Grey with Haldane, rather than uniting them.[26] But if any of them wished to bring a major proposal to the cabinet, then it made sense to try and gain the support of the cabinet's other heavyweights before it reached the full body. Before the cabinet discussed Lloyd George's Land Campaign in October 1913, he had secured the backing of all its senior figures, including the prime minister.[27] The cabinet discussed his plans over three days without changing them and succeeded only in exasperating each other with the long-windedness and irrelevance of many of the contributions.[28] Agreement was secured after the point of exhaustion was reached.

In fact, much to the disgust of their opponents, the 1905–15 cabinets proved, if not entirely harmonious, at least arenas where disagreements were kept from reaching the point of resignation or the kind of meltdown that had affected Unionism in 1903–5 or Liberalism in 1894–5. This was partly a matter of personalities within the cabinet and partly a matter of issues. Asquith made unity his highest priority and did everything he could to ensure that major disagreements did not escalate into disasters. But while Asquith did handle issues like naval spending skilfully, allowing endless discussions until acquiescence was reached, he also made some serious blunders, especially over his failure in 1909 to secure guarantees from the King to 'swamp' the House of Lords with Liberal Peers and his clumsy concealment from some members of the cabinet of the military discussions with France in 1911.[29] He was lucky that the cabinet did not contain an overmighty figure like Joseph Chamberlain who felt his last chance of the premiership could come by resigning from the cabinet and taking over the party. As Asquith had no obvious heir, in the way that he had stood in relation to Campbell-Bannerman, all his potential successors were unwilling to leave the cabinet and exclude themselves from the leading group. While they all had their likes and dislikes, there was little personal enmity between crucial figures like Grey and Lloyd George, certainly not enough to provoke a resignation from pique.[30] But the Liberals also found ways to manage the issues that divided them. Some contentious foreign policy issues, especially the commitment to France, remained ambiguous, at least until the crunch moment of August 1914. Naval expenditure remained a running sore, but Lloyd George's skill as a tax-raising chancellor meant the navy at least did not divert money from social reforms. In turn, the new agenda of direct taxation and welfare expenditure was pursued sensitively, without penalising the middle class and in conjunction with more traditional aims.[31] Ultimately, nobody in the cabinet was willing to break it up and the longer their unity lasted, the stronger it became, especially when the battle with Unionism intensified after the People's Budget was introduced in 1909. Nobody wanted to seem to aid the enemy by resigning at a time when Liberalism was close to long-cherished goals like ending the Lords' veto and Irish home rule. Without the experience of successful government it is doubtful the cabinet could have navigated the decision to declare war in August 1914.

The final reason for cabinet unity was quite simply the inefficiency of the cabinet itself. As the prime minister could not provide any effective oversight of what his colleagues were doing in their departments, it was left to them to run things very much as they thought fit, until they encountered difficulties, or brought major legislation to the cabinet.[32] The cabinet rarely sat more than once a week, usually on a Wednesday, and often not at all when parliament was not in session, so it was scarcely the ideal forum to co-ordinate the government's activities.[33] Most ministers were too busy and lacked the detailed knowledge to criticise their colleagues' proposals. This situation was addressed by referring important bills to *ad hoc* cabinet committees. The 1912 home rule bill was, for instance, considered by Birrell, Lloyd George, Churchill, Haldane, Samuel and Grey, with Loreburn as chairman.[34] This siphoned off contentious matters away from the cabinet table and provided the opportunity for agreement in a more informal forum. Whether it meant more informed or effective scrutiny of ministers' proposals must remain an open question, as very few records of committee deliberations have survived. The government remained, for most of the time, a government of departments, as some of its members remarked, and there was never any such thing as an overall Liberal strategy which was meant to be applied in each ministry. But while ministers ran their departments with little reference to each other, the tactics of how to approach the central political issues of the time was decided by the leadership as a whole in the cabinet.

The party in parliament

The effectiveness of the solidarity among the Liberal leadership played a crucial role in reducing the rest of the party to a supporting role in determining policy. This was true even of the second tier of the party – the ranks of the Liberal MPs and Peers. Of the two groups, the Peers were definitely the smaller. The mass defection of British landowners to Unionism over the home rule issue in 1886, left only a small group of Peers loyal to Gladstone.[35] By the late 1890s there were probably no more than a dozen or so Peers who were active in the party cause, while the Liberal whips had no feasible sanctions to stir perhaps 30 more general sympathisers.[36] However, the Liberal Peers contained a number of important, if elderly, figures in the leadership, like Spencer, Kimberley and Ripon who had held senior office under Gladstone. When Campbell-Bannerman formed his government, he was faced with the need to provide a Liberal presence in the upper house to present and defend the government's measures and to fill a number of offices based in the Lords. 18 Liberal Peers acquired office – a high percentage of the party's presence in the Lords. Indeed this figure was not achieved without some scraping of the barrel.[37] While none achieved a major post, Ripon and Crewe became close advisers of Campbell-Bannerman and Asquith, respectively.

Moreover, as the years passed in 1905–15, the Liberal presence in the Lords grew steadily stronger as peerages were handed out to Liberal stalwarts, mainly businessmen in return for donations to funds, local notables and ex-MPs.[38] These groups soon outnumbered the landowners in the Liberal peerage, though landowners continued to dominate office-holding as they were usually younger, had more time on their hands and, in some cases (Lord Acton and Earl Granville, for instance), needed the money.[39] The Liberal Lords mustered 75 votes for the People's Budget in 1909 and numbered, at least in theory, over a hundred by 1914. Moreover, a number of cabinet ministers, like Haldane (in 1911) and Morley (in 1908), accepted peerages to free themselves from constituency work and boost the party's speaking strength in the Lords. Whilst the Liberal Peers remained hopelessly outnumbered by their Tory opponents, they were stronger by 1914 than at any time since 1885 – a some-what paradoxical situation in a party that was increasingly hostile to landownership and privilege. But this antipathy does not seem to have extended to Liberal Peers. They remained in great demand for honorary positions in the party, especially the presidency of local Liberal associations.[40] Landowning Peers who could bestir themselves to local political activity could often find themselves in a leading role in the countryside, where wealthy and active Liberals were few and far between.[41] In other words, the Liberal peerage remained an integral part of Liberalism and a relatively quick route to government office. But this does not mean that the Liberal peerage as a body was influential in policy matters. Certainly, the existence of Liberal Peers and landowners did not stop Liberals abolishing the Lords' veto in 1911 or launching the Land Campaign in 1913–14.

But if the Liberal Peers were an important feature of the party, the MPs were absolutely crucial. They represented an important link between the activists in the constituencies and the leadership, provided one of the keys to efficient campaigning and organisation in the localities and, above all, their discipline and unity were crucial to sustaining the Liberal government in office. A good deal of research into the social profile of Liberal MPs has confirmed they consisted of two broad groups – businessmen and middle class professionals, with about half of the latter being lawyers.[42] Landowners were rare by 1914 and the working class 'Lib–Lab' element all but disappeared when most of the miners' MPs joined Labour in 1909. Educationally they were very varied, with public schools and Oxbridge well-represented, but not dominant. They were about evenly divided between Anglicans and nonconformists, with the Church of Scotland and a few Jews, Catholics and avowed freethinkers holding the balance.[43] Most were first elected between the age of thirty and fifty and a majority, though not an overwhelming one, had some sort of prior link with their constituency. This profile distinguished the Liberals from their Tory opponents, who had a significant landed contingent and were more homogenously Anglican, public school and Oxbridge.[44] In other words, Liberal MPs were mainly men who had enough wealth to contribute to their election expenses and to keep themselves while in parliament (MPs were not paid until 1911), they often had a local link to help their election chances and they represented a much wider cross-section of wealth and ability than the Tories.

Another way of thinking about Liberal MPs is to see them as divided into those who sought election to the Commons as a confirmation of their status and did not see it as a full-time job; and those who were hungry for office. This division bore some relationship to the social contrasts among MPs: businessmen often had too much to do outside the Commons and entered it too late to think of office; professional men were more likely to see the Commons as a route to the cabinet, or possibly legal preferment if they were lawyers. This was reflected in the fact that of the Liberal cabinet ministers with links to the business world, only Alfred Emmott had actually been in charge of a firm. For all the others their business connections provided an income which allowed them to devote themselves to politics. However, both 'amateur' and 'professional' groups had their difficulties. Though the average MP did not have to speak or ask questions on any onerous scale – indeed a few managed to avoid doing it altogether – the basic problem that many business MPs faced was that the requirement to attend the Commons was becoming increasingly burdensome.[45] Although the Commons did not sit until 2:45 in the afternoon and not usually after 11:30 pm, this still meant being in London from Monday to Thursday when government business was transacted. The number of bills being produced by government was rising inexorably and instead of the nineteenth-century model of a sitting of a few months in the spring and early summer, parliament had begun to sit all year, with breaks at Christmas, Easter and in the summer.[46] An autumn session was only once avoided in 1906–14 (in 1913). In 1906–9 a few businessmen were able to make a deal with the whips office that provided them with 'leave of absence', as the government majority was so big.[47] After 1910 this was no longer possible and the whips put immense pressure on MPs to attend.[48] This put a good deal of strain on business MPs and some were only able to carry on by delegating to family members and becoming less active in their firms – not always with happy consequences.[49] Many MPs felt they had been reduced to voting machines, trooped through the lobbies on the whips' orders. As one exasperated backbencher commented of his first two years in parliament, 'beyond voting I have done nothing'.[50] But it is a testimony to both the committed Liberalism of many back-benchers and the continued prestige of the postnominal letters 'MP' that there was no sign by 1914 of a mass withdrawal at the next election, though there was plenty of evidence of battle fatigue.[51]

The ambitious MP faced a different set of problems. There were only about 60 government posts to distribute in December 1905 and after the Peers had been accounted for there were not many more than 40 to distribute among 400 MPs. It was difficult for an MP to make his name with no Tory government to attack. It was even difficult to get a hearing when there were so many potential speakers.[52] Inevitably, some became disillusioned and started to think about careers elsewhere. But most ploughed on, hoping for a break. As the key to junior office was to attract the whips attention, this meant aiming either for a number of effective, well-informed attacks on the Tories, often after long study of the Blue Books and a suitable marshalling of facts and figures; or a carefully calculated act of rebellion. C. F. G. Masterman, for instance, owed his promotion in 1908 to persistent rebelliousness, while Ellis Griffith made his name with a devastating attack on the prominent Tory, F. E. Smith, in 1911.[53] Whichever route an ambitious MP chose, the key was to gain a reputation as an effective speaker and a master of parliamentary procedure and this was far from easy. The House was a notoriously difficult audience to please. The long-winded, abstruse or boring received short shrift and one misjudgement of the Commons' mood could be hard to recover from.[54] For every MP who started to climb the ladder, there were many more who felt excluded and by 1914 there was a core of the grumbling and discontented, leavened by those who had been dismissed from government office.

Despite this, the parliamentary party's discipline remained excellent. The government was only once defeated on an important issue in 1905–15 and that was on a snap vote on the Irish home rule bill on 11 November 1912. This was a tribute to the effectiveness of the whips office in cajoling MPs into attendance and obedience, with offers of rewards, threats of blacklisting and appeals to conscience. All of the chief whips of 1905–15 seem to have been reasonably efficient, if not, apart from Elibank, outstanding.[55] Their system for notifying MPs of divisions became even tighter after the defeat of November 1912, making use of the latest technology, including the telephone.[56] The long-term trend had been towards greater party discipline since the late nineteenth-century, but it should not be forgotten that the 1895 Liberal government collapsed when its MPs failed to support it on a routine issue and that Balfour's Tory government had been shaken by parliamentary divisions over tariff reform.[57] This simply did not happen in 1905–15. Part of the reason has to be the relative unity in the cabinet, which meant dissenters had no prestigious figures to look to for a lead. But MPs could also feel that the government was achieving key elements of the Liberal programme and that it would be a serious betrayal to endanger its life. As G. H. Radford proclaimed when ending his rebellion against the 1914 budget, 'I will not refuse my vote to a Government that carries the cargo of Home Rule, Welsh Church Disestablishment and Plural Voting.'[58] In fact, revolts that seriously threatened the government's plans were very rare occasions indeed and it is difficult to pinpoint any occasion on which backbench dissent changed the direction of an important policy.

Protests by Liberal MPs fell into two categories – those that complained the government was not going fast enough in pursuit of Liberal ideals and those that felt it was too hasty. The first group can be divided into protests about traditional ideals, mainly armaments expenditure, and about social reform.[59] Both reached their apogee in 1908–9, when the government's standing was at its lowest ebb and MPs were concerned about its perceived lack of direction and unpopularity. The largest rebellions were protests at naval spending, but there were also significant revolts over the failure to tackle unemployment. Many MPs took part in both revolts, though the naval issue also attracted a sizeable group who were not part of any other rebellions. The size and publicity these protests attracted was never repeated, though there were also large scale rebellions in 1912 in favour of a minimum wage. The significance of these protests is hard to quantify. They certainly emphasised to the cabinet that there was substantial disquiet on these issues, but the largest rebellions, on the navy, failed to influence government policy and the cabinet faced down their challengers in a decisive Commons vote.[60] On unemployment, it is true that more active measures were taken after 1908 but the key here was that John Burns's responsibility for the issue was superseded by a group of cabinet ministers who were determined to ensure the government was seen to be doing something. Perhaps it would be more accurate to say that many MPs shared ministers' concerns, rather than that Commons rebellions led to changes in policy.[61] Similarly, in early 1910 many MPs were unhappy about the cabinet's failure to press ahead with reducing the Lords' powers, but this was, at best, only a contributory factor to the decision that was finally taken to go ahead with the parliament bill.[62] Rather than continually being shaken by revolts, the government usually faced an 'awkward squad' of 25–30 MPs who wanted to press on faster with social reform, but who were too small to deflect cabinet policy even in alliance with the Labour MPs.[63] A group of similar size (and overlapping membership) continued to protest about arms spending and Grey's foreign policy and became increasingly well organised in 1911–14.[64] But they could hardly wish to defeat a Liberal government if the alternative was a much more jingoistic Tory administration and the rebels remained on the sidelines throughout this period.

Revolts from a 'conservative' direction were much rarer than these protests and only concerned a handful of figures in 1906–9, especially those who had a connection to the fallen ex-leader, Lord Rosebery, or who were rather unlikely Liberals who had been unexpectedly swept into parliament for what were usually safe Tory seats by the landslide victory of 1906.[65] In 1912–14, though, the situation became more serious. A number of MPs were unhappy about the disendowment provisions of the Welsh Church disestablishment bill and a much larger group had their doubts about home rule on a variety of grounds. It was on home rule that the whips had their finest hour. They managed to reduce the figures voting against the government on any part of the bill to a tiny group, while allowing a certain flexibility about unauthorised absence from divisions, as long as it could be covered by Irish Nationalist MPs.[66] As a result, the bill managed to grind its way through parliament in 1912–14, unhindered by Liberal doubts. If anything, MPs' enthusiasm for the measure probably grew as it became a crucial test of partisan identity and involved with other issues, like the authority of parliament against Tory attempts to subvert the army or provoke rebellion in Ulster.

Home rule attracted the most dissent in a 'conservative' direction. In contrast, there was no sustained opposition to social reform. The 'People's Budget' of 1909 provoked protests from perhaps 20 to 30 MPs, but Robert Perks's attempt to use the remnants of the Liberal League to organise the malcontents ended only in the complete collapse of this group.[67] The dissidents mostly retired from parliament in 1910 or quietly buried their opinions. In 1914 there was a further revolt against Lloyd George's budget, but this was more a protest from exhausted MPs who took the opportunity to raise a number of issues and complain about being kept at Westminster for another autumn session, than a backlash against social reform and taxation.[68] Of course, not all MPs were enthusiastic about this direction for the party, but it was not something many MPs were prepared to go to any lengths to oppose, especially as it was widely perceived to be popular.

In the end, the Liberal MPs proved remarkably cohesive and the pressures of Liberal solidarity helped keep them in line behind the cabinet. What they had in common was far more important than what divided them. This is usually seen as being a characteristic of Labour or Tory MPs, whose strong solidarities built on class identity and shared experiences and institutions has often been emphasised.[69] But Liberal MPs had equally powerful bonds to hold them together. This was partly a matter of their common experiences as MPs. An MP could not disappear into his office while he was at Westminster, because there were none, except for ministers and committee meetings.[70] He had to socialise with his peers, sitting with them in the chamber, wandering the corridors of Westminster, gossiping in the various rooms for dining, smoking or taking tea, or retiring to the nearby National Liberal Club, whose drawing room served many MPs as their common office. MPs who did not have a London home often used the Club as their hotel. But Liberal MPs did not just share the inconveniences of Westminster life. Most of them were part of wider networks that made up the warp and woof of Liberal life (at least at the elite level). A quite remarkable number of MPs had fathers, brothers and cousins who were also Liberal MPs.[71] Religious denominations, schooling, business enterprises and shared charitable endeavours constructed a dense web of relationships that defined Liberalism quite as much as shared ideology.

The party outside parliament

Liberalism, of course, did not just operate at Westminster. Officially the leadership was kept informed of the state of the party in the country by two organisations – the Liberal Central Association (LCA) and the National Liberal Federation (NLF). The LCA was the whips organisation. It raised money from party supporters, increasingly in this period by offering a deal of cash for honours. This was extremely lucrative and Whiteley, the chief whip in 1905–8, probably raised £500,000.[72] Elibank, the chief whip in 1910–12, pushed the system to what was thought to be its limit, though Lloyd George showed otherwise in 1918–22.[73] Whiteley and Elibank were only developing a system in place since at least the 1890s, but politics was becoming increasingly expensive. The Liberals were probably spending over £100,000 on an election by 1910 (possibly nearer £200,000) and the Unionists probably more.[74] The Liberal Publication Department poured out a river of pamphlets, leaflets and posters pushing the party cause – over 42 million publications in January 1910, for instance.[75] This tended to give Liberal election campaigns an increasingly homogenous look across the country. This was reinforced by the increasing number of auxiliary party organisations that intruded on the local level. This trend had started in 1903 when the Unionists founded the Tariff Reform League and Liberals set up its opponent, the Free Trade Union (FTU). The FTU was ostensibly non-party but it was kept going with Liberal money and staffed by Liberal organisers.[76] Its paid speakers toured the constituencies, promoting the Liberal message on free trade and distributing literature. Its perceived success produced a raft of imitations – the Budget League, the Home Rule Council, the National Insurance Committee and the Central Land and Housing Council (to promote the Land Campaign).[77] All of these were the creations of the whips and had the great advantage that they could work throughout the year, not just at elections, in spreading the good news about the party's policies and achievements.

All this activity meant that local party associations were no longer solely responsible for their own propaganda. The whips also started to play a larger role at local level through the eight regional Liberal Federations which were reorganised and set up throughout England in 1908.[78] The federations were theoretically controlled by delegates from the constituency associations, but were actually run by paid organisers who acted as their secretaries. They channelled money down to the associations in the form of grants to help with campaigns, paying agents and routine organisational work. They also alerted the whips to weak constituencies that might require extra help and reported on the success of national campaigns and the electoral implications of issues like women's suffrage. Again, the federations ensured that local politics was no longer so very local.

The final role of the LCA, though this was partly delegated to the regional federations after 1908, was to make sure the party would fight the next election with enough suitable candidates in winnable constituencies. This was a traditional role for the whips, but also the most sensitive. It firstly involved interviewing potential candidates and assessing whether they might make worthy Liberal MPs. Some would make their own way to the whips headquarters in Parliament Street, while others would be approached, sometimes in surprising circumstances. Sir Thomas Barclay found himself Liberal candidate for Blackburn in 1910 after what he thought was an inconsequential chat with the chief whip in the lift at the National Liberal Club.[79] The whips had to assess a potential candidate's opinions, his ability to financially contribute to an election campaign and his abilities. Once convinced on any of these points, the whips could consider recommending him to a constituency as their candidate. An impecunious figure might be offered financial help. In 1906 about 113 of the 400 Liberal MPs had received money from the whips to help with their election expenses.[80] Constituencies, though, had differing views on candidates. Some were such unattractive prospects for a Liberal and so short of funds they would simply rely on the whips office to produce a suitable, wealthy candidate.[81] Others were keen for help in finding a candidate, but set conditions about his views, background or finances. When Sir Frances Channing thought of standing down in East Northamptonshire he insisted he should be followed by 'someone of similar views to myself on all great issues, & especially "labour" questions', and that his local party wanted a candidate 'of fair means and they would like if possible a man of university training & good standing', with appropriate views on peace and temperance.[82] Yet others were confident they could find a suitable figure locally and if necessary raise the finance to conduct a campaign. Generally, the safer a seat the less open it was to persuasion from the whips, but they were still able to play a central role in determining the make up of the parliamentary party.[83]

If the LCA was the voice of the leadership in the localities, the official representative of the local parties was the National Liberal Federation. It consisted of delegates from all the affiliated local Liberal associations in England (Wales retained a separate National Council, and Scotland its own Liberal Federation). When it had been founded in 1877 there had been much talk of it being the 'parliament' of Liberalism and an alternative power base to the leadership.[84] Some commentators had feared it would come to dictate to the country's elected leaders. But by 1905 these ideas seemed fanciful. All the NLF was, in reality, was a talking shop. Delegates met once a year for a two day conference. They passed resolutions on Liberal policy, offered condolences to the families of deceased stalwarts and encouraged the faithful. In the interval between meetings, an elected Council performed much the same function. What was quite clear was that the NLF had no influence on the leadership. In 1911–19 the NLF President was the ex-MP Sir John Brunner. He attempted to use the organisation to change the cabinet's policies on naval spending, by prompting it to pass resolutions condemning the spiralling arms budget.[85] The impact on government policy was precisely nil. In fact, the NLF was declining in influence, if anything, as leaders no longer felt it incumbent upon them to address its annual gatherings. Any organisational role it had played was increasingly usurped by the whips office – Sir Robert Hudson, the LCA's secretary, was also the chief administrator of the NLF in the Edwardian period.[86] One Liberal MP's comment on the NLF was that the LCA was 'gradually sucking its life-blood and supplanting it'.[87]

The other significant connection between the localities and the centre was the body of MPs, who had direct access to the whips, if not always the leaders, at Westminster and were naturally concerned by the organisational state and opinions of their local parties and constituencies. This could be an important link, as when MPs from rural seats complained about the impact of proposed land taxation on agricultural land in 1909.[88] On this occasion the cabinet agreed with the MPs, but it was far from a foregone conclusion that the leadership would take their followers' views into account. It was, for instance, not always clear if MPs represented the opinions of their local parties in a straightforward way and an MP who disagreed with the cabinet could find his local party ranged against him. Most constituency associations left MPs to follow their own line in the Commons as long as they supported the current leadership. But a number of MPs who opposed important items of the Liberal programme found themselves being censured by their local parties and ultimately deselected as candidates, despite claims that they 'truly' represented local feeling, including anti-People's Budget MPs like R. L. Everett in Woodbridge and anti-home rulers like Sir Clifford Cory in St Ives.[89] In fact some MPs seem to have had little contact with their constituency at all – limiting their appearances to an annual speech and election times. Few took matters as far as Eugene Wason, the MP for Clackmannan and Kinross, who even failed to turn up for a meeting to re-adopt him as Liberal candidate.[90] This, however, seems to have been an older model of the MP-local party relationship that was in decline in the closely contested and partisan world of Edwardian politics. Younger and ambitious politicians like Charles Roberts at Lincoln were closely involved in their local party's activities, speaking regularly and even chairing party meetings, and many MPs of course lived in their constituency or had strong local links.[91]

The relationship between MPs and local parties naturally varied a great deal, if only because local parties did. By the Edwardian era all constituencies had a formally organised local constituency association, recognised by the whips and the NLF as the accredited representative of Liberalism. All had the duty of selecting a candidate for parliament and sending representatives to the NLF conference, if they wished. But beyond this their state of organisation varied wildly. In some very safe seats the association seems to have been dormant between national elections. This was particularly the case in parts of Wales where it was assumed everyone was a Liberal and that organisation was superfluous.[92] Over most of England, though, the situation was very different. Here the model was to have a formally enrolled membership, usually paying a low flat rate fee of as little as a shilling a year.[93] They elected a committee in every local government ward in the borough, charged with selecting municipal candidates and sending representatives to the council that was the governing body of the constituency association. The council, often known as the 'Five Hundred', or whatever its theoretical strength was, in turn elected an executive committee. If the parliamentary seat was one division of a larger city the council usually sent delegates to a wider body representing the whole of the city. The council, and often the executive as well, also contained representatives of affiliated local organisations.[94] The most important of these was the local Women's Liberal Association (WLA), whose members were vital voluntary workers and fundraisers. But the Young Liberals could also be significant in provoking their elders into activity and acting as a recruiting ground for members, while Liberal clubs solidified the social ties that bound local Liberals (though rarely providing much financial help to associations).

How active this organisation was depended on local circumstances. Not all towns conducted local politics under party labels, rendering the local ward's duty of selecting council candidates superfluous.[95] Safe seats and hopeless seats could easily become lethargic, while closely-contested ones became organisational models. Paying membership could be well over a thousand in some urban seats, but much smaller in Tory strongholds among the county seats.[96] Money was a constant source of concern as even local politics could be expensive. By 1914 many seats had a paid agent, a job that was becoming increasingly professionalized, with its own training scheme, pension fund, national organisation and magazine.[97] The agent's traditional duty was to 'look after the register'. This meant canvassing the constituency to find out who its potential Liberal voters were and ensuring they were registered to vote, while raising objections to the qualifications of Tory (or Labour) voters. This task was usually carried out with part-time paid help, but still occupied a good deal of the agents' time as it was crucial to success, especially in marginal seats. Each year agents assessed 'their' gains or losses in the hundreds of voters.[98] The agent also had the duty of overseeing the municipal and parliamentary campaigns and more generally of stimulating activity by organising meetings and expanding membership (and collecting their subscriptions). All this meant most associations needed to find more than £100 each year to function effectively, while an election could cost well over £1,000.[99] This was an astronomical sum – something like £50,000 in terms of purchasing power in the early twenty-first century. Party workers (apart from the agent) gave their services free, but the association still had to fund a share of the returning officers' expenses, posters, handbills, the hire of halls for speaking and conveyances to the polls for infirm or idle voters. Membership subscriptions were far too low to fund most of this activity. Candidates always contributed, in proportion to their own resources, and increasingly subventions filtered down from the whips and the regional federations.[100] Local Liberal worthies were frequently 'tapped' and the Edwardian era saw the flourishing of the 'bazaar', a day long combination of entertainment, stalls, refreshments and speech-making, which could be very profitable.[101] The latter was usually the responsibility of the local WLA, a factor that emphasised their significance in the existence of many associations. The proportion contributed by each of these sources varied according to the type of seat. Rural constituencies tended to depend heavily on the candidate, while well-populated urban seats had more wealthy Liberals and found it easier to organise fund-raising events.

Not surprisingly, most associations spent a great deal of their time worrying about organisational matters. Some do not seem to have discussed national politics at ward or divisional levels at all, though others were keen to badger their MP and the NLF with motions about specific issues.[102] All the key decisions, though, tended to be in a relatively small number of hands. Democracy in Liberal associations was largely theoretical. The divisional council, elected by the membership, met only once a year and its proceedings were largely ceremonial. Real power lay with the executive committee, or often a 'business' sub-committee of the executive. It was they who negotiated the selection of a candidate and then presented him to a meeting of the membership for approval, much as the Liberal cabinet presented their candidate for the leadership to the MPs.[103] Similarly, at ward level, candidates for the local council and boards of guardians were usually picked by the ward officers and committee. There was usually a considerable overlap between the inner group and the key Liberal figures on the local council, so they often made the important decisions about municipal policy, too.[104] The social structure of Liberal associations showed a certain similarity in most areas. About three quarters of the rank and file of the membership were working class, as in the population as a whole.[105] It also tended to reflect differences in the local economy. Liberal associations in mining areas were largely made up of miners. In the countryside agricultural labourers, artisans and even servants were well-represented. This pattern could be replicated on the council of many constituencies, but few working men held important offices at ward or constituency level, other than in some mining seats where their numerical preponderance and the financial muscle of their union allowed them to dominate.[106] Instead the elite tended to consist of retailers, small businessmen, professionals, especially solicitors, and a sprinkling of wealthier business figures. Essentially this class had the time to spare for meetings, the ability to make financial contributions to the party and the confidence and skills in public speaking and conducting meetings deemed essential for local office. While few big businessmen bothered with local politics, they could usually take a leading role if they did, as the Rowntrees showed in York.[107]

The views and concerns of the localities are hard to recover. The NLF was too bland and unrepresentative a body to act as a reliable guide.[108] Local party elites seem to have been largely concerned with local issues, but willing to follow the leadership at national level. Indeed, the attitude to Liberal leaders seems to have been close to hero worship. They were viewed as majestic figures who might occasionally descend from the Olympus of government to address a regional party gathering, but who could hardly be thought of in a critical way. Hence the bewilderment of many local parties when forced to choose between Asquith or Lloyd George after 1916. They simply were not used to thinking in this way. Certainly, there was no rank and file revolt over new initiatives like the People's Budget and the prominence of social reform, or old but tricky problems like home rule.[109] Essentially, the Liberalism of the rank and file, like that of the MPs' was driven by more than ideology. It represented a form of social identity, based both on generalised ideas about Liberalism as the party of progress, and the dense networks of family, friendship, locality, religion and occupation that tied Liberals together.

Outside the party's formal structures there were a host of pressure groups that looked to Liberalism to forward their programme and were largely staffed by Liberals. Some of them were of long standing and largely moribund by the Edwardian era, like the National Reform Union.[110] Others were very much alive, though their tactics differed. Some, like the Aborigines Protection Society concentrated on using their specialist knowledge to lobby the Colonial and Foreign Offices on behalf of native races.[111] Others, like the Scottish Home Rule Council, were essentially propagandist bodies who sought to spread their message among Liberals and the public at large through meetings, publications and the efforts of well-disposed MPs in raising the issue in Parliament.[112] Almost all MPs were recruited to the governing council of at least one such body. However, Liberalism was not plagued, as it had been in the late Victorian era, with pressure groups who felt they could further their ends by threatening to withdraw their support from the party, or put up their own candidates against it. Perhaps only the followers of Henry George's nostrum of the Single Tax on land values still behaved in this way and even they did not follow through on their threats.[113] The party system was simply too well-established and the loyalties of voters too entrenched for this tactic to seem feasible any more.

The final auxiliary of the party was the Liberal Press. Before 1914 the loyalties and attitudes of newspapers remained a matter of central concern for all politicians, as they remained the main means of communication with the mass electorate. While the populist formats pioneered in the *Daily Mail* had tended to reduce the amount of political coverage in the national dailies, most papers retained a distinct partisan identity and at election times would devote 25–40 per cent of their space to politics.[114] If anything the link between politics and newspapers was becoming closer as both parties sought to use their war chests to help out 'their' papers. The London evening paper, the *Westminster Gazette*, was rescued by a syndicate of Liberal businessmen organised by the whips office in 1908.[115] Journalists on national papers often enjoyed a close relationship with leading politicians. Lloyd George was not alone on the Liberal side in using newspapers as a conduit for his views, though he was exceptionally close to the editors of the *Daily News* and the *Daily Chronicle*, the two Liberal national 1/2d dailies.[116] These papers were outsold by their Tory rivals like the *Mail*, but the balance between the parties was somewhat corrected by the slight Liberal lead in the Sunday Press, where the *News of the World* leant towards them, and among provincial papers, which still counted for over half of newspaper readership.[117] Regional newspapers were also closely connected to the political parties and Liberal businessmen were encouraged by their party to support them and bail out their finances.[118] Indeed the Edwardian era saw a mini-revival in the Liberal Press which was much more healthy in 1914 than it had been in 1900.[119] While the differing perspectives of the social reforming, 'Little Navy', *Daily News* and the more cautious *Westminster Gazette* were repeated throughout the provincial press, the Liberal papers were never divided again as seriously as they had been over the Boer war in 1899–1902 and all pulled together for the common cause at Edwardian elections, eagerly accepting snippets from the Liberal Publication Department to boost their anti-Tory campaigns.[120] In effect the Liberal Press was an extension of the party and far less trouble than its Unionist counterpart. It certainly did not contain any figures like Garvin of the *Observer* with ambitions to dictate party policy.

The structure of the pre-1914 Liberal Party clearly marked it out as a modern political party, rather than a Victorian relic. It was dominated by its leaders, supported by a disciplined parliamentary party, a formally organised mass membership and a partisan Press. Its electioneering methods were well-funded, co-ordinated at the national level and as sophisticated as the technology of the times allowed. In 1906 and 1910 it validated its structure by defeating Unionism and holding Labour in a subordinate position. In this situation it was up to its leaders to determine in which direction they chose to lead their troops and how they wished to interpret the meaning of Liberalism in its application to government policy.

2
Foreign, Defence and Colonial Policy

Foreign policy

Liberal foreign policy in 1905–14 was the policy of one man, the Secretary of State for Foreign Affairs, Sir Edward Grey – the only cabinet figure appointed in December 1905 who held the same office for the entire lifetime of the Edwardian Liberal governments. By 1914 it seemed unthinkable to many that anybody else could fulfil this role. But even in 1905 it had proved impossible to appoint anyone but Grey. Campbell-Bannerman had not been eager to take this course as Grey seemed to be such a close ally of Rosebery, the prime minister's bugbear.[1] He considered Lord Elgin and offered the role to Lord Cromer before accepting there was no alternative to Grey. Grey, too, appeared to be reluctant to take office. He clung to the idea that his friend and ally, Asquith, should lead the Commons while Campbell-Bannerman was relegated to a figurehead prime ministership in the Lords, long after Asquith had abandoned the idea. But extraordinary measures were taken to make him change his mind, delaying the formation of the government. Finally, an entire evening of pleading from his other old political friends, Haldane and Arthur Acland, persuaded Grey to take office and the Liberal cabinet was finally completed. When its membership was publicly announced, Grey's appointment was almost universally considered in the Liberal and Unionist Press to be one of its strongest points.[2] Grey's removal from office was never considered by either Campbell-Bannerman or Asquith. Indeed his resignation was thought by Asquith to be such a disaster, that the government could not continue without him.[3] He was widely believed to be indispensable.

The source of Grey's authority sheds an interesting light on Edwardian Liberalism. He was certainly not a dazzling speaker, in the Commons or on the public platform. His orations were relatively few and his style prosaic, at best, if usually well-reasoned.[4] Nor did he have an outstanding record of public achievement. The only political office he had held prior to 1905 was as Rosebery's and then Kimberley's competent under-secretary at the Foreign Office in 1892–5. Outside of politics he had spent a year as chairman of his local railway company, written a book on fly-fishing and won the national real tennis amateur champion-ship five times.[5] But Grey did have the inestimable advantage of being a landowner (albeit a modest one) in a party largely deserted by his class over Irish home rule in 1886.[6] In the Edwardian era it was still considered essential that the Foreign Secretary should be a patrician – a pattern not broken until Ramsay MacDonald took the post in 1924.[7] This was because the world of diplomacy was still essentially an aristocratic preserve. Britain's diplomats and ambassadors were still drawn exclusively from the landed elite and so were their counterparts in all the other great European powers. It was argued that only people from this milieu could understand its codes and nuances and meet the representatives of other countries on an equal footing. Nobody at the top of the Liberal party seems to have challenged this idea in 1905 and its acceptance seriously limited Campbell-Bannerman's choices. In the very small field of Liberal landowners in parliament with previous government experience and some knowledge of foreign affairs, Grey was the outstanding candidate – of the two others seriously considered by Campbell-Bannerman, Elgin was a colonial governor rather than a politician (he had been Viceroy of India in 1894–9) and Cromer was not even a Liberal.

Grey thus owed his position at least partly to his rare position as a Liberal landowner, though he was, of course, also a full-time politician, just as much as someone like Lloyd George. It was just that the income to sustain his career came from his estates, rather than from a family law firm. He consolidated his importance by skilfully playing on positive stereotypes of his class. Some Liberals were bound to be impressed by Grey's lineage as the great-great nephew of the Earl Grey who had secured the 1832 Reform Bill. But, above all, Grey maintained the impression that he held office only with the greatest reluctance and that solely an overriding sense of public duty persuaded him to forsake the delights of his country estates, with their beech trees and trout streams, for the world of politics.[8] His, consciously contrived, image was of a man on a higher moral plane than the ambitious and grasping professional politicians around him. Liberals angrily denounced this pose in an opponent like Curzon or Balfour, but proved very susceptible to it in one of their own champions. It was accepted unquestioningly even by fierce critics of his policies like the Liberal journalist A. G. Gardiner, who referred to Grey's 'absolute purity of motive'.[9] It was a rare politician indeed who questioned the Foreign Secretary's honesty and straightforwardness.

Grey's other source of authority was the widespread impression that he was a very moderate Liberal – almost a sort of Conservative. This was only partly true. While Grey was lukewarm about home rule and wanted a powerful second chamber to balance the Commons he was also an ardent proponent of female suffrage and of most Liberal social reforms.[10] His image as a cross-party figure stemmed largely from his support for the Unionist government's prosecution of the Boer war in 1899–1902 and his abstention from partisan invective.[11] His tenure of the Foreign Office reinforced this impression by removing him from the forefront of controversial domestic issues and allowing him to play the role of the representative of the whole nation to foreign powers. Unionists who regularly denounced Liberalism and all its works were willing to exempt the noble figure of Grey from their condemnations. As Grey's constant critic, Arthur Ponsonby, observed, the Foreign Secretary 'has a great reputation in the country specially among Tories.'[12] Thus, Grey's resignation would have removed the most important figure in the cabinet who could appeal to a 'centrist' or moderate audience. His presence was a reassurance to cautious Liberals that the party remained respectable and sound on great issues, especially of foreign policy. His loss to the cabinet would have been heavy and Asquith for one would never have allowed this to happen. At crucial moments, Grey always got his way.

Grey used his indispensability to make sure that foreign policy followed the lines he favoured. This essentially meant that there should be continuity between the policies of the Unionist government and of their Liberal successors – something Grey insisted on with great force and clarity in his speech to the City Liberal Association on 20 October 1905.[13] Put simply, Grey did not believe that there was any such thing as a 'Liberal' foreign policy. The interests of the nation transcended party politics and were recognised by men in all parties. Grey, in office, would do much the same as his Unionist predecessor, Lord Lansdowne.[14] This was the view of Grey's mentor, Lord Rosebery, and the practice of previous Liberal administrations.[15] It was also widely supported in the party. The Liberal Imperialist strand of thought that had solidified in the late 1890s and early 1900s was committed to the idea of continuity.[16] One recent estimate has suggested there were more than twice as many Liberal Imperialist candidates at the 1900 election than 'pro-Boers' who criticised the Unionist government's actions abroad, especially its war in South Africa.[17] This development was partly stimulated by the feeling that Liberalism must not be seen to be 'unpatriotic' or weak in its foreign policy. As Grey said, the right of Liberal Imperialism 'to a share in Patriotism & Efficiency is a reply to the Tory claim of a monopoly of these'.[18] In a world of fiercely competing nations any other policy would threaten the country's security and ensure the Liberal party's political suicide.

However, Grey also had to contend with the reality that not all Liberals took this view. His doctrine of continuity could be interpreted as just accepting the tenets of Toryism in foreign policy. Many Liberals believed passionately that just as their party was the agent of liberty and progress in domestic policy, so it should be abroad. There were two distinct strands in Liberal thinking on foreign policy, though many Liberals mixed the two together in their views, even when they appeared to be contradictory. The first might be labelled the 'Cobdenite' position, as it often looked back to the mid nineteenth-century politician and patron saint of free trade, Richard Cobden, for validation. This was essentially an anti-foreign policy policy, or at least the belief that Britain should not enter into alliances and commitments with other European countries, especially ones that might drag Britain into war. As F. W. Hirst, editor of *The Economist*, put it, no Liberal government should ask its 'countrymen to give up their lives for a Continental squabble about which they know nothing and care less'.[19] Nor should Britain behave aggressively towards other nations, big or small. Instead the country should mind its own business and only enter into a war if its own survival was threatened. It should devote its energies to manufacturing and trade and above all to the promotion of free trade around the world, which would eventually lead to all countries recognising their mutual interdependence and the futility of war. As the *Manchester Guardian* put it, 'open markets' were 'a natural basis for understanding'.[20] This position was boosted by the publication of Norman Angell's book, *Europe's Optical Illusion* in 1909, which claimed to prove from a study of the world's economy that a war between the powers could only lead to the impoverishment of victors and vanquished.[21]

The other strand in Liberal thinking might be labelled 'Gladstonian', as the Grand Old Man of Liberalism was often invoked in its support. Rather than arguing against an active foreign policy, it suggested that a Liberal government should use British power to promote Liberal ideals around the world. This meant actively intervening to support constitutional regimes against reactionary opponents, to defend struggles for national self-determination and to prevent intolerable abuses, like slavery and wholesale massacre. A perfect example had been the Liberal agitation to intervene in the Ottoman Empire in 1895–7 to prevent the massacre of Armenians.[22] This position also meant defending moral standards of behaviour between the powers, especially the sanctity of treaties and arbitration of disputes. It did not necessarily mean a constant resort to armed force to preserve these ideas, though. Liberals preferred to see all the European great powers co-operating together to achieve these ends, through congresses and conferences – a process that was often described as the Concert of Europe.[23] Such collaboration would also make general warfare between the powers much less likely. Supporters of these ideals were able to point to the proliferation of international bodies devoted to world co-operation in the late nineteenth century, like the Inter-parliamentary Union, founded in 1889 and the series of peace congresses which started the same year. By the Edwardian era most European countries had societies devoted to these ends and even the governments of the powers were willing to participate in international congresses at The Hague in 1899 and 1907 to try and resolve issues of dispute. Campbell-Bannerman delivered a rousing peroration to the fourteenth conference of the Inter-parliamentary Union when it met in Britain in 1906, urging all the delegates to press their governments to work for greater international harmony at the second Hague congress.[24]

Grey, therefore, had a difficult task as Foreign Secretary. In addition to conducting the country's international relations, he had to convince his party that his own idea of 'continuity' was not greatly at variance with other Liberal views about foreign policy. This was particularly important because Cobdenite and Gladstonian views were also to be found to some degree in the cabinet, as well as in the party as a whole. In 1905 James Bryce, Burns, Lloyd George, Morley and Lord Loreburn, the Lord Chancellor, had all been 'pro-Boers' and thus were unlikely to automatically accept the doctrine of continuity with the foreign policy of the government's Unionist predecessors.[25] But Grey's task was made all the more difficult because of the ways in which British foreign policy had developed under his predecessor, Lansdowne, and which he wished to pursue. The Unionist governments of Salisbury and Balfour had concluded that it was impossible for Britain to sustain its worldwide colonial and trading interests without reaching an accommodation with the other powers. But, rather haphazardly, the only practical outcome of this desire was an 'entente' with France in 1904 to settle outstanding colonial disputes, especially over Britain's role in Egypt and France's position in Morocco.[26] Though this was not a formal alliance it rapidly acquired some of the characteristics of one. In particular, France could only value the British connection if Britain was prepared to support it against Germany in Europe, while Germany was likely to try and apply pressure to prevent the solidification of Franco-British relations. Their first attempt at this – a challenge to France's position in Morocco – was already disturbing the diplomatic waters when Grey took office in 1905. These events coincided with increasing popular and official fears of Germany as a rival. The rapid expansion of the German fleet produced worries in naval circles and the beginnings of a whole genre of 'invasion panic' literature exemplified by Erskine Childers's *Riddle of the Sands* (1903). Army officers ambitious to extend their service's role started to consider the possibilities of fighting a war with France against Germany.

Grey was committed above all to the entente with France.[27] He felt it was essential to relieve pressure on Britain's worldwide interests and that abandoning the French connection would turn France into an implacable enemy and leave Britain friendless and defenceless.[28] If that meant shoring up France's diplomatic position in Europe against Germany it was a necessary price. But Grey also extended this system by concluding a further entente with Russia in 1907.[29] This seemed to him a natural corollary of the French agreement. France and Russia were allies and Russia was believed to be a threat to Britain's Indian empire. By settling outstanding disputes in Afghanistan, Persia and Tibet he was relieving some of British strategists' most persistent worries.

To Grey this was an eminently practical solution to Britain's difficulties. But it deeply worried some in his party who felt it was incompatible with their notions of Liberal foreign policy. Essentially there were three areas of disagreement. The first centred around dislike of the idea of a concord with France and Russia against Germany, either on the grounds that this was a Continental entanglement which would unnecessarily involve Britain in other countries' quarrels and ultimately drag her into war, or on the grounds that it dissolved the Concert of Europe into mutually antagonistic blocs.[30] The second major criticism was that any involvement with Russia involved condoning its reactionary regime which was disliked by all Liberals.[31] Finally, it was alleged that lining up with France and Russia meant accepting the illiberal behaviour of these countries and their allies throughout the world.[32]

But on none of these issues was Grey to be shifted. Foreign policy remained his policy. But he did not have to constantly resort to the threat of resignation to get his way, either, because his critics were rarely in a position to mount an effective challenge. The central issue for Grey was the need to support France and Russia against Germany at moments of crisis and in this he had the backing of the cabinet. It was often suggested (sometimes with hindsight by cabinet ministers involved, like Lloyd George) that the cabinet was kept uninformed of his policies by Grey.[33] He was certainly unwilling to volunteer information. But the cabinet seems to have discussed foreign affairs with some regularity, if not always very profitably. The exchange of letters in November 1912 between Grey and Cambon, promising consultations if either country was threatened by a 'third Power', was extensively debated and altered in cabinet.[34] There was even a cabinet committee in 1911 to draw up a memorandum to Germany on terms for a possible settlement of differences.[35] What these discussions revealed was that a clear majority of the cabinet could not accept Germany's demand that Britain promise to remain neutral in any future Franco-German conflict, without first obtaining any concession from Germany. There was no alternative but to maintain the ententes. Moreover, Grey had the firm support of his old Liberal Imperialist friends, Asquith and Haldane, in the cabinet, and after 1911 of Churchill and Lloyd George.[36] The latter was crucial, especially when his Mansion House speech of July 1911 showed Germany that the British cabinet was united in resisting its demands. Grey's critics were much more lightweight figures like Lord Loreburn, Morley and Harcourt.

It was difficult for them and Grey's opponents in parliament to mobilise effectively against his policies at least partly because of the ways in which Ango-German tensions arose. When Grey took office in 1905–6 the key issues were being resolved at distance and with considerable secrecy and confusion at the Algeciras conference on the future of Morocco. At that time many enthusiasts for a Liberal foreign policy were still willing to support the recently-signed entente on the grounds that it had resolved the historic enmity with France and aligned Britain with a fellow-democracy.[37] In 1908–9 when Grey supported Russia over the annexation of Bosnia by Germany's ally, Austria, he was able to clothe his stand as a defence of the sanctity of treaties – something acceptable to most Liberals.[38] Even during the second Moroccan crisis in 1911 criticism of Grey was muted until after the affair was over. It occurred at the height of the government's conflict with the House of Lords, when few had the attention to spare from domestic politics or were willing to weaken the cabinet's hand against the peers. But even more importantly, the 1911 crisis revealed that when, however briefly, war threatened, the instinct of most of the Liberal Press and Liberal backbenchers was to rally behind the government.[39]

The scare of July 1911 left, however, deep suspicions amongst some of Grey's critics. In November 1911 about 80 MPs set up the Liberal

Foreign Affairs Committee to press for more open diplomacy and parliamentary supervision of foreign policy and a smaller core of anti-Grey forces developed, led by Arthur Ponsonby (himself an ex-diplomat).[40] But Grey was also able to disarm a good deal of the criticism of his policy. As he stated several times in the Commons, there was no *formal* commitment to support France against Germany, certainly no alliance, and Britain retained full freedom of manoeuvre – something that seemed to be confirmed by the publication in full of the Anglo-French entente on 24 November 1911.[41] There was, therefore, nothing tangible for his critics to campaign against. Much of their energy was diverted into trying to improve relations with Germany at an unofficial level, an activity that Grey saw as perfectly harmless. J. A. Baker, Liberal MP for Finsbury East, for instance, was central in setting up the Associated Council of Churches in the British and German Empires.[42] Grey was also adept at using the language of 'Liberal' foreign policy when it suited him. In March 1911 he promoted President Taft's idea for wide-ranging treaties of arbitration between the powers in a Commons speech which impressed many of his most long-standing opponents.[43] He was also able to use his role as host of the Conference of London in 1913 to put himself forward as the apostle of united action by the Concert of Europe in settling the affairs of the Balkans.[44] Indeed, most of the time Grey was happy for relations with Germany to be perfectly friendly – so long as they did not undermine the ententes. In 1912–14 Anglo-German rivalry at least seemed containable and agreements were discussed on issues as diverse as the Baghdad-Berlin railway and the future of Portugal's colonies.[45] While some Liberals had become profoundly alienated from Grey, most accepted he was not an aggressive Foreign Secretary, nor did he try to provoke war.

The other areas of disagreement about Grey's foreign policy remained, but they were merely irritants compared to the issues of Britain's relations with France and Germany. The Russian entente was always regarded with distaste by many Liberals, especially as Grey signed it at a particularly inauspicious time, when the Tsarist regime had just dissolved its parliament and was implicated in promoting pogroms against the Jews. There was a rather embarrassing incident in 1908 when Arthur Ponsonby was disinvited from the Buckingham Palace garden party for protesting too vehemently against Edward VII's meeting with the Tsar.[46] But there were benefits from the Russian agreement – in particular it removed some of the arguments for increasing spending on the army, as it would no longer be needed to defend India from a Russian onslaught. Grey could, and did, also argue that the entente allowed him to influence

Russia in a liberal direction and weaken the pro-German conservatives. Certainly the Russian liberals could be cited as warm supporters of the agreement.[47] Thus Grey could suggest he shared the aim of liberalising Russia and was merely approaching this goal in a much more practical way than his opponents suggested.

Finally, complaints about Britain's acceptance of the immoral behaviour of its entente partners and their allies in other countries remained very much the preserve of specialist pressure groups. The two most important disputes were over Persia and the Congo. In Persia, the Anglo-Russian entente allocated the north of Persia, including the capital, to Russia's sphere of influence. The Russians did their best to undermine the Persian forces pressing for constitutional government and to bring their sphere under close control. Grey was accused of complicity in this enterprise as the price for the entente.[48] In the Congo, the brutality and incompetence of Leopold II of the Belgians' rule led to calls for British intervention to rectify the situation. But Grey preferred a policy of pressure on the Belgian government, as he had no wish to alienate a strategically important European state and an ally of France. Again he was accused of condoning the indefensible in the name of the ententes.[49] However, these issues excited little public or parliamentary fervour and Grey was able to sidestep much of the criticism by suggesting that close relations with powers like Russia would produce more results than confrontation. After all, nobody wanted war for Persia or the Congo and most Liberals could accept Grey was an upright figure who genuinely disapproved of immoral behaviour by states. After all, it was he who finally ended exports of Indian opium to China in 1913 – an issue that had long been the subject of campaigns by Liberal activists in the Society for the Suppression of the Opium Trade.[50]

Defence policy

The Liberals faced the same kinds of difficulty with defence policy as they did with foreign policy. On the one hand there were strong pressures in favour of continuity between Unionist and Liberal cabinets, while on the other there were strident Liberal voices calling for changes in the name of Liberal beliefs and traditions. Moreover, defence policy was not separate from developments in foreign affairs and the new relationships with France and Russia introduced further strains into policy-making and complicated issues even more.

Senior Unionist politicians certainly had high hopes that the new Liberal government would follow in their footsteps. Balfour, the outgoing prime minister, had set up a Committee of Imperial Defence (CID), as a permanent sub-committee of the cabinet in 1902 to co-ordinate strategic thinking and this body was retained by Campbell-Bannerman, though it met less often under his aegis.[51] Both Tweedmouth, the new Civil Lord of the Admiralty, and Haldane, the Secretary of State for War, were regarded as 'safe' figures, unlikely to fall prey to wild ideas. Tweedmouth's predecessor, Lord Cawdor, briefed him extensively on naval affairs – indeed, owing to the slowness in constituting a new Board of the Admiralty, Cawdor remained at the Admiralty for two weeks after the Liberal government took office.[52] Haldane had already discussed military affairs with Lord Esher and Sir George Clarke of the CID in 1904–5 and was a friend of Balfour's, with whom he had co-operated before in politics.[53] Balfour's line in opposition was to support and strengthen those elements in the Liberal cabinet that he regarded as 'safe', rather than to engage in a head on assault on the new government's policies.[54] These overtures played strongly on the idea that defence policy should be 'above' politics and something all parties could agree on in the national interest.

This was a powerful argument and one to which Liberals were not immune. The Liberal Imperialist strand in the party argued that it should not be seen as weak or unpatriotic on defence, just as it should not in foreign policy.[55] But however appealing it might be, this line of thinking clashed with a long-held Liberal tradition that the party's duty in the field of defence was, above all, to reduce expenditure on the armed forces. Traditionally this had been defined by Liberals as 'unproductive' expenditure that took money out of the pockets of the people in order to finance the aristocratic elites who dominated the armed forces and wished to drag an unwilling nation into unnecessary wars for their own glory.[56] Liberals were also deeply suspicious of attempts to militarise society by expanding the role of the army. It was felt this must curb the liberties of Britain as a 'free' nation, especially if it ended in conscription.[57] These ideas remained important. In 1899–1900, during the Boer war, about half of the budget had been spent on defence and the Unionists had struggled to bring this figure down.[58] Both Liberals who wanted to reduce the role of the government in the economy and those who wanted to spend more on social welfare could agree that defence spending must be cut in the name of the old cry of 'retrenchment', which figured in 54 per cent of Liberal election addresses in 1906.[59] Moreover, once suspicions were aroused about the direction of Grey's foreign policy it seemed to some that increased defence spending would only heighten tensions with Germany and speed the path to war.

This clash between the consensual ideology of 'national defence' and alternative Liberal traditions was a complex and convoluted one, though, as the history of the army in 1905–14 reveals. Haldane was determined to hold down the army estimates to £28 million – a figure that was chosen because it was below Unionist expenditure in 1905, rather than for strategic reasons.[60] This was enough to hold off the advocates of retrenchment and allowed him to pursue his policies for the army unmolested. The direction of his reforms largely followed the unsuccessful attempts of the Unionists in 1901–5 to reshape the army to accommodate a home defence force and a body of soldiers who could rapidly be dispatched for service abroad. None of this interested most Liberals, or indeed anybody who did not have close connections with the army. But Haldane succeeded where his predecessors failed, largely by learning from their mistakes in upsetting a range of vested interests. He managed to remould the old part-time organisations, the Yeomanry and the Volunteers, into the Territorial Army to defend Britain, while six infantry divisions and a cavalry brigade became the British Expeditionary Force (BEF) for overseas service. This was widely acclaimed as a success, though it was fairly clear that the size of the BEF was determined by the ceiling of £28 million, rather than military considerations. But it was only able to make its way through the House of Lords because Haldane was following Unionist precedents. Indeed he largely recast his scheme for the militia, the army's reserve forces, in consultation with Balfour as his bill made its way through the Commons.[61] The Territorial and Reserve Forces Act of 1907 managed the remarkable feat of being both a consensual measure and one that reflected distinctive Liberal views about defence spending, though some Liberals objected to minor features of the scheme, like the Officer Training Corps in public schools, on the grounds that they increased military influence in civil society.[62] But to Haldane, the act expressed his hope to see 'the principle of continuity largely characterizing foreign affairs extended to our military organization.'[63]

This ambiguity in Liberal approaches to the army remained in place and was widely accepted by most Liberals down to 1914, particularly because army expenditure remained under control. Perhaps, just as importantly, MPs did not enquire too closely what the purpose of the BEF was. It was perfectly reasonable to believe that it existed to deal with an emergency in any of Britain's many colonies, or a threat to India, though the entente with Russia made this implausible after 1907. But the BEF could also be used to intervene in a war on the continent, perhaps by supporting France if it was attacked by Germany. Haldane may have thought of this possibility as early as January 1906. He and

Grey gave their approval that month to some existing, but unco-ordinated, discussions between British and French military officials about British troops holding the flank between the Channel and the far left of the French army in the event of a German assault.[64] These discussions were intensely controversial. They implied, though they did not definitely state, that Britain was committed to intervening in a Franco-German conflict. Once the formidable and devious Henry Wilson took over as Director of Military Operations in 1910 the BEF had only one purpose in army thinking – to help prevent a German invasion of France.

The Anglo-French military talks never became public. If they had, the cabinet would have been obliged to insist that they were not binding, but the secrecy surrounding them suggested that Grey and Haldane knew that they were risking a decisive split in Liberalism over foreign and defence policy. In fact, the discussions only slowly became known at the highest level. Campbell-Bannerman was initially given an edited version of events by Grey and when in early 1906 he was more fully enlightened (possibly by Haldane) is difficult to determine.[65] The rest of the cabinet were not told collectively of the military discussions.[66] But the Admiralty, some of the CID and the opposition knew nothing of the talks either, so they were in good company. This situation only changed in 1911 after the second Moroccan crisis concentrated minds about the need to be prepared for a possible war. At a CID meeting on 23 August 1911 Henry Wilson saw off rival naval plans to land elements of the army in lightening raids on the Baltic coast in favour of the army's scheme of a landing in France.[67] Reginald McKenna as Civil Lord was deemed by Asquith to be too closely connected to the navy's plans and was compelled to exchange jobs with Winston Churchill, the Home Secretary. Churchill ensured that greater co-operation with the army started to evolve and the navy concentrated on blockading German ports in case of war.

But the price for this greater clarity about possible war plans was that the military talks with France were revealed in particularly alarming circumstances. Asquith compounded this by clumsily omitting Morley and Harcourt from the CID meeting, word of which soon leaked out to them and the rest of the cabinet.[68] The result was two tense cabinet meetings on 1 and 15 November 1911 which insisted on adopting a formula that ensured the military talks were not a binding commitment to help France.[69] But the talks did not stop. As Haldane said, his strategy emerged 'unhampered in any material point'.[70] Henry Wilson continued to produce detailed plans for the transport and disposition of the army in northern France. In effect, the cabinet had reached a compromise.

They had agreed that it would not be automatic that the British army would intervene on the side of France in the event of a German attack. The cabinet would make a decision if the event arose. But should the decision be in favour of sending the army to northern France this would be militarily feasible. The key pro-intervention figures were Grey, the architect of the pro-entente foreign policy, and the service ministers Haldane and Churchill. But it was clear they had the ultimate support of Asquith and Lloyd George, so most of the cabinet's powerful figures favoured the policy. Ranged against them were those like McKenna who were prepared to support France in the event of war, but preferred Britain to concentrate on naval operations; and the outright critics of the whole entente policy like Loreburn and Morley.

Relating this division to ideology is complex. The pro-interventionists undoubtedly saw their strategy as in the tradition of 'national interest' defence policy and consensus with the opposition. Though military contacts between Britain and France had hardly started in December 1905, Balfour and the Unionist leaders fully endorsed this policy when they learned of it in 1911.[71] Liberals who favoured intervention in a European conflict did not usually emphasise the consonance of their ideas with party ideology, but with these broader concepts. As A. C. Murray, Grey's parliamentary private secretary, put it, support for France in a crisis was merely 'common-sense and patriotism'. These were universal categories that conclusively justified intervention. To deny them was to cast doubt on a Liberal's sanity and the connection between his Liberalism and reality – to put him among the 'cranks'.[72] This downgrading of Liberal ideology was not a new development in the thinking of men like Murray – all the pro-interventionists at the highest level, with the unique but crucial exception of Lloyd George, were Liberal Imperialists.

On the other hand, for men like Morley and Loreburn, their dislike of the military discussions was an outcome of their distrust of Grey's foreign policy and their insistence on the importance of elements of Liberal ideology, especially the Cobdenite dislike of 'entangling' foreign commitments, in determining strategy. Loreburn had no objection to an entente with France, but protested at Grey's 'perversion of the friendly understanding with France into an alliance.'[73] This meant that Britain would be dragged into war for the sake of 'a purely French quarrel'.[74] As Morley said, supporting France and Russia was not 'worth to us the body of one Territorial [soldier]'.[75] Finally, while McKenna's role was undoubtedly partly determined by pique at his removal from the Admiralty in 1911, he also represented another strand in Liberal thinking, which disliked increasing the role of the army in British life and preferred to rely on the navy.[76] It was clear to some that Britain's six divisions could make little difference in a continental war and the pro-interventionist strategy pointed towards the raising of a huge army and conscription.[77]

This was a shrewd suspicion. By 1913 the pro-interventionists Churchill, Haldane, Seely, and Lloyd George were all openly declaring their support for conscription in the cabinet.[78] But they did not do so on the grounds that this was a particularly Liberal approach to defence. The nearest they came to an ideological justification was Churchill's contention that conscription was a matter of 'the right of the State' to defend itself and 'the duty of the citizen' to respond.[79] In other words, the 'rights' of the state could in this case take precedence over the liberties of the citizen. This bore some relationship to arguments that Liberals like Churchill were endorsing about the need for state intervention and organisation in the fields of taxation and social reform. It is not perhaps coincidental that the pro-intervention group in the cabinet were also staunch advocates of important advances in the state's role in society like the 1909 Budget.[80] After all they could hardly will policies like conscription without supporting the means to pay for it. This shared enthusiasm for the state's powers might help to explain Lloyd George's otherwise anomalous presence among the Liberal Imperialists on the issue of conscription (and possibly also a pro-entente foreign policy). But while an increase in the state's role in fighting poverty could be, and was, explicitly derived from Liberal traditions, this was never the case with conscription.[81] Before 1914 no leading Liberal dared to make his support for this policy public and the Liberal case for conscription remained unmade.

This was because conscription was something most Liberals could not accept, as they regarded the absence of compulsory military service as a fundamental liberty, akin to freedom of speech and parliamentary government.[82] The whole idea conjured up images of a military state, quite apart from its obvious expense and immense practical difficulties. This was not just something Liberals could ignore as an impossibility, though. The Edwardian era saw an immense growth in propaganda for conscription with the National Service League, headed by the ex-Commander-in-Chief, Lord Roberts, allegedly boasting 250,000 members by 1914.[83] Prominent generals and many Unionists, like Lord Curzon, were ardent advocates of conscription and bills on the subject appeared with some regularity in the Commons. The movement fed on the 'invasion scares' that were periodically whipped up before 1914, but it also had the aim of producing an army that could take part in a continental war.[84] McKenna's navalist position tapped into the deep Liberal hostility to this whole movement and represented to some extent a distinctive Liberal position on defence policy. But, ironically, it was a position that was also shared by much of the Unionist leadership. Balfour for one did not believe a conscript army was needed to save Britain from invasion as long as naval supremacy was maintained and many Unionists were wary of conscription as electorally unpopular and likely to lead to massive tax rises.[85] These views were pragmatic rather than principled, but they indicated the extent to which defence policy produced overlapping positions within and between Liberalism and Unionism and complicated the whole idea of distinctively 'Liberal' views on defence. However, in 1913 the Unionists finally moved to support compulsory military training in schools, though not for adults, and this did open up a gulf between the two parties on the role of the army in civilian life.[86] But the key difference between the parties remained their attitude to military intervention in a Franco-German war. While the Unionists favoured this unequivocally, the Liberal attitude remained undecided.[87]

However, defence policy was only partly about the army. In many ways the navy was just as controversial an area in party politics throughout the lifetime of the Liberal governments. This was because naval expenditure was rising so rapidly. In 1885 it made up less than 13 per cent of government expenditure and cost significantly less than the army. By 1913 the navy was accounting for nearly 25 per cent of all expenditure and far outstripped the army.[88] This was largely because of developments in naval technology, especially the design of the new dreadnought battleships, which could outgun any previous ship. Trends in naval expenditure therefore clashed directly with Liberal beliefs about the need to control spending on the armed forces. This produced some of the most embittered public disagreements within Edwardian Liberalism, as well as some of the most bruising cabinet rows. But the party survived them, if with some difficulty.

One of the most important reasons for this was that naval expenditure was not a constant problem for the government. In fact the period 1905–8 was something of a honeymoon for the relationship between the Admiralty and the Liberal party.[89] Navy estimates were able to remain below the peak of 1904–5 because the government built fewer dreadnoughts than had been envisaged in the 'Cawdor plan' bequeathed to them by the last Unionist Lord of the Admiralty. This policy was broadly, if somewhat reluctantly, endorsed by the Sea Lords on the grounds that foreign shipbuilding programmes had been disrupted as they wrestled with how to respond to the new dreadnoughts. Unionist criticism was also far from all-embracing, largely because Fisher, the First Sea Lord, and effective service head of the navy, reassured Balfour about Britain's continuing naval supremacy. The government remained committed in theory to the 'two power standard', in other words that the British navy should be larger than the next two biggest naval powers, while in practice interpreting this policy with some flexibility – just as the Unionists had. Until the spring of 1908 the cabinet were able both to satisfy some of the Liberal demands for retrenchment and pursue what was effectively a consensual policy on naval building.

But this situation was fragile. In 1906–7 a quarrel over the navy estimates was only narrowly avoided by Haldane's suggestion that the building of one dreadnought should be contingent on the outcome of that year's Hague conference.[90] In 1908 the consensus period came to an end, when German plans for increased naval construction produced Unionist demands for a response from Britain. Asquith postponed the issue by stating that if the Germans seemed to be carrying out their intentions in 1909, then the British estimates would be increased.[91] By early 1909 this was clearly the case and the long-predicted fissure (or 'seam' as C. F. G. Masternan called it) opened up in the cabinet on the issue of naval expenditure.[92] The 'economists' wished to commit the government to only four new dreadnoughts, while the 'navalists' insisted on six, with the full support of the Unionist opposition and the Admiralty.[93] The difference was both several million pounds and symbolic. Should the Liberal ideology of retrenchment have any bearing on naval policy, or should it be subordinate to more widely defined considerations of national security? Once again an important division within Liberalism was perceived to revolve around the views of the Liberal Imperialists. Grey, Haldane, Runciman and Sydney Buxton were in the forefront of the 'navalists' and all had a Liberal Imperialist background. As Grey stated, on this issue, whatever Liberals had said about the virtues of retrenchment, 'promises must be subordinate to national safety'.[94] Many other members of the cabinet were aghast at the proposed scale of the expenditure and Asquith declared there was 'at any rate a temporary revival of the old pro-Boer animus' against the Liberal Imperialist members of the cabinet.[95] Asquith, despite his Liberal Imperialist past, seems to have sided more with the 'economists', though his primary aim was to patch up a compromise between the two groups.[96]

This division was replicated on the Liberal backbenches. Mounting dissatisfaction with the naval estimates had been apparent for some time and 136 MPs had signed a critical motion as early as 4 November 1907, while 82 'navalists' had produced a counter-motion on 19 February 1908.[97] This split was repeated in 1909 with 143 MPs lining up behind a call for reduced expenditure.[98] The vertical nature of the division in the party, from top to bottom, was especially threatening. Both groups on the backbenches could look to supporters in the cabinet to provide leadership and a collapse of the government was widely predicted in political circles.[99] Naval expenditure was the only important conflict on which this situation appeared, so it is worth reflecting on why the battle proved so divisive. On the 'navalist' side the issue was a test case of Liberalism's willingness to accept the supremacy of the agenda of 'national security'. The navy mattered far more than the army in this because it was the key to Britain's security from invasion and its ability to maintain its empire and world-wide trade network. Without a dominant navy, Britain's national survival could not be ensured. On the 'economist' side, there were a number of points of view sheltering under the banner of retrenchment. Some MPs insisted that naval expenditure was destroying Liberalism's historic role of holding down taxation.[100] In early 1909 the situation appeared especially critical as a large budget deficit was looming. This sense of crisis was reinforced by suspicions about Grey's foreign policy and the 'expert' advice from the Admiralty. The 'economists' feared that a great programme of naval building would ruin relations with Germany and set the two nations on a collision course, just as Grey's support of France was doing. Such a programme was totally unnecessary because, as Lloyd George wrote to Churchill, 'the Admirals are procuring false information to frighten us'.[101] The whole 'scare' was the result of interested parties imposing on the general public – another long-standing theme in Liberal rhetoric, but one that was reinvigorated by concerns about armament manufacturers and their connections to government policy across Europe.[102] By refusing to accept the official view that six new dreadnoughts were necessary many Liberals were registering their protest against the idea of a consensual defence policy which was determined without reference to Liberalism.

These positions produced interminable discussions in the cabinet in early 1909. But Asquith was not to be beaten. His ever-ingenious mind found a compromise – on 24 February 1909 he suggested four dreadnoughts should be built immediately and another four later in the year if they were needed.[103] This resolved the cabinet deadlock and prevented a split by assuring both parties they would obtain their objectives. But the truly significant developments were still to come. On 16 March 1909 the estimates were presented to the Commons.[104] Immediately, the bipartisan approach to naval spending collapsed, when Balfour demanded all eight dreadnoughts be built – the start of the famous 'we want eight, and we won't wait' campaign launched by the Tories.[105] But criticism of the estimates from the Liberal benches suffered an even more devastating blow and ultimately only 28 Liberals voted against the government's plans. Not only did backbench rebels lack cabinet leadership after the compromise of 24 February, but many felt the government had genuinely stood out against Tory demands for the 'eight', thus establishing a distinctive Liberal position on naval expenditure.[106] But, even more significantly, Asquith announced on 16 March that Britain was in danger of being outbuilt by the German naval programme.[107] The critics' position folded because most of them felt unable to oppose the cabinet when they were assured that Britain's national survival was imperilled.[108] It was one thing to be told this by the Tory press and the admirals; quite another to be solemnly assured of its truth by the Liberal leadership. In these circumstances, the need for more naval building was accepted by the party. This was at least easier than swallowing increased expenditure on the army. Liberals could comfort themselves that the navy was (at least in a European context) a purely defensive force. As Campbell-Bannerman had famously put it 'The sea power of this country implies no challenge to any single State or group of States.'[109] Moreover, expanding the navy did not risk militarizing civil society in the same way that increasing the army's role might. It was possible to think of relying on a great navy for defence rather than a great army as a specifically Liberal defence policy and this was certainly implied in McKenna's position in the cabinet. No doubt he felt it was his departmental duty as Civil Lord of the Admiralty to argue for more dreadnoughts, but he had no background in Liberal Imperialism and his determination to argue that any future war against Germany must be a primarily naval conflict could be seen as a development of his views on the need to increase naval expenditure.

After the crisis of March 1909 the situation was delicately balanced. But it was confirmed in July 1909 that the four contingent ships would be built, in response to the newly-announced Austrian and Italian dreadnought plans.[110] The eight ship programme of 1909–10 proved the start of a massive scheme of building, far beyond anything envisaged by the Unionists in 1905. Five dreadnoughts were built in 1910–11 and seven in 1911–12 (two paid for by the Dominions). In 1912 Churchill committed the government to a 60 per cent superiority over Germany's dreadnoughts and to build two ships for every extra dreadnought constructed in Germany. These developments effectively restored the bipartisan approach to naval building of 1905–8, leaving only minor differences between the Liberal and Unionist front benches.[111] Effectively, the 'navalists' had won. But the Liberal party did not split. Not only were there no cabinet divisions as serious as those of 1908–9, but only 37 Liberal MPs protested in the Commons against the decision of July 1909.[112] On the backbenches a group of 'irreconcilables' developed, much as on the issue of Grey's foreign policy, and 27 MPs opposed the estimates in 1913, for instance, and 35 in 1914. But they were a small, well-defined group, rather than representatives of an issue that split the parliamentary party down the middle. Sir John Brunner was forced to take his anti-naval expenditure campaign outside the Commons to the forum of the NLF – a sure sign of lack of support at the centre.

The cabinet were anxious that this outcome should be presented to the party as the inevitable product of concerns for national security after all other avenues had been explored. The 'economists' had to be satisfied with this continued sensitivity to their feelings – witnessed by the Haldane mission to Germany in 1912 and Churchill's proposal for a 'holiday' in shipbuilding in 1913.[113] But there was no disguising the fact that the promise of a distinctive Liberal policy on naval spending had proved a mirage. The reason why this did not lead to an even greater explosion in the party than the crisis of 1908–9 was the budget presented by Lloyd George on 29 April 1909. This finally revealed that Lloyd George had abandoned his position as an economiser, thus depriving the cabinet of its leading exponent of reduced naval expenditure.[114] But he had also produced a budget which destroyed the Liberal party's position as the party of 'economy', by making substantial rises in direct taxation and total expenditure central to Liberal party policy. In the political atmosphere of 1909–10, to reject this course and the 'People's Budget' was to cease to be a Liberal. The rhetoric of retrenchment was no longer available to the party and made no sense in describing their own position. When Neal Blewett analysed the election addresses of Liberal candidates at the January and December 1910 elections he found no significant mention of retrenchment.[115]

Furthermore, those Liberals who feared the navy would soak up the funds available for social reform could be reassured that there was plenty of money for both pensions and dreadnoughts, while those who worried about expenditure could focus their concerns on social welfare quite as much as the navy. These factors drained some of the explosive potential out of naval expenditure as an issue. Its most serious recurrence was in 1913–14 when Lloyd George, as Chancellor of the Exchequer, and

Churchill, as Civil Lord of the Admiralty, fell out over the naval estimates. This episode revealed that there was still considerable unease in the cabinet and among MPs at the ever-spiralling estimates. In December 1913 nearly a hundred MPs signed a letter protesting to Asquith at the scale of naval expenditure.[116] But once the two main protagonists had reached a compromise the issue again faded away and the usual core of Liberal MPs was left to protest against rising expenditure. The rest had become accustomed to accepting the government's plea that the country's defence was at stake. The 1909 estimates had established the precedent for Liberals that Britain had to outbuild Germany for its own safety and in 1913–14 Churchill was merely repeating the same argument. By 1914 the issue had lost the ability to wrench the party apart. At least, Liberals could comfort themselves, the big navy they had created was a powerful argument against the need for conscription.

Colonial policy

When the Liberals entered office in 1905, colonial policy was widely believed to be their most difficult problem. Though Liberal and Tory governments had behaved very much alike when it came to expanding and governing the empire, some Liberals had opposed new colonial acquisitions throughout the 1880s and 1890s and the party's attitude to the Boer war in 1899–1902 had threatened to split it apart, producing opposing Liberal Imperialist and 'pro-Boer' groups.[117] Once again, this was a matter of whether there should be a distinctive Liberal approach to the empire, or whether ideas of the national interest should take precedence. The Liberal Imperialist strand in the party had made rapid headway during the Boer war partly because they could argue that opposition to imperial expansion was electoral suicide and partly because they seemed to be urging the party to come to terms with the inescapable reality of European domination of Asia and Africa.[118] But the sceptics about imperialism had also been reinvigorated by the experience of enduring together the scale of public hostility evident in 1899–1900, and the subsequent lengthy, expensive and internationally criticised campaign against Boer guerrillas in 1900–2 convinced many that they had been right to stand out from the earlier public hysteria or 'Mafficking'.[119] Liberal critiques of empire were also becoming more sophisticated. In the late nineteenth century, anti-imperialists like Labouchere had criticised the expense of empire-building, argued that Britain gained nothing from new colonies and claimed that British conquest did little for native populations.[120] But J. A. Hobson had elaborated these ideas during the Boer war into an impressive economic analysis of imperialism as the policy of a few special interest groups looking for investments abroad.[121] The Boer war also convinced some Liberals that imperial expansion was deeply harmful to Britain itself, producing an increasingly aggressive, irrational and militarised population at home – something Hobson evaluated in *The Psychology of Jingoism* (1901).

These entrenched positions had been reflected in organisational divisions and personal antipathies at the top of the Liberal party. The Liberal Imperialists had founded a number of groups within the party, most importantly the Liberal League in 1902, which maintained its own funds and organisers.[122] Their leaders, especially Haldane and Grey, maintained open contempt for Campbell-Bannerman and there was constant talk of recalling Rosebery to the leadership. In 1901–2 there were mutterings about party realignments, with the Liberal Imperialists forming the nucleus of a new 'centre' group in politics. These developments, however intriguing, were cut short by the re-emergence of 'old' political divisions between Liberals and Tories, especially over the 1902 Education Act and tariff reform. Liberals rallied to defend the causes of religious equality and free trade. But party unity was also made more possible by the rapid decline of disagreements over the empire.[123] With the acquisition of the Transvaal and the Orange Free State in 1902 the empire seemed to almost everyone to be complete. Almost the whole of Asia, Africa and the Pacific had been divided between the European powers. There was simply very little more territory to acquire. This in itself resolved many of the disputes of the 1880s and 1890s as most of the 'new' empire could hardly be returned to independence as native power structures had been severely disrupted and these territories would merely become the easy prey of other colonial empires. Just as importantly, the adoption of tariff reform by the Unionists after 1903 gave the Liberals a distinctive concept of the empire to unite around. The Tories insisted that tariff reform would draw the empire together into one great trading bloc. By adhering to free trade the Liberals necessarily rejected this vision of closer integration through economic policy in favour of the existing ties of imperial rule, trade and sentiment that bound the empire together. The Liberal ideal became, in effect, the existing empire of the early twentieth century; one that was fairly loosely bound together, did not prove a drain on the mother country's resources and did not occupy the central role that it did in Unionist ideology. It was especially notable that Liberal MPs overwhelmingly turned down the idea of formally recognising Empire Day in 1910.[124]

This may not have been a very exciting ideal, but it was one the party could quietly unite around.

Thus there were already clear signs by 1905 that the empire would not be the millstone it had been for the party in the late nineteenth-century. But it left unanswered the question of whether there was a distinctive Liberal idea of what the empire should be, beyond the defence of the status quo against the innovation of tariff reform. There were, after all, strong pressures for continuity in colonial policy, just as there were in defence and foreign policy. The colonial office was still a relatively modest affair and had little day to day control over the actions of colonial governors, let alone the ministers of self-governing territories.[125] The rhetoric of 'national interest' was deployed frequently when discussing imperial affairs to justify congruence of opinion between Unionists and Liberals.[126] But some aspects of imperial policy offered the Liberals scope to differ from their predecessors in significant ways.

The most obvious of these areas related to those colonies dominated by settlers of European descent and especially to South Africa. There were some scores to pay off from the past and these were attended to first. Lord Milner, the Unionist High Commissioner in South Africa who was widely suspected of provoking the Boer war, received a very lukewarm defence against a motion of censure from the Liberal back-benches. The 'Chinese labour' that Milner had brought in to work the mines was phased out after the notorious role the issue had played in the 1906 elections.[127] But most importantly, the Liberal Colonial Secretary, Elgin, and Campbell-Bannerman decisively rejected the previous Unionist policy on the future of South Africa. The Unionists' proposed 'Lyttelton constitution' had suggested that the defeated Boer republics of the Transvaal and the Orange Free State would receive only very limited self-government in the immediate future. To the Unionists the Boers were the defeated enemy and would have to accept subjugation to British rule. But, under the Liberals, the two republics obtained full internal autonomy in 1906–7.[128] As Churchill put it, 'We on this side know that if British dominion is to endure in South Africa it must endure with the assent of the Dutch [Boers] as well of the British'.[129] This was a huge gamble, though one that paid off when the Boer leaders agreed to co-operate in the formation of a new Union of South Africa with Cape Colony and Natal in 1909–10. To Liberals this represented not only a determination to reverse Unionist policy but a commitment to self-government, rather than central control, in the colonies of settlement that the Unionists could not match. On this issue the Liberal Imperialist members of the cabinet had long been in full agreement with their colleagues. Haldane had argued in 1904 of the South African republics, 'Our duty was to make them self-governing as soon as we can.'[130] This was because, while Liberal Imperialists accepted the Unionist case that war was necessary to defeat the Boers, they could not agree to the idea of prolonged authoritarian rule over a people who were accustomed to run their own affairs through elected institutions. At this point Liberal Imperialists acknowledged their Liberalism had to take precedence over their Imperialism, because self-government was such a central tenet of Liberalism. If a politician did not accept the virtues of elections and parliaments over rule by proconsuls like Milner it was doubtful if he could continue to describe himself as a Liberal.

For many Liberals, this South African policy of local control rather than rule from the centre was also reflected in their attitude to formal links between Britain and the colonies of settlement. The Unionists had proposed in Lyttelton's Despatch of December 1904 that the periodic conferences of colonial premiers should become an Imperial Council, with the British prime minister as its president and a permanent commission.[131] Elgin dissociated the Liberals from this approach and instigated a weaker version of these proposals, which removed the connotations of an embryo imperial authority that so excited many Tories. Instead, Elgin set up a dominions section in the colonial office and agreed the colonial premiers would meet once every four years.[132] Later on the Liberals refused to remove colonial office control of the dominions section, to give any role to a committee of colonial High Commissioners in London or to appoint permanent colonial representatives to the CID.[133] The route to imperial federation was firmly blocked, to the distress of many Unionists. Instead the Liberals retained the model of *ad hoc* co-operation between the self-governing colonies and Britain. Again, Liberal Imperialists had long accepted this approach, fearing that tightening the imperial bonds would only result in quarrels and strains between Britain and the colonies of settlement.[134] This approach was reinforced by the Liberals' determination to avoid any structures that would pave the way for the introduction of tariffs and imperial preference.

The question of whether there was a distinctively Liberal approach to the directly ruled colonies which were dominated by their native peoples is much more complex. The largest and most controversial of these colonies was India, whose governance raised some key questions in the Edwardian era. The central Liberal initiatives were the 'Morley-Minto' reforms of 1907–9, named after the Liberal Secretary of State for India, John Morley, and his (Unionist-appointed) Viceroy.[135] Essentially, the reforms increased Indian participation in the government of India. Morley appointed two

Indians to the Secretary's Council in London in 1907 and one Indian to the Viceroy's executive in 1909. The Indian Councils Act of 1909 ensured that non-officials, many of whom were elected, were a majority in all provincial councils and that these councils could discuss all aspects of the provincial budget. But these reforms could be seen in a number of ways. They could be represented as part of a consensual approach to India in British politics. After all, the last major reform in Indian representation, the 1892 Indian Councils Act, was the work of the Unionists and the Morley-Minto reforms built on these earlier institutions.[136] Moreover, Lord Curzon, perhaps India's most controversial Viceroy, had been recalled by the Unionist government in 1905 and this could be seen as an indication that Tory policy was already turning against Curzon's style of heavy-handed intervention in India's economy, society and foreign policy, which had provoked considerable unrest. The Morley-Minto reforms in some ways continued this reaction by seeking a more collaborative and less confrontational approach to ruling India. Moreover, the limits of these reforms need to be emphasised. While they offered Indians a role at the provincial level, they retained the official majority in the central Indian legislature, while Indian presence in central government remained largely token. Congress was also dismayed by the institution of separate Muslim electorates for the provincial councils – something that was widely seen as a policy of 'divide and rule' and a concession to reactionary elements in the Indian administration.[137] The reforms were accompanied by restrictions on freedom of the press, like the Press Act of 1910, and executive deportations and internments to counteract armed resistance. These contraventions of basic civil liberties appalled many backbench Liberal MPs, and Morley sometimes had to rely on Unionist help to fend off this criticism.[138] Finally, Morley did not intend his policies to pave the way for Indian independence in the foreseeable future – indeed he sometimes doubted whether representative institutions could be exported to Asia at all. As he wrote to Minto, 'Not one whit more than you do I think it desirable or possible, or even conceivable, to adapt English political institutions to the nations who inhabit India.'[139]

However, this is not the whole story. While the reforms were always presented as a 'Morley-Minto' collaboration, perhaps to disarm opposition by suggesting their consensual, administrative nature, they were clearly instigated by Morley. Left to his own devices it is not clear that Minto would have agreed to take this direction. Indeed he, like Curzon, wished to place much more emphasis on the role of the Indian princely rulers in developing Indian institutions and to outflank middle class 'politicians and agitators'.[140] Morley effectively ruled this out. Similarly, it is not clear that the Unionists would have produced any reforms on the lines of those enacted in 1909. Curzon was resolutely hostile to the Councils Act and while Lansdowne conceded that reform was necessary 'he showed a pretty direct antipathy to the whole thing'.[141] Moreover, while Morley supported the Indian administration in its suspension of civil liberties when dealing with 'terrorists', he disliked many of its actions and successfully pressed to modify some of them.[142] Thus it can at least be argued that there was a distinctive Liberal approach to India, which involved adopting a more collaborative and representative approach, though not necessarily believing that Indian self-government was likely to result in the near future. Those, if any, who believed this on the Liberal side were a very small group indeed. Most of the concerns raised by Liberal backbenchers centred on the idea that practices that they disapproved of in Britain should not be permitted in India – hence the significance of debates about temperance, the export of opium to China and the operation of legalised brothels.[143] In other words, many Liberals could not accept the argument that because India was a different society, different standards of morality in legislation could be permitted. This at least contained the germ of the idea that India and England should be governed in comparable ways, with due concern for local opinion and civil liberties. Morley hinted at this himself. When he told Minto that English institutions were inappropriate in India he went on to say 'the *spirit* of English institutions is a different thing, and it is a thing that we cannot escape.... The party of ascendancy fought that spirit in Ireland for a good many generations; but at last ascendancy has broken down.... Cast-iron bureaucracy won't go on for ever, we may be sure of that'.[144]

No other part of the empire raised the question of constitutional developments for native peoples in quite the same way. The nearest parallel was Egypt, which was not formally a colony and where Grey's directions to the British agents showed a good deal of similarity to that of his Unionist predecessors.[145] Over most of Africa, the question was to what extent the empire was protecting the interests of native Africans. Some Liberals had developed a distinctive approach to this problem in the 1890s, based on British relations with West Africa. It grew out of a combination of the commercial interests of Liverpool traders, the early ethnographic work of Mary Kingsley and the propagandist talents of E. D. Morel.[146] Essentially, it insisted that the key issue was to avoid making concessions to monopolistic European companies to develop African resources. Instead, Africans should be left to develop the land as peasant proprietors, ruled by their chiefs in a system that later became known as 'indirect rule'. Above all, Africans should not be forced, either directly through slavery, or indirectly through taxes and economic pressure, to work for European interests. This argument tied in very strongly with the historic Liberal antipathy to slavery and was advanced forcefully by Liberal pressure groups like the Aborigines Protection Society. All of these ideas seemed to be validated when the abuses by rubber companies licensed by Leopold II to work in the Congo were exposed in the early 1900s, precipitating a massive international campaign of condemnation.

However, by 1906 it was doubtful how distinctively Liberal these ideas were any more as they became part of the political consensus and the official outlook of the colonial office. It grew increasingly suspicious of concessions in West Africa, even refusing one to the eminent Liberal and philanthropist, William Lever.[147] In Nigeria, Frederick Lugard raised indirect rule to the status of an ideology. But at the same time, Liberal governments were forced to recognise that these policies clashed with their desire to devolve power to the colonies of settlement and leave them to conduct their own affairs. Reluctantly, Elgin conceded the colonial office could not prevent the exclusion of non-whites from the Union of South Africa parliament, nor the suppression of Zulu autonomy by the government of Natal.[148] To try and do so would wreck South African autonomy and federation. This was very much the colonial office line, too. Thus it was difficult to determine if there was a distinctive Liberal approach to Africa's non-white races by 1905–14 other than the orthodoxies of the administrators.

In external affairs, the Liberal party faced repeated internal clashes between powerful ideologies of national interest and national security and attempts to apply types of Liberalism to government policy. This was profoundly distressing for many Liberals and produced much soul-searching. Grey successfully avoided all attempts to make him pursue a distinctive foreign policy, though he was able to convince many Liberals that his line was not incompatible with some versions of Liberalism. In the arena of defence, Liberals could perhaps believe that the expansion of the navy was a particularly Liberal policy, though it was an aim shared by their Tory opponents, and one that had caused many problems for Liberalism. Beneath the surface, huge rifts existed in the cabinet about whether and how Britain should intervene in a continental war. Only in the empire was there much that was unequivocally 'Liberal', especially the rejection of tariff reform and imperial federation. Other than perhaps in India, the Liberals found themselves as defenders of the status quo against Tory innovations to revive Britain's power in the world. Ironically, while Liberals in the late nineteenth century had been the party suspected of undermining 'official' views of Britain's relations with the world, by 1914 men like Grey, Haldane and Harcourt stood for the orthodoxies of their departments against both some of their own supporters and the Tory opposition.

3
Liberals and the United Kingdom

The background to Irish home rule

The Liberal party believed itself to be a party that was committed to the principle that nations had the right to govern themselves. This association of liberalism and nationalism was the result of the party's memory of events in the early and mid-nineteenth century. Then, many Liberals (though not necessarily Liberal governments) had avidly supported the unification of Italy and Germany and independence for Greece, Poland and Hungary.[1] It had seemed unproblematic to associate the creation of nation states with liberal ideals. In all these situations, nationalists were struggling against what seemed to be reactionary and intolerant regimes that Liberals could only despise, and asserting the right of peoples to govern themselves, rather than live under the despotism of autocratic and obscurantist regimes like the petty princelings of pre-unification Italy or the Tsarist or Ottoman empires. Nationalism as a political programme appeared to be the twin of liberalism. This was a position to which most Liberals still adhered in 1914, bolstered by their interpretation of nineteenth-century European history.[2] But its application to Ireland caused the party more difficulties than any other issue before the First World War.

In some ways this was to be expected. The creation of nation states had not always fitted in neatly with British interests and this had created problems for the attitudes of the Liberal party. Gladstone's career exemplified these difficulties. He had returned as a leading Liberal in the late 1870s, after a temporary retirement, at the head of a campaign protesting about the Conservative government's support of the Ottoman empire as a bulwark against Russian expansion, even though Ottoman troops had massacred Christian subjects in the Balkans.[3]

Gladstone became associated with the idea that the Turks should be cleared out of Europe, 'bag and baggage' and new nation states like Bulgaria should be created in their place. But this caused intense disagreements within Liberalism as it was feared the new states would fall prey to Russian influence. When Gladstone was back in office he sanctioned the occupation of Egypt in 1882 to protect British interests there, even though this meant suppressing a nationalist uprising by force.[4] Again, this was deeply controversial within Liberalism and John Bright, another icon of Liberalism, resigned from Gladstone's cabinet, rather than accept this policy.

These contradictions within Liberal approaches to nationalism came to a crisis point in a particularly devastating way in 1886 over Irish home rule.[5] The British political system had been rocked in the 1880s by the combination in Ireland of agrarian protest and political nationalism. In 1885 Parnell's Nationalist party won 85 of the 103 Irish seats and held the balance of power at Westminster between Conservatives and Liberals. At the end of 1885 it leaked out that Gladstone had become convinced of the justice and necessity of conceding to the Nationalists' major demand and instituting a form of home rule for Ireland. He formed an administration with Nationalist support in 1886 and brought forward what became the first Irish home rule bill. The effect on the Liberal party was devastating. About one-third of Liberal MPs rebelled and joined with the Conservatives in voting the measure down. Gladstone dissolved parliament and fought an election on the home rule issue. The Liberal dissidents coalesced into a new party, the Liberal Unionists, who contested the election in alliance with the Tories and in later years gradually merged with their larger ally. The result was a crushing defeat for the Gladstonians, who were reduced to 191 MPs. They did not win a majority of seats again until 1906.

This disaster coloured all further Liberal thinking on home rule, because it convinced most Liberals that the issue had no appeal to the British electorate and was deeply divisive for Liberals. Its unpopularity seemed to be demonstrated by the 1886 election results, but its divisiveness was more complicated to unravel. Undoubtedly, this was linked to the way in which Gladstone dealt with home rule.[6] He gave no indication that his mind was moving in this direction during the 1885 elections and very few Liberal candidates had endorsed home rule in their election addresses. His intentions emerged gradually and haphazardly and he took few in the parliamentary party or even his cabinet into his confidence. When the home rule bill was defeated in the Commons, Gladstone did not retire, drop the measure or even go into opposition to allow the party to regroup. By calling an election on this one issue, he solidified the divide in his party, drove the dissident.Liberals into the arms of the Tories and decisively identified the Liberal party with home rule. In a sense, attitudes to home rule became enmeshed with attitudes to Gladstone. Liberals who trusted him became home rulers. Those who did not, or simply saw him as a rival, or an 'old man in a hurry', became Liberal Unionists.

But the Liberal division was about more than Gladstone. It was also about the nature of Liberalism. Gladstone was able to take most Liberals with him over home rule, not just because he was a revered (and ancient) Liberal leader, but because he was able to convince his party that home rule was an authentically Liberal approach to Irish issues. Fundamentally, he suggested that the Irish were a nation seeking to govern their own affairs, just like the many continental nations whose cause Liberals had supported (Norway and Hungary seem to have been particularly on his mind).[7] The separate Irish identity within the United Kingdom deserved to be respected and home rule would do this, while reconciling Ireland to remaining part of the wider unit. This approach linked in with the world-view of many nonconformists that it was up to each community, just as much as each congregation, to choose its own path and with current academic thinking about the continued significance of the past in determining collective identities and the need to take account of these forms in government.[8] The demand for home rule, in this approach, was entirely compatible with Liberal principles of liberty and popular consent on which government should be based. If Liberals did not accept home rule, they would be driven to rule Ireland by coercion and the suspension of civil liberties in order to suppress popular discontent and no Liberal could tolerate this outcome.[9] This was an extremely powerful argument and one that the majority of Liberals could accept.

However, it was opposed by a significant minority of Liberals. For some, these arguments could not be allowed to override Britain's national interests, which should prevail over party ideology, just as they had done over the invasion of Egypt in 1882. To these Liberals, home rule was merely a stage on the way to separation and the creation of an Irish state which would potentially be a hostile neighbour in a vital strategic position. Moreover, it would be a symbol of Britain's weakness to other powers and might begin the process of disintegrating the empire from the centre.[10] At the very least, Ireland might impose tariffs that would harm British trade or the country might be so impoverished by home rule that destitute Irish migrants flooded into Britain.

But in addition, home rule divided Liberals about what was the appropriately Liberal response to Irish demands. This was because it seemed clear that Irish nationalism was not a liberal movement and a home rule Ireland might not be a liberal state. Irish nationalism was very closely associated with the Catholic church and might be intolerant of Protestant minorities. As the Nonconformist paper, the *Christian World*, warned, 'as soon as the Catholics have their own Parliament, the bitterest persecution will commence'.[11] The Nationalist party was widely believed to intimidate political opponents and to settle arguments with sticks and fists and there were doubts whether it would preserve civil liberties in an Irish state it would seek to dominate. Even a committed home ruler, like Robert Reid, the future Lord Chancellor, warned 'If I could believe in the honesty and purpose of the Parnellites I should feel very happy. What I fear is that they would use the Executive power, if they got it, to inaugurate a reign of terror in Ireland'.[12] Moreover, Irish nationalism seemed to have little respect for the rule of law and in its 'land war' against Irish landowners had been connected to everything from encouraging the withholding of rent to cattle maiming and even murder. In contrast, the British state in Ireland promoted liberal values. It upheld religious and civil liberty and enforced a fair system of justice. The Irish were not the equivalent of the Greeks in the 1820s with Britain as the Ottoman empire. Instead the British state was like the Italian state after the Risorgimento, confronted with a 'backward' region, like the Italian South, which required liberal values to be enforced upon it. Ireland had to be saved from 'priests and Fenians and professional agitators supported by the votes of an ignorant peasantry'.[13] In this reading, the Irish were not a nation, but part of the wider United Kingdom, and their identity would merge into that state in time, just as Scottishness had become accommodated to Britishness.

This range of arguments ensured that it was not just cautious Liberals, exemplified by the Marquess of Hartington, who deserted Liberalism in 1886, but many Liberals whose views on other issues were indistinguishable from those who remained with Gladstone.[14] The division of 1886 broke many Liberal friendships and even fractured family ties. A. E. Pease, Liberal MP for York, claimed 'families were broken up, fathers and sons ceased to speak to each other, and brothers were at daggers drawn'.[15] He was speaking from experience – his uncle and a cousin were Liberal Unionist MPs after 1885, while he, his father and younger brother all sat in the Commons as Liberals. Home rule became a deeply sensitive subject for Liberals, associated with division and failure, and anti-home rule sentiments continued to have some appeal in the party. Gladstone's continued dominance kept Ireland to the fore, though, and a second home rule bill was attempted in 1893, only to be rejected by the House of Lords. But from this moment the party started to retreat on the issue. Gladstone's colleagues refused to launch a campaign against the Lords over Irish home rule. After Gladstone retired in 1894, the new Liberal premier, Rosebery, suggested that home rule would only be enacted when there was a clear majority for it in England – as there had not been in the 1892 election.[16] At the next election in 1895 home rule proved to be only one of the issues promoted by the Liberal leadership.[17] Then, in 1899, the new chief whip, Gladstone's son Herbert, persuaded the leadership that home rule should not be promoted at the next election as a policy that Liberals were committed to enact in the near future – certainly not in the next parliament.[18]

Even this did not prove enough of a watering-down of the home rule commitment for some, though. The Boer war produced another crisis in the party about attitudes to Ireland. The years 1899–1902 saw the height of popular imperial sentiment in Britain and some debate about closer union between Britain and the colonies of settlement. Home rule seemed out of touch with these ideas and even potentially treacherous as the Nationalists loudly sided with the Boers. Rosebery, having retired from the leadership in 1896, returned to politics in 1901 to demand that Liberals not only embrace imperialism as the creed of the day but adopt a 'clean slate' for domestic policies – in particular he implied, if not quite stated, that home rule should be abandoned.[19] This caused uproar among Liberals, as Rosebery was effectively asking the party to repudiate the last fifteen years of its history. He received the backing of a number of prominent MPs and peers, but not of Asquith, Grey and Haldane, the front-line Liberal Imperialist politicians who had supported the Unionist government over the Boer war, and whom Rosebery had hoped to recruit. This was a crucial moment for Liberalism because it ensured that Liberal Imperialism became associated with a cautious attitude to home rule, rather than its outright rejection. Its leaders adhered to a formula worked out by the ingenious Asquith, that the party should take a 'step by step' approach to home rule.[20] This meant offering the Nationalists a series of concessions, like administrative devolution, short of home rule, but not ruling out home rule for the more distant future. Campbell-Bannerman stuck to the policy suggested by Herbert Gladstone in 1899 that home rule was Liberal policy but not an immediate issue. The three positions provided the substance of the main inter-party argument in 1902–5 until finally

Campbell-Bannerman adopted the 'step by step' strategy in his speech at Stirling on 23 November 1905 to unite Liberals for the next election.[21]

There was an air of unreality about the debate, though, as Rosebery's view was clearly a minority one and Asquith and Campbell-Bannerman's position had much in common. The bitterness and prolonged nature of the controversy said much about how it had become entangled with struggles over the leadership of the party and the extreme sensitivity of Liberals about home rule once Rosebery publicly opened the issue up again in 1901. It was clear that most Liberals remained unenthusiastic about home rule given its painful role in the party's history. But only a small group were prepared to repudiate the policy altogether. This was because it was still one of the defining policies of the Liberal party – after 1886 to fail to support home rule was to cease to be a Liberal and to become a Liberal Unionist and ally of Conservatism. It also meant repenting Gladstone's and the party's actions since 1886 – what Campbell-Bannerman contemptuously called the policy of the 'white sheet' – and accepting that Ireland might have to be governed by coercion rather than consent.[22] Instead, Campbell-Bannerman insisted Liberals must acknowledge that home rule was an important expression of their belief in 'the virtues and efficacy of self-government' and 'the appreciation of national sentiment.' Gladstone's arguments about the importance of recognising Irish nationality were quite as important in the 1900s as in 1886. Ireland was still dominated by Nationalism despite Unionist attempts to weaken the movement's hold and it could be argued only home rule would reconcile Ireland to the empire. Even more practically, the party needed the support of Irish voters in Britain. So, in the end, it proved relatively easy for Campbell-Bannerman to unite the leadership around the 'step by step' policy of no home rule in the next parliament, but some measure of devolution. Rosebery's final attempt to split Asquith, Grey and Haldane from this agreement, with his Bodmin speech of 25 November 1905 against home rule, failed and the party went into the 1906 election clustered under the 'step by step' banner. About 10 per cent of Liberal candidates repudiated home rule in their election addresses and another 6–7 per cent declared unequivocally in its favour as an immediate objective.[23] Everyone else, including all the leaders, played a variant on Campbell-Bannerman's formula.

Rosebery was unable to persuade his party to abandon home rule and draw Liberal policy on Ireland into line with Unionist policy. But, ironically, Liberal and Unionist policies on Ireland had grown closer together anyway by the time the Liberals took office in 1905. Home rule remained the great divide between the parties, but this was something the Liberals did not intend to implement in the near future. Some Unionists, though, had become interested, like the Liberals, in the idea of Irish self-government that fell short of home rule. The Unionists had passed power at county council level to the Nationalists through the 1898 Irish Local Government Act. In 1904–5 the Irish Secretary, George Wyndham, and his permanent under-secretary, Sir Antony MacDonnell, became embroiled in a scheme to introduce a form of devolution into Irish government.[24] The policy caused a huge controversy and Wyndham's resignation, but when James Bryce took office in December 1905 as the Liberals' Irish Secretary, he inherited MacDonnell as head of the Irish civil service and MacDonnell's ideas could provide one basis on which to begin planning the as yet undefined first step of the Liberals' 'step by step' devolution policy. Indeed, some Liberals had been happy to give the impression during the 1906 election that their Irish policy would merely be a continuation of the MacDonnell-Wyndham scheme.[25]

MacDonnell's first draft proposals showed a remarkable continuity with his scheme of 1904. He had then proposed a financial council of 12 elected and 12 nominated members. On 3 February 1906 he presented Bryce with a plan for an executive council of 20 indirectly elected and ten nominated members to advise the lord lieutenant and oversee some aspects of Irish administration.[26] MacDonnell's idea was to persuade moderate Irishmen of wealth and standing to co-operate in governing Ireland and to build up a less radical alternative to the Nationalists. He was also keen to ensure Unionist co-operation and produce a scheme that could pass the House of Lords. Unfortunately for him, a Liberal Irish administration could not just acquiesce in his approach. In direct contrast to the Unionists, the Liberals' intention was to govern Ireland in co-operation with the Nationalists, thus ensuring that even if there was no home rule bill, Ireland would be ruled with the consent of its elected leaders. As Campbell-Bannerman had stated, in Ireland Liberals could not ignore 'the popular will constitutionally expressed through the people's representatives'.[27] Campbell-Bannerman had seen Redmond in November 1905 and promised him administrative devolution, no reduction in Ireland's representation in the Commons and consideration for Catholic education interests, in return for Nationalist help in returning Liberal candidates in Britain.[28] Bryce had continued this policy by assuring the prominent Nationalist, John Dillon, that the devolution proposals would be shown to the Irish leaders. When they saw the lines MacDonnell was working on in October 1906 they were horrified and pressurised the cabinet committee overseeing the bill to amend it and produce a scheme that promised much more popular control and bore some resemblance to a proto-parliament.[29]

The committee obliged, suggesting a council of 100–120 members, directly elected by the parliamentary voters. In cabinet, though, the issue proved divisive. Asquith, Grey and Haldane, the Liberal Imperialist proponents of the 'step by step' policy, argued for a council that more nearly resembled MacDonnell's original ideas, in opposition to the committed home rulers, Burns, Loreburn and Morley, thus reopening the quarrels of 1901–5.[30] The eventual compromise provided for a council of 107, with 82 members directly elected on the local government franchise.[31] Birrell, who had taken over from Bryce as Irish Secretary in January 1907, hoped this would be acceptable to Redmond and the Nationalists, though he can have been less sanguine about it passing the Lords. However, the draft bill published in May 1907 did not meet Redmond's views on a number of crucial issues and in the weeks leading up to a special Nationalist convention on the bill on 21 May it became clear that opinion was decisively against the measure. Redmond did not feel his position was strong enough to challenge this situation and moved the bill's rejection at the convention. In response, the cabinet scrapped the measure.[32] No doubt those who shared Asquith's approach were glad to do so, but this decision also confirmed that the main outline of Liberal policy in Ireland was to co-operate with the Nationalists and not to pursue ideas they rejected.

Birrell was happy to accept that administrative devolution was dead. He took the lesson of the episode to heart and ensured that subsequent legislation took even more account of Irish conditions and reflected Nationalist opinion. In 1908 the Irish Universities Act recognised Queen's College in Belfast as a separate university and incorporated the colleges in Dublin, Cork and Galway as a new National University. It was implicitly assumed that the first would be dominated by Ulster Protestants and the second by Catholics – something that went against the spirit of non-sectarian university education dominant in the rest of the United Kingdom, but which reflected the reality of the Irish situation.[33] Birrell consulted John Dillon and William Walsh, the Catholic Archbishop of Dublin, closely over this measure. Land legislation reflected Nationalist aspirations as much as the Lords and the Treasury would allow. In particular, it departed from the Unionist view that all transfers of land from landowners to tenants must be voluntary.[34] The 1907 Evicted Tenants Act enabled the state to compulsorily purchase land for those evicted during the land disputes of previous decades. The 1909 Land Act introduced compulsory purchase of land in the congested districts of western Ireland. Furthermore, Birrell refused to suspend civil liberties to deal with agrarian unrest in Ireland in 1907–9, and repealed the Unionists' Arms and Coercion Acts.[35] It also became clear that many appointments to the middle ranks of the civil service and county courts were going to Nationalists.[36] All of this enraged Unionists and ensured there was no consensus policy on Ireland, even without home rule. Birrell could claim that though home rule seemed as far away as ever at least Ireland was being run on 'Irish' lines and readied to govern itself. Rather than trying to undermine the Nationalist party, as the Unionists had done, the Liberals had accepted them as the legitimate representatives of Ireland who deserved to be consulted in its government. The long term trend, at least, was still towards home rule.

The home rule moment

This unstable equilibrium that Liberal Irish policy had reached in 1907–9 was overthrown by the political crisis of 1909 when the House of Lords rejected the 'People's Budget'. The election called for January 1910 was widely expected to be much closer than the Liberal landslide of 1906. It raised the question of how the Liberals could secure Irish support in Britain and, if necessary, the backing of Nationalist MPs in the Commons if they failed to obtain an overall majority. Redmond insisted that nothing less than a pledge to tackle home rule in the next parliament would do, especially as the spirits and land taxes in the budget were not popular in Ireland. The crucial cabinet meetings were on 30 November and 1 December 1909.[37] It was decided to give Redmond something like the promise he requested and Asquith intimated in his speech starting the Liberal campaign on 10 December 1909 that home rule was something that future Liberal governments would feel free to enact.[38] Though this was not an unequivocal commitment, it was a development of tremendous significance because it indicated that the shifts that had been underway since the 1890s to shelve home rule could, if required, be abandoned in the next parliament. It confirmed that, when the Liberal leadership was under pressure, it was willing to reaffirm home rule as Liberal policy and something that was still central to Liberal identity.

However, it was also obvious that the issue was not one that Liberals were willing to emphasise to the electorate. Only 39 per cent of Liberal election addresses mentioned home rule at all in January 1910 and 41 per cent in the December election of that year.[39] In the first election of 1910 ministers seem to have agreed not to deal with the subject in their speeches and they only did so in December because of Balfour's challenge to submit constitutional legislation to a referendum. This suggested Liberals still believed home rule was a difficult subject which alienated the electorate, raised innumerable difficulties and divided the party, even if it was Liberal policy. However, it was a policy that at last seemed practical after the results of the January 1910 elections were announced. The Liberals and Unionists had almost equal numbers of seats and the Liberals depended on the Nationalists and Labour to remain in office. Home rule was the obvious price for Nationalist support. The Liberal government would also have to tackle the reform of the House of Lords after it had vetoed the 'People's Budget' and this raised the prospect of removing the final legislative barrier to achieving home rule.

But events in 1910–11 revealed that many in the Liberal leadership remained unwilling to face the prospect of home rule. There was a crisis in Liberal-Nationalist relations immediately after the January 1910 elections, when Redmond insisted the government should set out its plans to end the Lords' veto of legislation before it reintroduced the budget.[40] Grey headed a group of ministers who were unwilling to rely on a Nationalist alliance to remain in power and wanted to reform the Lords, rather than end its veto – a policy that might, of course, have still blocked the way to home rule, especially if it was carried in agreement with the Unionist opposition.[41] Grey was supported by his old Liberal Imperialist colleagues, Haldane, Runciman and Samuel as well as most of the cabinet's Peers.[42] Only the threat of an imminent loss of office allowed their arguments to be overcome in favour of a policy of attacking the Lords' veto at the cabinets of 12–13 April 1910.[43] The key figure in the cabinet who argued against Grey's position was Lloyd George.[44] But when, in the summer of 1910, there was a conference of the party leaders to try and reach a settlement of the constitutional crisis over the role of the Lords, it was Lloyd George who suggested in his memorandum on a possible coalition that home rule might be replaced by a general scheme of devolution.[45] On this basis, home rule had very few firm friends in the Liberal cabinet. It was ultimately being proceeded with because it was the price of the Nationalist alliance. The doubts about home rule came from two directions – those, like Lloyd George, who feared the policy would be troublesome for the Liberals and those Liberal Imperialists, headed by Grey, who had long sought to postpone the issue, perhaps in the hope it would never come about.[46] But neither group could deny that home rule was an authentically Liberal solution to Ireland's place in the United Kingdom and on that basis the cabinet turned its mind to producing a home rule bill in 1911.

The first stage was to commit consideration of the bill to a committee, made up of Birrell, Lloyd George, Churchill, Haldane, Samuel and Grey, with Loreburn as chairman.[47] It looked into the matter in a fairly leisurely way and the bill was then discussed at several cabinets at the end of 1911 and beginning of 1912. Deliberations largely focused on the previous Gladstonian scheme of 1893 and it was never really disputed that there would be an Irish executive, responsible to a bicameral parliament and able to legislate in areas other than those reserved to the Westminster parliament. Consideration of the bill raised a number of thorny questions, like the financial arrangements for Ireland under home rule, which produced a tortuous solution from Herbert Samuel.[48] But the most important issues were whether home rule should be part of a wider federal scheme to devolve powers to the constituent parts of the United Kingdom, and if the Protestant population of Ulster should receive some kind of special treatment in the home rule legislation. Both raised fundamental questions about Liberal attitudes to nationality in the British Isles.

Federalism, as a general scheme of devolution was usually (and inaccurately) described, was promoted in 1911 by both Churchill and Lloyd George. Churchill suggested an elaborate plan of separate parliaments for not only Ireland, but Scotland and Wales as well, together with seven regional assemblies for England.[49] More modestly, Lloyd George proposed that Irish home rule should be accompanied by a provision that future Westminster legislation which dealt only with one part of the United Kingdom should be debated and voted on by a grand committee of English, Scottish or Welsh MPs as appropriate.[50] While Churchill's scheme never gained much support, Lloyd George's survived almost until the introduction of the home rule bill in April 1912.[51] Indeed, when Asquith introduced the bill he prefaced it with some remarks suggesting he hoped it would only be the first such measure in a larger and more comprehensive policy and one of the few amendments of substance to the home rule bill in its first circuit of parliament in 1912–13 was to cut out the Irish parliament's power to reduce customs duties – something that was seen as inimical to future federal projects.[52]

This interest in federalism can be interpreted in a number of ways. Irish Nationalists were always deeply suspicious of this idea and it was partly their pressure which secured the deletion of Lloyd George's grand committee scheme from the home rule bill.[53] They saw federalism as an attempt to wreck home rule by associating it with a vast, complex scheme that would lead to an interminable debate and probably never come to anything. But federalism also presented an avenue whereby home rule might be diluted. It was not clear that Scotland or Wales, let alone the English regions, would need a parliament with full legislative powers and if Irish home rule was enmeshed in a wider devolution project it, too, might find its powers scaled down. Moreover, federalism was sometimes linked with projects to associate the parliaments of overseas colonies of settlement with the United Kingdom parliament, so Ireland might find itself merely one link in a strengthened imperial chain. This was precisely why federalism had some supporters among Unionists, especially Austen Chamberlain and the editor of the *Observer*, J. L. Garvin.[54] It might, therefore, offer a way of agreeing a settlement of the home rule question with the opposition and cutting out the Nationalists.

There is no doubt that some Liberals had these 'negative' reasons for favouring federalism. Grey's opinions on the subject probably fall into this category and Asquith's pro-federalist remarks in April 1912 may well have been designed to keep a line open to the Unionists, should this prove fruitful.[55] Some prominent Liberal backbench federalists, like R. C. Munro Ferguson, had a long history as 'doubters' over Irish home rule and the movement in 1913 and 1914 to settle home rule by a conference with the Unionists on federalist lines was obviously open to the accusation that this was an attempt to sideline the government's bill.[56] However, this is not the entire picture. Some Liberals genuinely were committed to a wider scheme of devolution and attempted to use the home rule bill as an opportunity to further their schemes. The most powerful element in the 'positive' view of federalism among Liberals was provided by Scottish Liberals who had become advocates of Scottish home rule, and, to a much lesser extent, of Welsh Liberals, who favoured self-government for the principality.

Scotland had retained a plethora of separate institutions after the abolition of its parliament in 1707.[57] But many nineteenth-century Scottish Liberals had little time for the Established Church of Scotland, the Scottish legal system or the four ancient universities, seeing them as strongholds of privilege and corruption. Increasingly, Scottish identity was reforged around conceptualisations like the heroic Scottish past, Scotland as the home of industry and enterprise and the Scottish role in creating and running the British empire in partnership with England. These ideas did not necessarily require any institutional expression and many Scottish Liberals remained content with the existing union. But others did not and a home rule movement emerged among Liberals in the 1880s. This was obviously stimulated by the question of home rule for Ireland and it fed on the idea that Scotland's needs were being neglected and its institutions were inadequate to meet the country's needs. But among enthusiasts it was also an echo of developing nationalisms elsewhere in Europe and a reaction against the cosmopolitanism and modernity of urban life in favour of a simpler, nobler Scottish past. In 1889–95 seven Scottish home rule motions were introduced into the Commons and all but the first were approved by a majority of Scottish MPs, mainly Liberals.[58] Liberal governments were pressurised to improve Scotland's system of government and a Scottish Standing Committee was set up in 1894 and again in 1907 to debate purely Scottish legislation. The operations of the Scottish Office were continually criticised and it gradually started to gather the various Scottish boards and departments under its aegis. Increasingly it resembled a Scottish executive which could be held responsible to a Scottish parliament.

The Edwardian era witnessed an intensification of Scottish Liberal feeling in favour of home rule. The main carrier of this idea was the Young Scots Society, a sort of equivalent of the Young Liberals in England, though much more independent and aggressive.[59] But home rule feeling also drew on the increasing level of legislation, particularly on social issues, emanating from Westminster. Some of this was not well adapted to Scottish circumstances and law and seemed to show that Scots needed to govern themselves.[60] Scottish Liberals were also frustrated by the fact that while they dominated Scotland's representation they had to wait for the Westminster parliament to find time to enact the Scottish Liberal programme. Liberal governments proved increasingly sensitive to the need to accommodate the separate policies of Scottish Liberals and produced a Scottish Land Act in 1911 and a Temperance Act in 1913. But neither of these measures was entirely satisfactory to Scottish Liberals, who felt they had been watered down to suit English tastes and the opposition of the House of Lords.[61] Moreover, some Scottish Liberals, especially in the Young Scots, were eager to press on with a more far-reaching programme of social reform than the Liberal cabinet seemed likely to produce.[62] There was also the consideration that antipathy to the significant Irish population in western Scotland made some Scots virulent opponents of Irish home rule.[63] If it was combined with Scottish home rule it might be more palatable.

All of these feelings were brought to a head by the government's Irish home rule bill. Scottish MPs attempted to pressurise the cabinet committee to produce a Scottish measure in tandem with Irish home rule. When this failed, on 6 May 1912 a delegation of 32 Scottish Liberal MPs saw Asquith to demand a home rule bill in 1913.[64] All this was to no avail. The cabinet could not accede to these requests. To do so would have been to involve Irish home rule in precisely the difficulties that 'negative' advocates of federalism hoped. But this was a tactical matter. It did not mean that Liberalism was unwilling to deal with Scottish home rule in the future. Liberal governments had become increasingly willing to produce legislation to meet the particular demands of Scottish Liberalism. The demand for home rule within the party north of the border was clearly growing and Asquith was careful not to rule this measure out in his reply to the Scottish Liberal MPs. They introduced their own home rule bills in May 1913 and May 1914 to remind the government they had not gone away and were planning to increase the pressure on the government on the eve of the war.[65] Given the need to 'sell' Irish home rule to the Scottish electorate at a 1915 election, it is by no means impossible that Scottish home rule would have been a formal commitment by that stage if war had not intervened in 1914.

Most of the enthusiastic 'positive' federalists in 1912–14 were found in Scotland. Welsh Liberalism was not as committed to self-government for the principality, even though it was closely identified with Welsh national feeling. Liberalism had dominated Welsh politics since the 1880s at least partly because it represented a national revolt against the dominance of anglicised landowners and the Church of England as the established church in a largely nonconformist country.[66] Welsh Liberalism was also closely connected with a vigorous cultural renaissance, much of it in the Welsh language. Owen Edwards, a leading figure in this movement, was even briefly a Liberal MP.[67] In some ways Welsh Liberalism was as much a nationalist party as a liberal party. But this national feeling did not translate automatically into demands for self-rule. This had been debated in the 1890s, but it had proved impossible to rouse much enthusiasm among Welsh Liberal MPs.[68] Wales did not have the separate legal and administrative system that persisted in Scotland and formed the core of much of the logic for Scottish self-rule. Moreover, Welsh Liberalism's most long-standing and important demand was the disestablishment of the Anglican Church in Wales and this provided a powerful alternative focus for nationalist feelings. Ironically, Lloyd George's prominence in the Edwardian Liberal party seemed to demonstrate to Welsh Liberals that they could have an important influence on the British government, rather than needing their own assembly.

However, Welsh Liberals did expect their party to provide separate institutions and legislation for Wales, when this was necessary to reflect

Welsh conditions. Liberal governments had a record of acceding to at least some of these demands, while Unionists usually opposed them – Balfour was almost apoplectic when Lloyd George mentioned the need for a 'Minister for Wales' in 1906.[69] Gladstone's second government had passed the Welsh Sunday Closing Act in 1881 and the 1892–5 administrations had appointed a Royal Commission to look into the Welsh land system and incorporated the federal University of Wales in 1893.[70] A separate Welsh section of the department of education had followed in 1907. Some examples of separate treatment for Wales had, therefore, built up by the Edwardian era and suggested there might be some point to Welsh self-government. E. T. John, the MP for East Denbighshire, launched a campaign on these lines in 1910. But he had only a handful of backers in the parliamentary party.[71] What transformed the situation in Wales was the Scottish campaign for home rule in 1912–14. When it seemed the government might look favourably on this, Welsh Liberals were indignant that their country might be left behind. This was not the equality of treatment and consideration they looked for. The Welsh National Liberal Council was galvanised into calling for 'an equal measure of self-government' for Wales and organising a campaign with this objective.[72] E. T. John produced a Government of Wales Bill in February 1914, supported by eight Welsh Liberal MPs.[73]

Asquith could be no more sympathetic than he was to the Scottish home rulers. But the Welsh Liberals had a trump card in Lloyd George. When Welsh self-government had been a controversial issue in the 1890s, he had at times associated himself with the cause, especially when he had spearheaded the Cymru Fydd movement in 1895–6.[74] One of his jobs in government was to look after the interests of Wales and it seemed impossible to Welsh Liberals that he would allow Wales to be slighted when the other Celtic nations were pressing forward to self-government. It was noticeable that Lloyd George's grand committee scheme of 1911 included Wales as well as Scotland. Lloyd George was not a consistent advocate of federalism, of either a 'positive' or 'negative' variety. But he was not opposed to the idea either, as his activities in the 1890s showed, and given his role as Wales's semi-official political leader, it was not surprising that he at least attempted to combine Irish home rule with greater self-government for Wales and, necessarily, Scotland as well in 1911. That he was not successful was dictated by the tactical considerations of the moment and the overriding need to pass Irish home rule as the price of the government's survival.

But what was clear in 1912–14 was that for many Liberals, federalism was not just a decoy. The Liberal party had increasingly associated itself with separate treatment for Scotland and Wales, as well as Ireland, in its legislation and by 1914 there were strong pressures for the party to move towards self-government for Scotland and probably Wales as well. In this context Irish home rule was not just an irritating debt to the Nationalists but part of a developing commitment to the plurality of the United Kingdom and a recognition of the need to give non-English nationalities institutional expression of their identity. The Liberals had consistently been stronger in Scotland and Wales than in England since 1886. By 1914 they seemed more than ever a party for the 'Celtic fringe' – in December 1910 84 of the Liberals' 272 MPs were elected in Scotland and Wales and they relied on the further 84 Irish Nationalist MPs for their majority in the Commons. As Unionists never tired of pointing out, they had won a majority in England in 1910 and were deprived of government by the 'log-rolling' coalition of Irish, Welsh and Scottish MPs. One Tory MP claimed 'There is a widespread movement on foot among the Celtic elements in the U.K. to assert predominance over the Anglo-Saxon.'[75] The Conservatives, on the other hand, were the truly English party and stood for England's continued leading role in the United Kingdom.

However, if the Liberals were the party who stood for the national rights of the non-English nations in the United Kingdom, this raised the question of what their attitude should be to Ulster Protestants in the context of Irish home rule. This proved one of the most dangerous issues the party faced in the Edwardian period and also one of the most difficult. Liberals simply could not make up their mind how to apply their views on nationality in the United Kingdom to Ulster. Initially, the home rule bill made no special provision for Ulster.[76] Its rights were protected to some extent in the legislation, but only in so far as the rights of all Irish Protestants were – as in the provision that the Irish parliament could not make any laws that discriminated on the grounds of religion. But this decision was always troubling for Liberals. On 6 February 1912 Churchill and Lloyd George had proposed that Ulster counties should be able to 'contract out' of home rule and the cabinet had been deeply divided on the issue. Asquith's report of the cabinet meeting suggested they had decided Ulster might have to be excluded from home rule and felt they were free to change the home rule bill in this respect in the future.[77] Debates on whether Ulster should be excluded during the first passage of the home rule bill in 1912 produced considerable disarray on the Liberal backbenches, particularly when the

Liberal MP, Thomas Agar-Robartes, moved that Antrim, Armagh, Londonderry and Down should be left out of home rule.[78] Then, in autumn 1913 Asquith began discussions with Bonar Law to see if a compromise could be reached that did involve special consideration for Ulster.[79] Eventually, on 9 March 1914, the cabinet offered Ulster counties the right to vote themselves out of the jurisdiction of a home rule parliament for six years.[80] Discussions on the time limit of exclusion and the precise area to be excluded were continuing fruitlessly when the First World War intervened.

This sequence of events can be viewed purely as the result of tactical considerations by Asquith. To keep the Nationalists in line he had to produce a home rule bill that was acceptable to them and pass it, despite the House of Lords's ability to delay the legislation for two years. This militated against separate treatment for Ulster. But, on the other hand, once it became clear in 1912–13 that the Unionist campaign against home rule's most powerful argument was the plight of Ulster and that Ulster Protestants were preparing armed resistance to rule from Dublin, Asquith began to look for a settlement that would be acceptable to Unionists and Nationalists.[81] Those Liberals who urged Ulster exclusion sooner than Asquith came round to it were just more willing to try and deal with trouble before it came to a head. But Liberal ideology also played a part in this scenario which should not be ignored. Firstly, Asquith was only able to keep his party together while the Irish home rule bill laboured through Parliament in 1912–14 because he could be certain that, however worried some Liberals were about the difficulties of passing home rule, the party was overwhelmingly committed to the principle of recognising Irish nationality within the United Kingdom. The cabinet did not fragment on the issue and only two or three MPs could be labelled opponents of Irish home rule as a principle.[82] The party still believed the arguments of 1886 held good and that to be a Liberal was to be a home ruler, even if some Liberals wanted home rule to be part of a general scheme of devolution or preferred Ulster to be excluded from the project. Most Liberals actually believed the case for home rule was stronger in 1912 than in 1886. Nationalists had dominated local government in Ireland since 1898 without Ireland descending into anarchy. Moreover, home rule in the dominions had been a great success, even in South Africa, where Boer and British had been fighting as recently as 1902. There was no reason to believe self-government would not work in Ireland.

In fact, as the Irish home rule bill wound its way round the parliamentary circuit, most of the party became more committed to it, not less. This was largely because of the scale and intensity of Unionist opposition. Liberals believed that Bonar Law's association with armed resistance in Ulster was undermining the whole concept of parliamentary government and respect for the rule of law. The most fundamental of Liberal principles were being attacked by an irresponsible demagogue. Liberal anger reached new heights with the 'Curragh mutiny' of March 1914, when it seemed that sections of the army would refuse to take action against the Ulster Unionists, and the inter-party Buckingham Palace conference on home rule, hosted by George V on 21–4 July 1914. It seemed to many ordinary Liberals and backbench MPs that the Unionists were attempting to use the army and the monarchy to frustrate the will of an elected parliament. As R. D. Holt complained, 'The officers in the Army are Tories almost to a man and no doubt the Tory party have calculated that if Ulster resists Home Rule by force the Army will refuse to support the Government'.[83] The Buckingham Palace conference was not much better to many Liberals – 'a dangerous constitutional innovation' which allowed too much of a role to George V, whose 'personal friends are almost without exception Unionists'.[84] Nothing less than parliamentary government itself was at stake with the home rule bill. In these circumstances the party just had to press on and pass the measure, come what may.

Liberal belief in home rule was the bedrock of Asquith's strategy in 1912–14. But the most important doubts among Liberals always centred on the treatment of Ulster and Liberal attitudes to Ulster and nationality provided a framework for Asquith's options on how the province should be viewed. Initially, Asquith rejected the idea of separate treatment for Ulster and this remained the position, unofficially until autumn 1913 and officially until March 1914. This line seemed to violate Liberal principles about recognising the claims of non-English nationalities in the United Kingdom in a particularly flagrant way. If Ireland could determine its form of government, why shouldn't Ulster? This worried many Liberals, particularly Methodists who had links with their co-religionists in Ulster and advocates of federalism who argued Ulster should receive the same treatment as Wales and Scotland.[85] It was not an accident that Lloyd George and Churchill were the leading protagonists of both federalism and Ulster exclusion in the cabinet in 1911–12.

One important reason why the cabinet and parliamentary party were able to go on opposing concessions to Ulster in 1912–13 was because they could make a case that a united Ireland did not transgress Liberal ideas about nationality. It was still possible to suggest in 1912 that

Ulster Protestants were not a nation. This of course raised the thorny problem, 'what is a nation?' But there was a fairly ready Liberal answer to this question. A nation was a group of people who made a persistent claim to be a nation. That was precisely why the continuing Nationalist dominance of Ireland, despite Unionist attempts to undermine it, was such a powerful vindication of Ireland's nationality. But, as the leading Liberal theoretician, L. T. Hobhouse, put it, 'does Ulster claim to be a nation? ... Not if its desire is, what we have always understood it to be, to remain directly subject to the British Parliament. It is, in fact, the focus of an old, but decayed Ascendancy caste, and its desire is to retain what it can save from the wreck of the Ascendancy system'.[86] In other words, Ulster Protestants were not a separate 'Ulster nation', but a part, albeit the largest part, of those, mainly Protestant, Irish people who saw themselves as primarily British rather than Irish. Their aim was to stop any form of home rule, against the wishes of the majority of the Irish people, and Ulster exclusion was only one of their tactics to forward this aim. This could be confirmed by reference to the public position of Carson, Ulster's leader, which was indeed to oppose any form of home rule.

Not all Liberals were convinced by this argument, but it allowed Asquith's strategy some purchase in Liberal tradition and made it feasible for him to state that there was only one nation in Ireland and therefore no justification for dividing the country.[87] However, this position was gradually undermined in 1912–13. The Unionist case came increasingly to focus on Ulster, rather than opposition to home rule as such.[88] Bonar Law's private discussions with Asquith in 1913 confirmed that Ulster was the key to the whole situation. Even more compellingly, the Ulster Protestants furnished every possible indication of their determination to resist home rule, including by arms, while being quite ready to abandon Protestants elsewhere in Ireland.[89] Ulster was willing to fight for Tyrone and Fermanagh, but not Dublin or Cork. It became very clear that there was a separate Ulster Protestant identity that was distinct from Irish nationality and did not wish to be ruled from Dublin. In these circumstances it was increasingly difficult to sustain the case Hobhouse had outlined in 1912. In fact, he had suggested that if Ulster exclusion was put forward 'as a substantive proposal seriously intended, it will constitute a new fact. Belfast will then be, indeed, claiming recognition as a miniature nationality, and the claim will be duly weighed'.[90] By late 1913 Asquith was not alone in weighing Ulster's claim and finding it proven. This allowed the prime minister and Lloyd George to convince the cabinet on 4 March 1914 to make the offer to exclude some Ulster counties for a limited period.[91] Once this decision had been made the Liberal party had accepted that Ulster Protestants did deserve recognition of their national identity within the United Kingdom.

In addition, to go on with the policy of a united Ireland would have meant facing the reality of using armed force against Ulster. Some cabinet members, like Grey, were always utterly opposed to this course.[92] But other Liberals said they would be prepared to use the army in the name of upholding parliamentary sovereignty, most famously when Churchill declared there were 'worse things than bloodshed'.[93] However, statements like these need to be treated with care. The cabinet never did order the army to suppress the Ulster Protestants' private army, the Ulster Volunteer Force. It now seems clear that even the troop movements that preceded the 'Curragh mutiny' were intended to safeguard arms depots and possibly to overawe Ulster, rather than to provoke a conflict.[94] This forbearance was obviously intended to ensure a dangerous situation was not further enflamed, but it also reflected elements in Liberal belief. Many Liberals were happy to call for the law to be used against Ulster's leaders and in particular for Carson to be arrested for some of his statements.[95] But they recoiled from the idea of suppressing Ulster Unionism by pitched battles in the streets of Belfast, which would 'float Home Rule in blood'.[96] The veteran home-ruler, Morley, responded to Churchill's remark that ' "there are worse things than bloodshed" ' by damning the phrase as ' "a platitude, and worse, a Tory platitude" '.[97] Like many of his colleagues, Morley could not accept that drastic measures of coercion against Ulster Unionism were authentically Liberal, just as he opposed coercing Irish nationalism or, indeed military government anywhere. Imposing the rule of law in Ireland at the point of a bayonet was not Liberalism to many Liberals. That definition of their creed had been rejected by the party in 1886.

Asquith's tactics over home rule have been much criticised, but in terms of Liberal ideology, they make some kind of sense. However, he could also have justified concessions to Ulster in 1912, given the scale of the party's divisions on the issue. He could at least claim that by July 1914 he had brought home rule to the brink of enactment. Ironically, he had also brought Liberals and Unionists closer together on Irish policy than at any time since 1886. Both parties tacitly accepted that home rule for most of Ireland would happen and that Ulster would be excluded. Their only disagreement was over Ulster's borders and the time limit for exclusion – and even the last issue was theoretical as everyone knew an excluded area would hardly be likely to change its mind, or be coerced by Westminster. The Liberal party had finally accepted that at least two definitions of Irishness should be given institutional expression within the United Kingdom. From that point it was a smaller and less controversial step to extending this policy to Scotland and perhaps Wales as well.

4
Liberalism and Democracy

One of the most important ways in which Liberals thought of their role in extending the bounds of freedom and liberty was in the context of expanding the right of people to participate in legislation and government. When Gladstone's second administration produced the Reform and Redistribution Acts of 1884–5, and extended the householder franchise that already existed in the boroughs to the counties, it was widely assumed that this work was complete. As a system had been set up under which the great majority of adult males could expect to qualify to vote at some stage of their life, Britain had witnessed 'the success of democracy'.[1] Many politicians spoke and acted as if this was a commonplace of British life. The electorate was over five million strong after 1885 and political parties spent much of their energies marshalling their votes for the general elections required every seven years. Whichever party achieved a majority of seats in the House of Commons elected by the voters formed the country's government and enacted its policies in the name of the electorate who had placed it in power. However, many Liberals rapidly became convinced that democracy had not been produced by the reforms of 1884–5. In particular, two features of the British system still stood in the way of full representative government and the sovereignty of the people: the ability of the hereditary House of Lords to veto legislation approved by the elected Commons; and the fact that householder suffrage did not automatically enfranchise all adults – indeed it specifically excluded all women from voting. Tackling these issues proved two of the party's most difficult and controversial tasks in the Edwardian era.

The House of Lords

Once nineteenth-century Liberalism moved away from the previous century's idea of a balanced constitution of Monarchy, Peers and Commons and embraced the sovereignty of the people, it was bound to look on the role of the House of Lords in the legislative process with disfavour.[2] It was difficult to see how the existence of a body that was made up of hereditary Peers, with a leavening of judges and Anglican bishops, could be justified in Liberal terms, unless it was willing to accept the supremacy of the Commons and confine itself to ancillary and ceremonial functions, like the Monarchy, which had not dared to veto an act of parliament since 1707. Until the mid-1880s this had seemed at least feasible as a constitutional development. The Peers had accepted all the major political and religious reforms of the nineteenth century, including the reform acts of 1832, 1867 and 1885. The last instance seemed to show that they would not hold out against a Liberal policy that was backed by a great popular campaign. Liberals continued to make up over 40 per cent of the Lords and to wield considerable influence there.[3] Many leading Liberals, like the Marquess of Hartington, heir to the Duke of Devonshire, were closely connected to the peerage and showed that the Lords were not devoid of popular sympathies.

However, this hope that the Lords might co-operate in their own demise was dashed in 1886 by the home rule crisis and the split in the Liberal party. The Liberal peerage overwhelmingly opposed Gladstone and refused to acquiesce in a policy that meant abandoning the Irish members of their order to Nationalist rule from Dublin. As a result, while there were 203 Liberal members of the Lords in 1880, there were only 38 in 1887. Thereafter, Liberals remained a small minority in the House of Lords and had to face the prospect of continuous Unionist opposition to measures produced by a Liberal government. It was no surprise that the 1887 NLF conference called for the removal of the Lords' power to veto legislation.[4] The issue became critical during the 1892–5 Liberal governments, when the Lords rejected the second Irish home rule bill in 1893. In his last speech to the Commons, Gladstone insisted the issue of the Lords had to be tackled and the Liberal MPs were so incensed that they carried an amendment to the address, against the wishes of the cabinet, to demand an end to the Peers' veto.[5] Rosebery, Gladstone's successor, took up the issue of Lords reform in a number of speeches and the matter was second only to Irish home rule in Liberal election addresses in 1895.[6]

The experience of 1892–5 fixed the House of Lords in Liberal minds as the great barrier to popular government which had to be removed and hostility to the Lords became a staple of Liberal speeches. This attitude was not just based on the actions of the Lords, but their composition. Nonconformists had long objected to the role of Anglican bishops as legislators in the Lords and regular backbench bills had tried to remove them.[7] But, more importantly, the House of Lords was very much still a house of great landowners in the late nineteenth century. Liberals had always been less closely associated with upholding the system of great estates than the Tories, as they had seen this as merely one interest among many in society, and the Liberal party.[8] In the 1880s it had been the Liberals who had been prepared to legislate on behalf of Irish tenants, Scottish crofters and, to some extent, English farmers, to rebalance their relationship with their landowners. In 1885 Joseph Chamberlain attempted to put the provision of allotments for agricultural labourers at the forefront of the Liberal programme. But any general anti-landowner tendencies, which had deep roots in working class radicalism, had been held in check by the prominent role of landowners within Liberalism. In 1886, though, the Liberal Peers became only the most prominent members of a mass exodus from the party by the landed elite. This allowed and encouraged Liberals to support anti-landlord policies and to construct an entirely negative picture of the role of landowners in society and politics.

Liberalism had always been susceptible to the idea that society was not being run for the general good, but in the interests of a corrupt and self-serving clique, from the 'Old Corruption' of the pre-1832 political system onwards. In the later 1880s landowners started to fulfil this role for many Liberals. They increasingly built up a picture in which landowners were accused of exercising a consistent policy of political and economic pressure in the countryside to enforce Tory dominance. Agricultural labourers were believed to be particularly susceptible to this 'feudal screw' and Liberals attempted to investigate and expose 'the intimidation which in rural districts was terrorising or penalising Radical voters.'[9] Thoughtful young men in the Liberal camp, like Herbert Samuel, made their own studies of rural life, which revealed a society rife with intimidation, starvation wages and insanitary hovels.[10] Great urban landowners, especially in London, like the Dukes of Bedford and West-minster, were also accused of exploiting their leaseholders, avoiding local rates and being responsible for slum conditions.[11] Thus Liberal antipathy to the Lords was steadily reinforced by the conviction that they represented a class whose interests were profoundly antipathetic to that of society as a whole. This was in marked contrast to much Unionist writing of the 1880s and 1890s which vigorously defended the Peers as wise and beneficent statesmen whose judgement on what was best for Britain was far superior to the demagogues and wire-pullers of popular politics.[12]

Hostility to the Lords was deeply ingrained within Liberalism by 1905 and unlikely to be rescinded. But the issue did not play a great role in the 1906 election, which concentrated on the record of the Tory governments of 1895–1905. Issues like free trade and the 1902 Education Act were of far more immediate significance than the Lords, which were mentioned by less than a third of Liberal candidates.[13] But once the Liberals started to try and enact their longed-for programme, their Lordships returned to the centre of the political stage with a vengeance. In particular, they used their power of veto to destroy some major government measures, especially the 1906 Education Bill and the 1908 Licensing Bill, as well as other bills on plural voting and Scottish land reform.[14] This reignited Liberal hostility to the Lords, which could draw on the accumulated resentment and arguments of the late nineteenth century. But it also posed the question as to what the Liberals intended to do and how they wished to reconstruct the relationship between the Lords and the Commons.

This issue had caused some difficulty for Rosebery's government in 1894–5. The majority of the cabinet and the annual conference of the NLF had declared for a simple restriction of the Lords' power of veto, to allow the upper house to delay, but not to prevent, legislation passed by the Commons.[15] But Rosebery had favoured a number of different schemes, including reforming the composition of the Lords and instituting joint conferences of the Commons and Lords to resolve disputes. These disagreements had been one of the reasons why no great campaign to reform the Lords had been launched in the 1890s. They were no closer to being resolved when Campbell-Bannerman's government faced the issue. A cabinet committee was set up in early 1907 to try and produce a solution. Its members were Loreburn, Ripon and Crewe from the Lords, plus Asquith, Haldane, Lloyd George and Harcourt and its deliberations were complete by 19 March 1907.[16] The committee's conclusions were based on a memorandum from Crewe, as amended by Asquith. It suggested that when the Lords and Commons disagreed, matters should be decided by a joint vote of the two houses, but with the Lords represented by a delegation of 100 members, 20 of whom would be government ministers and the rest chosen by the whole House of Lords. Rather misleadingly, this became known as the 'Ripon plan'.

This idea naturally involved rejecting the suspensory veto, which hitherto had been the most canvassed Liberal solution to the problem posed by the Lords. Crewe's reasons for doing so were clear. The suspensory veto was only a 'paper check' on the dominance of the Commons and was far too close to abolishing the Lords' veto altogether and instituting unicameral government.[17] It would also involve a huge constitutional conflict with the Lords, who would resist it to the last, and this could drag in the Monarchy, as Edward VII might have to be asked to threaten the creation of enough Liberal Peers to overcome the Unionist Peers' intransigence. By implication, Crewe's plan was much more moderate and consensual, and would retain a more significant role for the Lords – it was the 'line of least resistance' as the cabinet committee put it. Crewe's ideas also had links with Rosebery's thinking in the 1890s, which was not altogether surprising as Crewe was Rosebery's son-in-law and Asquith had been a leading Liberal Imperialist. It was noticeable that Liberal Imperialist leaders like Haldane had, in the past, been much less enthusiastic than many other Liberals about the benefits of unrestricted popular government.[18] This was undoubtedly linked to their lack of enthusiasm for Irish home rule, the major Liberal legislation the Lords had rejected in 1892–5, and their wish for a consensual approach with the Unionists on foreign and defence policy.

Rather surprisingly, though, the 'Ripon plan' was approved by the whole cabinet committee and then the cabinet itself.[19] It is unlikely that they had all come to see the benefits of co-operating with the Lords, but there were tactical reasons that may have outweighed any ideological objections. Most importantly, the Liberal Commons majority in early 1907 was so huge that even if the 'Ripon plan' added 60 or so votes to the Unionist side in a joint sitting with the Lords, the Liberals would have a majority. If the Liberals called an election in 1907 and put this plan to the country, they might still be returned with a massive enough majority in the Commons to outvote the Unionists. However, even with these factors in its favour, Campbell-Bannerman was profoundly uneasy about the 'Ripon plan' and continued to 'hanker after the more drastic method of the one year's veto', referring to the cabinet committee's ideas as 'this milder scheme'.[20] Before the cabinet's ideas were announced on 24 June 1907, Campbell-Bannerman managed to reverse its position and restore the idea of the suspensory veto as Liberal policy – or the 'C-B veto plan' as it became known.[21] This extraordinary turnaround was only possible because Campbell-Bannerman's ideas retained an inherent reservoir of support in the cabinet, which had been temporarily overwhelmed by the cabinet committee's report. In particular, most

Liberals remained reluctant to allow the Lords a continuing place in legislation that in any way shared the Commons' role.[22] The Commons were the representatives of the people and it was their responsibility and right to decide which legislation should become law. The Lords had to accept that 'the voice of the Commons must be taken to represent the popular will'.[23] The Lords could only be permitted the quite separate and subordinate role of suggesting revisions and allowing time for reflection on particularly controversial measures, as with the suspensory veto. But they could not be allowed to participate in the Commons' role.

The 'C-B veto plan' was put to the Commons and duly passed in 1907 as the policy of the Liberal cabinet. But it was not proceeded with and given the contradictory stances the cabinet had taken in 1907 it was not clear whether it remained government policy. This became more than a theoretical issue in November 1909, when the Lords rejected the government's budget and the cabinet was compelled to call an election on the issue of the Lords' actions. As Asquith made plain in his keynote speech of 10 December 1909 at the Albert Hall, the Liberals' policy was not only to secure electoral backing for the budget, but to reform Commons-Lords relations. This meant not only securing the Commons' supremacy in financial matters like the budget, but 'the absolute veto ... must go...'.[24] However, Asquith went into no more detail than these rather ambiguous words, which actually stated no more than that the existing situation had to change. The cabinet had no definite plan when it went into the election – possibly a sign that attempts to formulate such a design would not have been easy.

However, the Liberal divisions that were plain in the January 1910 election did not recreate the arguments of 1907. While all Liberal candidates condemned the Lords' actions as an attack on representative government and often threw in some abuse of the Lords and great land-owners as well, there was no unanimity on what action to take after the election. As Neal Blewett has calculated, 20 per cent of Liberal manifestos made no suggestions at all.[25] Just over half favoured the 'C-B veto plan'. The 'Ripon plan' was not mentioned at all, which was not surprising as it was not public knowledge outside of the cabinet. But the remainder of candidates insisted the composition of the House of Lords must be reformed, with or without the suspensory veto. These divisions became acute once the election results were known. The Liberals lost their overall majority in January 1910 and found themselves reliant on the Irish Nationalists to remain in office. The Nationalists insisted the cabinet proceed immediately with a proposal for the suspensory veto, which, of course, would open the way to Irish home rule and the two issues of the Lords and home rule remained entwined thereafter. Grey, however, rallied the forces of the reformers and until mid-April it was possible their arguments would prevail.[26]

While reform of the Lords had not been a major issue in 1907 it had, like the conference plan embodied in the Ripon proposals, been raised by Rosebery in 1894. Grey had become an enthusiastic advocate and it had remained a thread in Liberal thinking ever since.[27] The great argument against it had always been its complexity and the difficulty of reaching agreement on who should replace the hereditary Peers, an issue still unresolved nearly a century later. As Loulou Harcourt suggested, ideas to reform the Lords were prone to take 'the form of fanciful schemes (like the Abbe de Sieyes) for a new heaven & a new earth' and were about as likely to come to anything.[28] But the idea had two, rather different, ways of attracting Liberal support. The first saw it, like the Ripon plan, as a more moderate proposal than the suspensory veto, as a reformed Lords would be justified in retaining its veto powers, thus allowing it to block, for instance, home rule. This was undoubtedly the scheme's main attraction for Grey, and probably for Haldane, who was the other cabinet minister who had committed himself to reform in his election manifesto.[29] Grey always insisted that his aim was to avoid the dominance of a 'Single Chamber' and that he wanted his reformed upper house to 'have more influence than the House of Lords'.[30] It was even possible that reform was a policy that could be agreed with the Unionists. Though they had noticeably failed to change the composition of the Lords in 1895–1905, Unionist leaders were on record as theoretically favouring some sort of reform of the Lords' composition.[31] This bicameralist strain in Liberal thinking was thus part of a wider, cross-party suspicion of the actions of the Commons and in favour of a series of checks and balances on its proposals. But it could also be justified within Liberal thinking by referring to the fear that an elected assembly might act in an illiberal way and therefore a mechanism was needed to block popular proposals which breached fundamental liberal principles. It was no accident that those who favoured this approach, like Grey and Haldane, were also lukewarm home rulers, because the primary objection to home rule within the Liberal tradition was the fear that a Nationalist Ireland would be an illiberal state, which promoted religious and political persecution. Over both home rule and a reformed second chamber they were trying to preserve liberalism from popular assault.

However, this was a minority position within Liberalism, which favoured the idea that popular sovereignty must be defended. This concept had been reinforced by the events of 1909–10, which had been simplified in Liberal eyes to the question, 'Shall the People be Ruled by the Peers?' Most Liberals saw the battle as one of Commons v. Lords and had no wish to strengthen the Lords. But Grey's idea had a certain amount of tactical purchase in the spring of 1910. This partly stemmed from an analysis of the January election results. If, as most Liberals believed, they had lost a good deal of the moderate, middle class support they had won in 1906, the party must not seem to be 'extreme' in its policies, especially as a second election was probable in 1910, either because of disagreement with the Nationalists, or as part of an assault on the Lords' veto powers.[32] The party needed to advocate House of Lords reform to convince moderate voters that a Liberal government would not indulge in controversial adventures. Implicitly, this also meant breaking free from a Nationalist alliance, which would alienate moderates. This strategy appealed not only to Grey and Haldane, but also to Crewe, Runciman and Samuel – again revealing the policy's relationship to Liberal Imperialism.[33]

But reform also appealed to the cabinet for other reasons and McKenna, Churchill and Lloyd George all flirted with the idea.[34] This was because reform could be seen as a far-reaching as well as a moderate proposal. After all, if Liberals were deeply opposed to the whole idea of a hereditary House of Lords, it seemed difficult to justify retaining the current House, even if its powers were reduced. An all out attack on the domination of the Lords by great landowners and the hereditary principle might suggest the need to replace the Lords with an entirely or largely elected chamber. This was clearly what Grey proposed in his memorandum of 31 January 1910 which set out the case for Lords reform and Churchill initially supported him on the grounds that the great idea which Liberals must combat was 'the principle of hereditary legislators'.[35] By arguing for an elected second house Grey gave his reform proposals a much wider appeal in Liberal ideology. It was an approach that was adopted in 1912 under the Irish home rule bill, which provided for a senate to be elected by proportional representation. In different circumstances it is not inconceivable that Grey might have been able to win the argument, even though most Liberals favoured abolishing the Lords' veto.[36] But the inescapable fact was that if the cabinet did not attack the Lords' powers they would lose Nationalist support and the government would be out of office.[37] Gradually, this swung the cabinet behind the suspensory veto plan, though the idea of reforming the Lords remained in the preamble to the Parliament Act passed in 1911.

However, this was not the end of the Liberals' debates over the Lords. When Edward VII died in May 1910, the Liberals agreed to a 'truce of God' with the Unionists and a conference to see if an agreed settlement could be produced to the Lords crisis.[38] The Liberal delegates were Asquith, Lloyd George, Crewe and Birrell. Asquith ignored the suspensory veto, to which he was publicly committed, and the idea of House of Lords reform which had been widely debated, in his cabinet in the previous few months. Instead, he returned to the Ripon plan which he and Crewe had produced in 1907.[39] The Unionists were more than willing to negotiate on this basis and the conference broke down only because of the Liberals' reluctance to accept a separate category of constitutional legislation (including home rule), which the Unionists suggested should be the subject of a referendum if the two Houses disagreed.[40]

None of this was known to the rest of the Liberal party, let alone their Nationalist allies, and it raises the question of why Asquith took this course, given the difficulties he would have faced in persuading his party to accept the Ripon plan and the fact that nobody had canvassed the idea publicly before. Possibly Asquith had a deep ideological attachment to the scheme. But, as he would not agree to include home rule in the Unionists' list of constitutional legislation, he was not even offering his party an escape route from the Nationalist alliance through an agreed settlement with the Unionists. As this meant Asquith ultimately accepted the Liberals were committed to the Nationalists and home rule, it was illogical for him not to insist on the suspensory veto and the explanation of his attitude may be found in this paradox. No doubt, Asquith was curious to explore the Unionists' attitude to the Lords and what proposals they might make on the subject at a future election. But as he accepted his party's commitment to passing home rule he may not have expected the conference to succeed. However, Asquith did not wish talks to break down immediately or in acrimony. Above all he needed to be seen to have been 'reasonable' and to have tried to reach a settlement, to win over moderate and wavering voters. He may also have wished for a respite to rest the Liberal forces after the great electoral campaign of 1909–10 and give them the option of fighting the next election on a new and more accurate electoral register.[41] Even more importantly, he needed a decent interval after Edward VII's death, before he could pressurise George V to guarantee he would create enough Liberal Peers to swamp the Unionist majority in the Lords if they rejected a future Liberal parliament bill after another election.[42] To achieve this, Asquith had to convince the king as well as the voters that he had tried for a settlement and the Ripon plan was ideal in this respect as the Unionists could accept parts of it, but not all of it. If Asquith had produced the suspensory veto as his main negotiating ploy, the conference would have collapsed immediately. But if he had genuinely wanted an agreement, it might have been far better to have concentrated on Lords reform, which had wide support in his cabinet and at least theoretical Unionist agreement. The revival of the Ripon plan by Asquith in 1910 was probably a tactical ploy rather than a reflection of deep belief in its proposals.

The final ideological battle over the Lords took place at the December 1910 election, called after the breakdown of the conference. The Liberals were at least officially united around the suspensory veto.[43] But the Unionists did not just support the right of the Lords to reject legislation, as they had done in January. Instead, they presented their own proposals. First, on 17 November 1910, they suggested a species of House of Lords reform, based on the ideas of Rosebery, the ex-Liberal leader.[44] This plan proposed a Lords consisting of some hereditary peers, some office holders and an element which might be directly or indirectly elected. While this distanced the Unionists from a simple defence of the hereditary principle, it failed to divide the Liberals. Grey had moved to the position of a wholly or largely elected second chamber and this had been the basis of cabinet discussions in January–April 1910. The Liberals simply could not accept the Unionists' scheme, though it might have been a starting point for negotiations at a private conference, like that of June–November 1910. Then, on 23 November, Lansdowne suggested that, in addition, the Ripon plan should be adopted, with the extra proposal of a referendum on constitutional issues. Rapidly, the debate in the final days of the election campaign came to centre on the referendum. Not surprisingly, the Liberal leaders had no wish to discuss the Ripon plan, which, unbeknown to their followers, they had put forward at the constitutional conference, and the referendum focused debate on the key issues of home rule and tariff reform.

The remarkable conversion of the Unionist party to the referendum had been foreshadowed at the constitutional conference.[45] The idea had obvious tactical advantages. Some obnoxious Liberal proposals, like Irish home rule, roused little interest in Britain and might be rejected in a referendum of the whole United Kingdom. The referendum also still allowed the Lords to play a crucial role in blocking important legislation. Most importantly, it allowed the Unionists to respond to the suspensory veto with an alternative that was not hostile to democracy and popular sovereignty. Indeed, it took these ideas further than the Liberals proposed.

For this reason, it had not been suggested by the Unionists until a dire emergency arose and, in private, it was heartily disliked by many who felt it was a cynical manoeuvre which was incompatible with Tory principles.[46] Indeed, the referendum had been advocated before 1910 on the Unionist side primarily by thinkers like A. V. Dicey and William Lecky who were Liberal Unionists.[47] Though they vigorously defended the Union, both men were still sufficiently Liberal to believe that only a measure which embraced popular sovereignty would ultimately be justified in blocking measures like home rule.

Herein lay the Liberals' difficulty. The referendum was an eminently liberal proposal, which was supported by leading Liberal intellectuals like J. A. Hobson.[48] Many Liberals distrusted it as a distraction from the Commons v. Lords battle and as an idea that was primarily associated with Unionist thinking. But they found it very difficult to attack in principle. Almost all the Liberal criticism of the referendum in 1910–11 focused on points of detail about how it would function in practice.[49] The Liberals found themselves in 1910–11 defending the Commons as the only appropriate depository of the popular will and spurning elections to the second chamber and the referendum. But this was the outcome of the tactical situation in 1910–11 and the exigencies of the Irish alliance, even if it could be justified by referring to the distinctive traditions of British history. It was not, however, the only possible alternative for Liberals. Once they had accepted it in April 1910, though, there was no going back and it proved the basis of the Parliament Act of 1911 which was finally passed by the Lords under the threat of a mass creation of Liberal Peers. The period after the election merely saw a rehearsal of the arguments of 1910, though, as the two sides found it impossible to move from their entrenched positions.

Franchise reform

The party's difficulties over the House of Lords were a sign that while all Liberals thought they were democrats, the practical application of that belief to the British constitution was problematic. However, the Lords was not the only obstacle to the achievement of democracy. In 1884–5 Britain acquired a genuinely mass electorate, but one with an exceptionally complex system under which adult males had to qualify to vote. As J. A. Pease put it in 1912 'The intricacy of our franchise laws is without parallel in the history of the civilized world.'[50] Essentially, most men gained their vote as householders, which effectively meant the male head of the household in a separate dwelling.[51] But this made it difficult for adult sons living at home and lodgers to qualify. Certain groups, like those in receipt of poor relief, were disfranchised and everyone was inconvenienced by the cumbersome process of drawing up the electoral roll. Electors had to be in residence for a year in the same constituency to register (in effect, at the same address) and this disqualified millions of men each year. As a result, no more than two thirds of adult males were on the register to vote at any time. Most men moved on and off the register depending on their circumstances. The system certainly discriminated against younger, single men and anyone who moved regularly. Whether it was biased in terms of class is more debatable. Certainly, many politicians of the early twentieth century believed the poorest had least chance of voting.

One aspect of the system which did display obvious class bias was the continued existence of plural voting, which accounted for six to seven per cent of all votes. The rules governing this practice were exceptionally complex, but it occurred mainly in the counties and consisted of men who qualified to vote in one seat through their residence, but were allowed to vote in one or more other constituencies by virtue of owning property there worth 40 shillings per annum (in a county seat) or occupying as owner or tenant any land or building worth £10 per annum (in an English borough). Most of these people were probably small property owners or businessmen. There were also nine seats where only university graduates could vote, in addition to their residential qualification. There were not many plural voters, but they could easily turn the result of a close contest, especially as they tended to be concentrated in particular seats.

The 1884–5 reform acts which embedded this bizarre combination of systems had been a compromise between Liberals and Tories. Many Liberals always regarded them as undermining the principle of democracy and the equal value of all men's contribution to the political process. In 1888 the NLF called for a complete overhaul of the system on the basis of a simple residency qualification.[52] Gladstone accepted the need for some change that year, the issue was promoted heavily by the leadership at the 1892 election and there was an abortive registration bill in 1893–4.[53] Thereafter it remained an object to which Liberals were committed and which was regularly mentioned in Liberal election addresses.[54] Analysis of the voting system by Liberal and Conservative agents confirmed widespread beliefs that it worked against Liberals, especially in the case of plural voting, which delivered nearly 50 seats to the Tories at the close election of December 1910.[55] This clearly distinguished the Liberals from the Unionists, who mounted a robust

defence of the existing system, especially the plural vote as a recognition of superior talents and wealth which might be overwhelmed in a
democracy.[56] Reforming the electoral system mattered profoundly to
Liberals, but it took a long while to force its way up the agenda of the
Edwardian Liberal governments.

This was partly because no clearly definable class of adult males were
excluded from the franchise – most men appeared on the register
periodically. It was also obvious that the Lords would block any change
detrimental to Unionism, as they did with a bill to abolish plural voting
in 1906. But there were also tactical difficulties. Any change to the
voting system raised the question of the distribution of constituencies,
which had not changed since 1885. While Liberals might hope to
benefit from more seats being allocated to expanding working class
suburbs, the falling population in rural seats in Ireland, Scotland and
Wales would result in the disappearance of safe anti-Unionist constituencies. In particular, Irish representation would have to fall by nearly 50
seats to take account of Ireland's declining population since the Act of
Union and this would mainly hit the Nationalists.[57] Neither they nor
their Liberal allies would agree to this until home rule was a real prospect.
Finally, electoral reform also raised the issue of women's suffrage, on
which Liberals were very deeply divided. It was, therefore, no coincidence
that Asquith's government delayed bringing forward a comprehensive
electoral reform bill until 1912, when not only had the House of Lords'
absolute veto been abolished, but home rule was about to be introduced
and pressure had grown intense for an initiative on women's suffrage.[58]
The bill provided for a simple system, based on a six month residence
qualification and continuous registration. It could be amended to apply
to women as well. Plural voters would only be able to exercise one of
their franchises and redistribution would follow the bill, but not until
home rule was law. This bill only failed because it was torpedoed by the
Speaker's ruling on a technical point and it was replaced in 1913 by
simple bill outlawing plural voting, as there was no parliamentary time
for a more complex measure, which would undoubtedly be delayed by
the Lords for two years.

On the issue of the adult male franchise, the Liberals were strongly
committed to a democratic solution, and only the complexity of the
subject and tactical considerations prevented them acting more successfully and urgently. Sweeping plans for proportional representation (PR)
or the alternative vote (AV) were more divisive. PR had a number of
Liberal advocates since the 1880s, partly on the grounds that it would
allow a better representation of minority opinion (this also appealed to

a few Unionists) and partly that it was a more accurate representation of the electorate's wishes.[59] Liberals were certainly not opposed to the measure on principle – it was 'excellent in theory' as Churchill said and it was applied to elections for the Irish second chamber under the 1912 home rule bill, in order to ensure a fair representation of southern Unionist opinion.[60] A Royal Commission looked into the matter in 1908–10, but the leadership was unwilling to take it any further forward.[61] The Liberals benefited from dominating certain areas as well as suffering from under-representation in Tory parts of the country, so any commitment to PR would have been a huge gamble and unlikely to receive backing from many Liberal MPs. Its most enthusiastic supporters in the party seem to have been in London, where the (Liberal) Progressives were increasingly angry at small (Unionist) Moderate majorities in local elections producing an overwhelming preponderance on local councils.[62] But in January 1910 PR would probably have reduced the overall anti-Unionist majority from 124 to 56. The party organisation, on the other hand, favoured AV in order to avoid losing seats to the Unionists when Labour and Liberals split the 'progressive' vote. This was seriously considered in 1912 and possibly only shortage of parliamentary time prevented its appearance in the reform bill of that year.[63] The matter was probably not thought urgent as Labour's progress in by-elections was strictly limited and AV might anyway encourage more Labour candidacies. But the party was not irrevocably committed to the first past the post system, despite its deep roots in history. All Liberals accepted that the electoral system had to reflect the voters' wishes and that might mean radically changing the way voting happened.

Democracy was one of the party's motifs in the early twentieth century and popular control was regarded as a sovereign remedy, not just at the national level, but in the locality, too. Liberals had championed the school boards abolished by the Tories in 1902, many argued for the local veto to control the drink trade and Liberalism was associated on many councils with those who wanted to extend the powers and functions of local government. An argument that referred back to the need for popular participation was difficult for Liberals to resist. Or at least it would require compelling reasons for it to be rejected. However, in one conspicuous area, that of women's suffrage, the Liberal party noticeably failed to prove itself the 'democratic' party. Instead, the issue proved one of the party's most agonising quarrels of the Edwardian era.

Women's suffrage was an eminently Liberal cause. At a parliamentary level the movement had really begun in the 1860s among a circle of high-minded Liberal intellectuals and MPs and under the patronage of

John Stuart Mill, the presiding intellectual genius of mid nineteenth-century Liberalism.[64] For the rest of the nineteenth century its best-known protagonists were leading Liberals like Henry Fawcett, Sir Charles Dilke and James Stansfeld and there was far more support for the measure among Liberal MPs than among Tories. This Liberal genesis was not surprising. Liberals were associated with wishing to extend the vote to excluded groups. As more and more men were given the franchise it raised the question of whether women should be included, too. After all, many women owned property, paid taxes, were formally educated or acted as the head of a household and thus fulfilled all the attributes that were commonly associated with justifying extending the vote to new groups of men. As J. S. Mill eloquently put it in 1867, 'Can it be pretended that women who manage a business – who pay rates and taxes, often to a large amount, and frequently from their own earnings – many of whom are responsible heads of families ... are not capable of a function of which every male householder is capable?'[65] The argument for female suffrage was, in fact, fundamentally the same set of reasons that had been put forward for allowing more men to vote. Naturally, it appealed more to Liberals than to Conservatives. However, after 1885, when most of the male electorate was propertyless and working class, some Conservatives also came round to the idea that it was illogical to exclude women from the franchise. The crucial distinction between Tory and Liberal suffragists, though, was that most of the former only wished to give the vote to a minority of propertied women, while Liberals usually favoured the principle of a much wider enfranchisement.[66]

The other argument for women's enfranchisement which was associated with Liberalism concentrated on women's difference from men, not their similarity. It suggested that women were interested in separate subjects than men and if they were allowed to vote this would make an important contribution to changing the agenda of politics. It was, for instance, commonly asserted that women were more interested in temperance and aspects of social reform, especially those concerning children, than men were. Certainly many women who were involved in local government were closely connected with these issues.[67] These were also subjects associated with important strands of Liberalism and this made women's enfranchisement particularly attractive to many Liberals.

Thus there were two kinds of argument in favour of women's suffrage that appealed directly to Liberalism. However, it was clear in the late nineteenth century that the cause had prominent enemies in the Liberal camp. Gladstone, Rosebery and Asquith were all opponents of women's suffrage and in the eleven votes on the subject in the Commons before

1900, a majority of Liberal MPs were against in five of them.[68] An examination of the arguments used by Liberals in opposition to women's suffrage is revealing, though. As with the 'pro' position, the 'antis' had two broad categories of argument. The first centred on the concept of separate spheres. This was essentially the idea that nature (or sometimes God) had ordained men and women to different roles in life. Man's proper function was the public aspect of life, including politics and voting. Women, on the other hand, should reign in the home and family life and the genders should each respect the other's role. Whether or not women owned property or paid taxes was irrelevant to this fundamental natural division. As Asquith put it, 'the natural distinction of sex' was central to human life and 'ought to continue to be recognized, as it always has been recognized, in the sphere of parliamentary representation.'[69]

The other set of arguments against women's suffrage focused on the deleterious effects of allowing women to vote. These could be expressed in a number of ways. For instance, following on from the separate spheres idea, Gladstone suggested that if women entered the political arena this would change the whole role of women in society, injure family life and undermine women's femininity.[70] Asquith argued that it was not equitable for women to vote as they could not be required to take part in enforcing laws they had helped to make and female enfranchisement would therefore endanger the whole structure of politics.[71] Moreover, he stated that women did not want the vote and were not interested in politics, so their judgements would be faulty in political matters. Women were adequately represented in parliament already by their fathers and husbands and parliament had dealt with any real grievances that women had. Female suffrage was, therefore, superfluous and could only bring dangers in its wake.

All these arguments were advanced at the highest level of Liberalism. But it became increasingly clear that they had less and less purchase in the Liberal party. In 1905 a NLF resolution sponsored by the executive in favour of women's suffrage passed easily.[72] A majority of Liberal MPs supported backbench bills on women's suffrage in 1906–9, including one introduced by Henry Yorke Stanger in 1908 which passed its second reading with a majority of 179. Asquith seems to have made the question an open one in his cabinet.[73] In 1911 the government offered parliamentary time to the 'conciliation bill' to enfranchise some women and in 1912 it brought forwards its own reform bill, which could be amended to include women's suffrage.[74] By then Asquith was in a minority in his cabinet. The leading 'anti', apart from the prime minister, was Harcourt, essentially a second rank figure, while Lloyd George, Grey and Haldane were all pro-suffrage.[75] Leading historians of the suffrage movement, like Martin Pugh, have speculated that the Liberals would have gone into a 1915 election committed to giving women the vote.[76]

The gradual ascendancy of the suffrage argument within Liberalism was probably unstoppable by 1914 and this slow triumph had an important ideological dimension. This was because anti-suffrage Liberals suffered from a major handicap in putting their case. While pro-suffrage arguments could appeal directly to Liberal ideas, anti-suffrage arguments were not distinctively Liberal. They were the same arguments that anti-suffrage Tories used.[77] In effect, the 'antis' were suggesting that in the field of women's suffrage Liberal ideas had to give way to other ideologies, just as, for instance, in foreign affairs and defence many Liberals believed ideas of national interest took precedence over Liberal approaches. However, this point was much more difficult to sustain when discussing the suffrage. All Liberals regarded their party and ideology to be especially associated with extending the franchise. It was problematic, to say the least, to suggest that Liberal arguments should not apply to some parts of this issue. Moreover, on defence and foreign affairs the Liberal Imperialists provided a coherent strand in the party who stood for the primacy of national interest arguments. No such grouping existed to resist women's suffrage.[78] Ultimately, it was an individual decision and may well have been closely linked in many cases to deeply personal views about the role of women. Asquith's anti-suffragism, for instance, can be connected to his two marriages, as his first wife took no interest in public life, while his second, Margot, was given to interventions in politics which were occasionally embarrassing and potentially disastrous.[79]

Anti-suffrage Liberals knew their cause was in retreat for most of the Edwardian era, though. The essential difficulties of making the anti-suffrage case within a Liberal framework were increasingly compounded by the problems of relating anti-suffragism to political and social realities. The whole idea of separate spheres just did not seem to describe the situation within Liberalism in two important ways. Firstly, women had been allowed to vote in some local government elections since 1869 and had first served on some authorities in 1870.[80] After 1907 they could vote for and sit on every body up to and including county councils. Many women Liberals took advantage of this opportunity and served on local authorities. This practice could be accepted within the separate spheres idea on the understanding that local politics was essentially an extension of women's caring and nurturing role in the home and excluded the 'masculine' topics dealt with by parliament. But in the 1900s this seemed an increasingly artificial distinction. Bodies like the London County Council were responsible for a huge range of functions in one of the world's greatest cities. If women could help decide issues connected to tramways, gasworks and land purchase at the local level it was hard to see why they could not do so in parliament. Moreover, the welfare functions traditionally ascribed to local government and the feminine sphere were increasingly intruding into national debates. If it was helpful to have women's contribution to running the poor law, then surely they could also contribute to debates on pensions, national insurance and minimum wages.

Secondly, even if the separate spheres ideology insisted women Liberals should not take part in parliamentary politics, they already did. With the creation of a mass electorate in the 1880s and the restrictions on candidates' election expenses, all parties required an army of voluntary helpers to make speeches, canvass voters, raise funds and deliver leaflets. A number of local Women's Liberal Associations were set up and they coalesced into a national Women's Liberal Federation (WLF) in 1887.[81] By the Edwardian era women were a vital part of most active constituency associations and all politicians were familiar with the sight of women performing every political function that men did, except voting. The separate spheres idea increasingly described an ideal world that had long ceased to exist in the Liberal party. To make their feelings clear on the matter, the national executive of the WLF refused to give aid to Liberal candidates who were anti-suffragists after 1902, thus giving Liberal MPs another incentive to support a female franchise.

Given the clear trend in the party towards women's suffrage, historians have taken some care to analyse why the party did not produce an enfranchisement bill before 1914. One problem was always parliamentary tactics. In the period 1906–9, when the demand for voting rights for women was building up, the government line was always that a major measure of electoral reform could only be considered towards the end of a parliament, as it would have to be followed fairly closely by an election, which would allow the new voters to participate in the political process.[82] But a government bill on women's suffrage would deeply divide the cabinet, so Asquith always insisted such a measure could only be the result of an amendment on a free vote to a franchise bill.[83] But when the government's bill appeared in 1912, the attempt to amend it was ruled out of order by the Speaker in January 1913 and it was abandoned. This meant there was no parliamentary time left before a 1915 election for a complex bill, which would undoubtedly be opposed by the Lords and take two years to pass.

The only other way a women's suffrage bill could pass was as an agreed measure between pro-suffrage Liberal and Unionist MPs in the Commons, which would then have a good chance of being accepted by the Unionist-dominated House of Lords. This was the strategy adopted by the conciliation committee of MPs from all parties in 1910–12.[84] It was certainly not a far-fetched or naïve idea. The bill they produced in 1911 passed the Commons by 255 to 88. This was possible because, like the Liberals, the Unionists were divided about women's suffrage and there was a distinguished Tory minority of supporters of the cause, including Balfour and Bonar Law. As the conciliation bill was drawn up on the basis of satisfying the maximum number of MPs it took their views into account and only proposed to enfranchise the minority of women who could describe themselves as householders. This was the same classification that was already in use for most male voters, but when applied to women it would exclude most married women, because their husband would already be qualified to vote as the householder. Thus only widows, separated and unmarried women who were heads of households would be able to vote, together with richer married women, whose husbands owned or occupied two or more buildings or pieces of land, thus allowing them both to qualify for one of these properties.

Many Liberal MPs were prepared to vote for such a measure in order to establish the principle of female enfranchisement. But this could not disguise the fact that Liberal suffragists could not accept the conciliation bill as a final settlement of the women's suffrage question. Most of them favoured a very broad franchise for women, as embodied in W. H. Dickinson's bill of 1907, which wanted to give the vote to wives of male householders, as well as female heads of households, or Geoffrey Howard's adult suffrage bill of 1909, which imposed a simple residence requirement on all adults. As Liberals believed in the efficacy of popular participation and control for men, most of them who were suffragists could not accept a restricted female enfranchisement bill as other than an interim measure. The committed suffragist Arnold Rowntree noted of the 1910 conciliation bill, 'Bad though the Bill is, I shall vote for it hoping that if it was passed it would be followed by an Electoral Reform Bill widening the franchise...'.[85]

This Liberal-Conservative coalition on women's suffrage was broken by the increasing suspicion in the Liberal party about Tory motives. In particular, several members of the cabinet, especially Churchill and Lloyd George, and figures in the party organisation came to believe that the conciliation bill was merely an attempt by the Unionists to enfranchise a small group of wealthy women who would be likely to vote against the Liberals. Lloyd George complained the bill would 'on balance add hundreds of thousands of votes to the strength of the Tory Party'.[86] Extensive enquires among Liberal agents and the regional federations confirmed this impression, though it was hotly disputed by some of the bill's proponents.[87] But it was overwhelmingly these considerations of party advantage which motivated the suffragists in the Liberal cabinet to turn against the conciliation bill in 1911 and promote instead the government's reform bill of 1912, which they hoped could be amended to secure a wide female franchise. In 1912 the conciliation bill was defeated by 222 to 208 and one of the crucial factors was that while the Liberal majority for it in 1911 was 109, in 1912 it was only 44.[88] The anti-suffragists were relieved by this turn of events and some advocates of women's suffrage felt the party had betrayed an excellent opportunity to establish the principle of female enfranchisement. But this manoeuvre was only possible because politicians like Lloyd George could appeal to the party's commitment to democracy as something that superseded any belief in the principle of women's suffrage.[89] This was just too powerful an argument for most Liberal MPs.

Thus a combination of tactics, party advantage and ideology prevented women's suffrage becoming law, despite its widespread acceptance in the Liberal party by 1914. There can be little doubt that this prolonged wrangle and inertia did the party harm. Defections from the WLF were becoming noticeable in 1912–14 and the National Union of Women's Suffrage Societies (NUWSS), the main non-violent suffrage organisation, which contained many active women Liberals, formed an Election Fighting Fund in 1912 to sponsor Labour candidates against anti-suffrage Liberal ministers.[90] Historians have only been surprised that there was not even more disaffection among women Liberals. That there was not is testimony to the way in which the Liberal party was associated with promoting an agenda that politically active women could identify with, even if it did not deliver women's suffrage.

Some women Liberals, like those in the Women's National Liberal Association (WNLA), which withdrew from the WLF in 1893 over its suffrage pledge, found it possible to identify with Liberalism in an unproblematic way.[91] But the WLF was an independent organisation that was not controlled by the party leadership and had its own slate of policies – in contrast to Tory women's organisations. In the Edwardian era it became increasingly vocal on the suffrage issue and only narrowly rejected pleas for local branches to refuse help to any anti-suffragist

Liberal MPs.[92] That most women Liberals stayed with the organisation can only be explained by referring to the other activities that female Liberals were involved in apart from suffrage campaigns. It was for instance noticeable that Rosalind, Countess of Carlisle, the President of the WLF in 1891–1901 and 1906–14 was also a famous temperance activist, as well as a suffragist.[93] Many women Liberals were also active in local government and through their experience of administering the poor law had become active social reformers.[94] Others were involved in 'social purity' movements that tried to eradicate the double standard in sexual behaviour.[95] On this kind of issue the Liberals seemed to offer the best hope of progress. This was obviously true on temperance and social reform and even on 'social purity' issues which governments tended to shy away from, the Liberals showed some movement, as in 1912 when they provided time for a Criminal Law Amendment Act to tighten up the law on prostitution.[96] Many feminists were also campaigning for government action on the prevalence and treatment of venereal diseases and the Liberals appointed a Royal Commission on the issue in 1913, taking care to rule out any return to the Contagious Diseases Acts of the 1860s which had so enraged many women.[97] To many female Liberals these were feminist issues, just as much as the suffrage was, and Liberalism was willing to identify itself with them, even when it meant attacking entrenched forms of masculine behaviour, as with temperance. This convinced enough women Liberals that the party remained on their 'side' and in particular that it was prepared to rebalance gender relations away from an endorsement of masculine behaviour that harmed women and towards a much more responsible idea of masculinity.

Democracy was a concept all Liberals could agree on, yet it managed to divide them profoundly in the Edwardian era in any number of ways. This was always partly a matter of tactics. But it also represented ideological disagreements. There was no simple answer to whether a suspensory veto or an elected House of Lords was more democratic, or whether PR or AV should be preferred to the first past the post system. On women's suffrage Liberals disagreed about whether arguments surrounding the nature of gender identity should have preference over their concern for democracy. Ironically, certain forms of female enfranchisement were even opposed in the name of democracy. This confusion has often been skated over by historians in favour of an examination of the party's attitudes on the 'new' agenda of social reform. But, in fact, Irish home rule, Lords reform and women's suffrage were all far more problematic precisely because they caused disagreement about the party's core beliefs and how these should be applied.

5
A Nonconformist Party?

One of the truisms about nineteenth-century Liberalism was its identification with religious nonconformity.[1] This had deep roots that could be traced back to the late seventeenth century and the association of Toryism with the Church of England and Whiggery with religious toleration for dissenters. Many Victorians assumed the continuing connection between religion and political allegiance to be one of the fundamental aspects of their public life. But in the twentieth century this link steadily weakened as religion was increasingly consigned to the world of private opinion and conscience.[2] Precisely when this occurred and why has proved a matter of considerable historical controversy, but the Edwardian era has attracted a good deal of attention as one of the crucial moments in this process. This is partly because it saw the emergence of the new Labour party and the agenda of social welfare and redistributive taxation at the national level and partly because it witnessed the last great church versus chapel struggles.[3] To many historians, religion seemed much less important to politics in 1914 than it had done in, say, 1906. One significant way of investigating this idea is to examine in what senses Edwardian Liberalism functioned as the 'party of nonconformity' in this period and how this concept related to the wider ideological concerns of Liberalism.

Nonconformity and Liberalism

Liberalism and nonconformity were bound together by more than memories of the seventeenth century. In a very general, but fundamental, sense their ideologies meshed.[4] Firstly, Liberalism stood for freedom of speech and assembly and this naturally included the right of people to worship in their own way, unmolested by the state. Similarly, nonconformity, by its very name and origins, was an assertion of people's rights and liberties not to conform to the doctrines of the established church and to organise and practice their religion outside of its control. Secondly, Liberals disliked hierarchies that claimed a divine sanction for their role in society, whether they were monarchs or bishops. To Liberals, the only legitimate source of political authority was popular consent. Nonconformity fitted in neatly with this approach. Denominations and congregations organised their own affairs and all allowed considerable lay participation. Ministers were not intermediaries between the human and the divine, but lecturers and teachers. Liberalism and nonconformity often appealed to people for much the same reasons and were seen by their followers as naturally complementary.

These ties were confirmed during the nineteenth century. It was mainly Liberals who associated themselves with campaigns to free nonconformists from what they regarded as penalties consequent upon their faith, like the obligation to pay rates to the Church of England, which was finally abolished in 1868. On the other hand, most nonconformists saw the struggle to keep the state out of religion as anomalous to other campaigns to free society from state interference and they generally favoured Liberal causes like free trade. To many nonconformists, extending the franchise was no more than endorsing the popular participation seen in governing the chapels. Analysis of Victorian pre-secret ballot elections confirms that by the mid nineteenth century there was a strong correlation between being a nonconformist and voting Liberal.[5]

However, the relationship was never unproblematic. Most active and committed nonconformists may have been Liberals, but they were not the only components of Liberalism. Moreover, the particular interests of nonconformists did not always match the tactical concerns of Liberal governments or all the elements in Liberal ideology. Finally, nonconformists did not agree, even about policies that directly affected the role of their denominations in society. This meant that numerous arguments disrupted the nonconformist–Liberal relationship in the nineteenth century. For instance, Gladstone's Education Act of 1870 was popular with many Liberals, because by allowing the establishment of elementary schools under the control of local boards elected by ratepayers, it enhanced local democracy. But it outraged some nonconformists because it failed to eliminate the leading role of the Church of England in providing mass education.[6] The Liberal commitment to Irish home rule in 1886 may have been compatible with Liberal notions of nationality and self-government, but it offended some nonconformists, who disliked the idea of setting up a Roman Catholic-dominated parliament in

Dublin.[7] While there was a close link between Liberal and nonconformist worldviews, this did not mean that the party simply reflected nonconformist opinion. The relationship between nonconformist ideas and attitudes and the specific policies pursued by Liberal governments was always fraught and complex. This situation was also reflected in the Edwardian era.

Church versus chapel

Some of the most important grievances that nonconformists held against the established churches had been settled in the nineteenth century. Nonconformists could hold public office, they no longer required an Anglican clergyman to officiate at their weddings and they could enter higher education, even at Anglican foundations like Oxford and Cambridge. But two issues rumbled on and played important parts in Edwardian politics; education and disestablishment. Between them they ensured that the battle between church and chapel remained crucial to political identity.

Education was one of the key issues facing the new Liberal government of 1905. A committee was appointed to prepare a bill on the subject at the cabinet's first meeting and the subsequent 1906 education bill was the major, and most controversial, government measure of the year.[8] This priority reflected the need to respond to Balfour's Education Act of 1902 and the furore it had produced. This act was in turn the first major piece of educational legislation since Gladstone's act of 1870 and a determined attempt to alter the terms of that settlement.[9] Since 1870 there had been two systems of public elementary education for the mass of the population. The first consisted of 'voluntary' schools founded by religious denominations and supported by direct grants from the Treasury – though these grants did not meet all the schools' costs. This type of school was overwhelmingly Anglican, though Catholics and some Wesleyans also had their own schools. As well as general education, they provided instruction in the faith of the denomination that ran and owned the school. The second type of school was those set up under the 1870 act, to provide schools where the churches had not met local needs. They were entirely funded by local ratepayers and responsible to locally elected school boards. They, too, could provide religious instruction, but only in the basic ideas of Christianity, drawn from reading the bible. This was acceptable to nonconformists, but not to Anglicans or Catholics, who insisted on the need for their church's guidance on how to interpret the bible.

Many nonconformists had disliked Gladstone's 1870 act for leaving the Church's position in schooling intact. But they had come round to seeing the merits of the system.[10] If they organised efficiently, they could dominate the school boards and ensure more schools were built, that they kept out any hint of Anglican instruction and that they were better-funded and equipped than the voluntary schools. Gradually, they could hope the board schools would squeeze out their Anglican rivals and indeed by the later 1890s it seemed that the increasing expense of teachers' salaries, the upkeep of buildings and rising expectations of educational provision was condemning the voluntary schools to a slow death. They were saved from this fate by Balfour. His 1902 act replaced the dual system by making both voluntary and board schools eligible for full support from local ratepayers. The school boards were abolished and all schools were placed under the authority of committees of the local county or county borough council. However, councils could only nominate two of the six governors on the boards of ex-voluntary schools. This ensured they could retain control of their denominational religious teaching and only appoint teachers of their faith.

Nonconformists rightly interpreted this as a blatant attempt to shore up the position of Anglicanism in education. They particularly objected to the idea of paying rates to support denominational teaching that they regarded as erroneous. It seemed like a return to the old days before 1868, when nonconformists could be compelled to pay rates towards the upkeep of the parish church. By the end of 1905, over 65,000 had protested by refusing to pay their local rates and suffered distraint of their goods by the bailiffs and over 150 had been imprisoned.[11] The outpouring of anger played an important role in dissolving the Unionist government's popularity after 1902 and Liberals were happy to side with the forces of nonconformity. As Campbell-Bannerman stressed, the 1902 act was 'a mere Church bill in disguise', which only served to privilege the interests of Anglicans at the expense of other denominations.[12] 86 per cent of Liberal election addresses in 1906 demanded the amendment of the offensive act.[13] Only free trade was mentioned more often by Liberal candidates. However, exactly what this amendment would be was rarely spelt out in any detail – an approach also favoured by the Liberal leadership.

The reasons behind this reticence soon became apparent when the government began to shape its education bill. The nonconformist demand to abolish rate support for denominational instruction in ex-voluntary schools that were now part of the local authority system was compatible with Liberalism. It certainly seemed an infringement of the liberties of citizens to compel them to contribute to religious instruction whose content they could not endorse. But most nonconformists and Liberals, like almost everyone in Edwardian Britain, accepted that religion was a crucial part of a child's education. This was not disputed even by notably irreligious figures in Liberalism, like John Morley, and the idea of a purely secular state education system had very little support – it was backed by only 63 MPs when the 1906 bill was debated in the Commons.[14] It followed, therefore, that parents had a right and duty to have their child educated in the form of Christianity which they accepted. Nonconformists could approve of the biblical instruction being given in ex-board schools, but conscientious Anglicans and Catholics could not and wished for their children to be taught the particular approach of their denomination. Anything else would be an infringement of their religious liberty, just as much as it was to compel nonconformists to pay rates for Anglican or Catholic religious teaching. Therefore, Liberals had to find a way of accommodating both the nonconformists' objections to supporting denominational teaching and the right of Anglicans and Catholics to have provision for such teaching in the local authority system. Liberal concern for religious liberty could not just be concern for nonconformist liberties.

If this were not complex enough, the church versus chapel argument was not the only Liberal approach to education. The party contained some people who believed that the religious conflict was a distraction from the real issues in education.[15] Liberalism stood for the realisation of the self's potential, free from artificial constraints. It could be argued, therefore, that education was central to this goal, because nobody could develop their talents without the fullest possible access to a system of teaching which allowed them to recognise and develop their abilities. Liberals' aims in education should concentrate on extending educational provision, by, for instance, reducing the size of elementary school classes, raising the school leaving-age to fourteen, making more free secondary school places available or expanding university education. This approach found much to recommend in the 1902 act, which had definitely improved the resources available in ex-voluntary schools and moved closer to a single national education system. At the leadership level, Haldane was particularly associated with these ideas and he had openly approved of Balfour's act, much to the rage of nonconformists.[16] When Campbell-Bannerman formed his government, he offered the parliamentary secretaryship at the board of education to T. J. Macnamara, a Liberal MP and prominent figure in the National Union of Teachers.[17] But Macnamara refused, because he knew any attempt to undo the

1902 Education Act would split elementary teachers, as many of those in ex-voluntary schools had benefited from the legislation and approved its aims.

Finally, even those Liberals who accepted the necessity of a new education bill did not always share the priorities of nonconformist protestors. What had enraged many Liberals about Balfour's act was its lack of respect for the principle of public control and accountability. Not only had it abolished the school boards, it had allowed ex-voluntary schools to receive rate support, while representatives of the local authority were only a minority on their boards of governors. These schools could, therefore, continue to act in ways which local ratepayers disapproved of, even though they paid for the children's education. Liberals particularly disliked the idea that they could maintain a religious 'test' when employing teachers, thus excluding any applicant who was not from the denomination who controlled the school. This seemed to many Liberals to be an infringement of religious liberty and often an arbitrary exercise of clerical power, as local priests were usually prominent on such boards of governors. The key for many Liberals was, therefore, to make these schools ultimately accountable to the people, if they wished to receive public support, rather than necessarily to concentrate on the issue of denominational instruction.[18]

All these problems made the education bill of 1906 a minefield of potential divisions within Liberalism. The cabinet committee who considered the bill struggled along for two months, revealing deep disagreements. Crewe wished the bill to be part of a wider overhaul of the whole elementary system, but was worn down by his colleagues' insistence on the overriding political imperative to tackle the religious issue.[19] Birrell, the President of the Board of Education, argued forcefully that the key issue was that all rate-supported schools should be controlled by the local council, and in this he was supported by the whole committee. But he wished to find a compromise between the liberty of nonconformists to refuse to support denominational education and the liberty of parents who wished their children to receive this teaching.[20] His suggestion was that denominational instruction should no longer be financed from the rates. But, in return, denominational instruction could be provided by private means and outside school hours on two mornings a week in any school, ex-voluntary or ex-school board, for any child whose parents wished it to attend ('ordinary' facilities or clause 3). It was expected that this option would mainly be exercised by Anglicans. But Catholics needed their schools to have a much more specifically Catholic regime. So Birrell took up Haldane's suggestion that in any school where 80 per cent of parents requested the measure, there could be denominational instruction on every day of the week and no non-denominational bible instruction at all ('special' facilities or clause 4). Birrell hoped this would satisfy both sides of the denominational argument and thus provide the bill with a chance of passing the Lords and providing a final settlement of the issue.

But in cabinet, Birrell's careful balance was modified to make the bill more acceptable to nonconformists. Denominational instruction was confined to ex-voluntary schools and excluded from ex-board schools and clause 4 was restricted to urban areas with over 5,000 people, to ensure rural Anglican schools could not take advantage of its provisions.[21] This represented a clear victory for those like Lloyd George who wished to ensure nonconformist support for the bill, but it also divided the cabinet precisely because acceding to nonconformist demands was not the only priority for many Liberals. In the Commons, though, the bill was generally accepted by Liberal MPs. Most believed it was still a genuine attempt to satisfy the conflicting elements in the Liberal approach to educational controversies. But it was also subjected to intense pressures. Catholics among Liberals and Nationalists wished to extend the operations and terms of clause 4 and some MPs, including a segment of nonconformists, wished to amend it so that Anglicans could have a better chance of taking advantage of its provisions.[22] On the other hand, many nonconformists were aghast at the provision for denominational education, especially in clause 4, which aroused considerable anti-Catholic feeling. The Wesleyan Conference refused to support the bill and the Baptists and Congregationalists demanded significant amendment.[23] There could be no clearer indication that Liberalism was not merely a mouthpiece for nonconformist interests. Most Liberals could appreciate hostility to rate-aided denominational education, but by taking this stand, the nonconformist bodies seemed to be motivated by nothing more than hostility to Anglicanism and Catholicism.

The bill's greatest hurdle, though, was the Lords, which passed the bill's second reading, but then proceeded to amend it out of all recognition to protect the denominational schools. Pressure was brought to bear, though, from sources as various as the Monarch, the Archbishop of Canterbury, the Duke of Devonshire and John Morley to try and reach an agreement.[24] There were numerous private consultations between the parties and a formal conference on 18 December 1906, before peace talks finally collapsed and the bill was withdrawn because the Lords insisted on their amendments. But the government's behaviour was instructive. It was definitely prepared to make further concessions on denominational instruction, particularly by allowing teachers employed in local authority schools to provide this sort of course, but only if the local council agreed. The Unionists demanded teachers in any school have the right to undertake denominational teaching, but Crewe insisted that the cabinet could not compromise on councils' ultimate control.[25] Thus the government was prepared to increase the amount of denominational instruction in schools, even though this horrified many nonconformists and seemed to nullify the whole point of their struggle since 1902. But they were not prepared to reduce the amount of popular control of ex-voluntary schools. The key point was local democracy, rather than the victory of one side in the church versus chapel argument. This attitude bore some resemblance to the Liberal-nonconformist argument over Gladstone's education act of 1870, which had introduced popular control of board schools but not directly assaulted the Church's position in education.

The convoluted events of 1906 had revealed the real difficulties of producing legislation that accommodated nonconformist interests, accorded with other Liberal ideas and priorities and had any chance of passing the House of Lords. McKenna, who succeeded Birrell at the Board of Education in 1907, attempted a different approach. First, he did what he could through administrative regulations, rather than legislation. Most importantly, he tackled the teacher training colleges, which were state-funded but largely Anglican or Catholic foundations, and which only admitted trainees of their own denomination.[26] McKenna insisted they abolish religious tests if they wished to continue to be state-funded. This move made it much easier for nonconformists to train as teachers and accorded well with Liberal notions of religious liberty. But on the central question of amending the 1902 Education Act, McKenna had much less success. He initially introduced a short bill which required ex-voluntary schools to refund to the local council one-fifteenth of the salary of all teachers who had undertaken denominational instruction. This was an ingenious measure, designed to ensure that nonconformists were no longer paying rates to support denominational teaching, but most nonconformist MPs demanded a wider settlement of the issues raised by the 1902 act.[27]

McKenna responded by withdrawing his bill and introducing a more comprehensive measure on 24 February 1908, which drew on some of the ideas of a committee of backbench nonconformist MPs.[28] Much of it was familiar. Once again it insisted that all schools funded from the rates should come under full control of the local council and have no religious tests for teachers. Denominational teaching was allowed on two days a week, as long as it was not given by the school's teachers and was outside of normal hours. The most important innovation was that ex-voluntary schools could return to their pre-1902 situation by 'contracting out' of the local authority's control. They could receive a state grant, but this would be much less than rate-aided funding. This would mean the state was still funding denominational instruction, but only on the terms it had done so before 1902, and nonconformists could hope that the less generous financial provision for contracted-out schools would gradually force most of them to agree to local authority control in return for funding from the rates. This bill in turn was withdrawn when it seemed unlikely to secure much enthusiasm from nonconformists or agreement from the Church or House of Lords.

But the next President of the Board of Education, Walter Runciman, used it as a basis to explore an agreement between the churches.[29] By this time the government was increasingly desperate to prove it could settle the long-running sore of the education issue and it pushed its nonconformist supporters to the limits of their patience in order to produce a bill that could be accepted by the Church of England and the Lords. Runciman's bill of 20 November 1908 repeated many of the features of McKenna's proposals, but it went further to appease Anglican feelings. Crucially, it suggested all schools could have denominational teaching in school hours and this instruction could be given by the school's teachers (though local authorities would not pay them for this work). To many nonconformists this was a victory for the Church because it ensured Anglican schools could keep their denominational character within the rate-aided system – the very issue that had so outraged them in 1902. The other side of the coin was that, given these concessions, it was expected that most Anglican schools would agree to accept local authority control (this would have been compulsory where the only school in a district was a denominational school) and that there should be no religious tests for teachers in these schools. This was the absolute limit of the government's concessions and once again it showed that the key issue for Liberals was to establish the principle of local democratic control in schools that local ratepayers paid for, rather than to reduce the amount of Anglicanism taught in those schools. On this basis it seemed a compromise was possible, but it was torpedoed by an Anglican revolt against the Archbishop of Canterbury's proposals.

This was the last significant attempt to revise the 1902 act. After the failure to reach an agreed settlement Liberals shied away from the issue as far too difficult and divisive. Education was mentioned in only

22 per cent of Liberal election addresses in December 1910.[30] But if the government accepted only parts of the nonconformist agenda, the weight of nonconformist opinion inside the Liberal party was still strong enough to prevent the government adopting any strategy for education that did not deal with their demands. This was graphically demonstrated when Jack Pease, who had taken over as President of the Board of Education in 1911, drew up an elaborate proposal in 1913 to overhaul the whole educational system, including an increase in central grants, improving teachers' pay and conditions, raising the school leaving age and introducing continuing education classes.[31] Pease's plans had strong support from Haldane and Crewe and from the Liberal education group, led by the backbench MP, J. H. Whitehouse. But, under nonconformist pressure, the scheme was gradually scaled down to a proposed bill to make all ex-voluntary schools, in areas where they were the only school, subject to full council control.[32] The only way the kind of educational agenda that Liberals like Pease and Haldane supported could make headway was through administrative regulation. For instance, in 1907 new rules ensured that any secondary school receiving state grants had to reserve 25 per cent of its places for ex-elementary school pupils. Lloyd George's 1914 budget at last reformed and increased state grants to elementary schools and opened the way to develop further education.[33] But, as Haldane lamented, while the issue of religious education remained unresolved it continued to dominate all discussion of education.[34]

The great education quarrel between church and chapel troubled politicians down to 1914. But the two sides' other great dispute, over disestablishment, did seem capable of settlement in the Edwardian era. The Anglican Church of Ireland had been disestablished in 1869 and disestablishment of the Church of England had been a central demand of nonconformists in the 1870s and 1880s.[35] It reflected their growing self-confidence and political involvement and the belief that Anglicanism was no longer powerful enough to deserve special recognition from the state, but would always treat nonconformists as second class citizens while it remained the establishment. The issue had even played a significant role at the 1885 general election.[36] By that time about half of Liberal MPs were prepared to support the idea, at least in principle. This reflected a conviction that all the manifestations of Anglican privilege that prevented the operation of total religious liberty could be traced back to the fact of the establishment. This was reinforced by the solid hostility of most of the Anglican hierarchy and many politically active priests to the Liberal cause. The desertion of many prominent

Anglican landowners to Liberal Unionism only strengthened this feeling and by 1895 virtually all Liberal MPs approved of the principle of disestablishment.[37] But by this time the issue was rapidly losing its political importance. Nonconformists increasingly felt that the idea had little relevance, as their remaining practical grievances against aspects of the Church's role as the establishment were eliminated, as with the Burials Acts of 1880 and 1900. By 1900 very few nonconformists could have felt oppressed in any way by the fact of establishment. As the issue became less pressing for nonconformists, the commitment of most Liberals to the cause was revealed as largely theoretical. A disestablishment motion was carried 198–90 in 1907, but it excited little comment and only one cabinet minister (the ex-Baptist, Birrell) was present.[38] In December 1910 the issue was mentioned in precisely three per cent of Liberal election addresses.[39]

Disestablishment of the Church of Scotland had been an equally controversial issue north of the border. Its driving force came from those Presbyterians who had left the Church, mainly over issues arising from the workings of establishment. Many of them were active Liberals and the party went into the 1892 election more or less committed to the idea of Scottish disestablishment.[40] However, most of these Presbyterians had drawn together in the United Free Church in 1900 and it increasingly began to explore whether reunion might be possible with the established Church of Scotland, on the basis of that Church changing its constitution to give it complete independence from the state on spiritual issues. This would solve most of the difficulties that had led to the Presbyterian secessions in the first place. Discussions began in earnest in 1908–9 and by 1913–14 there seemed every possibility of success.[41] These developments effectively ended any enthusiasm for disestablishment in Scotland and the issue rapidly faded from sight for Liberals, despite having been one of the most controversial political topics of the 1890s.[42]

This left the issue of Welsh Church disestablishment in lonely eminence. Initially the campaign against the established Anglican Church in Wales had been dominated by the leading pressure group in favour of disestablishment, the Liberation Society, and had been run as part of the general campaign against established churches throughout Britain. However, during the 1880s a new generation of Welsh Liberal MPs and leaders had broken away and started to advocate the merits of disestablishment in Wales, whatever happened in England.[43] Their argument was based on the fact that while nonconformists and Anglicans were fairly equally divided in England, in Wales nonconformists outnumbered

the established church by about three to one. The true 'national religion' of Wales was nonconformity, not Anglicanism. In effect, therefore, this became an argument about the need to recognise the distinct
national character of Wales, rather than a dispute between Anglicans
and nonconformists. On this basis, the measure was akin to a less
controversial cousin of Irish home rule. A bill on the matter was lost in
1895 with the fall of Rosebery's government.

Campbell-Bannerman knew there was no chance of such a bill passing
the Lords and that Welsh nonconformists were more immediately
exercised by the need to reverse Balfour's education act, so he shunted
the issue off to a Royal Commission in 1906–10.[44] But pressure from Wales
was intense and Lloyd George was only able to keep Welsh Liberals in
line by promising a disestablishment bill by 1909 at the latest.[45] Moreover,
the failure of the education compromise in 1908 produced a need for a
bill to satisfy restive nonconformists. A bill on Welsh disestablishment
duly appeared and was read for a first time in 1909 before being lost in
the furore over the People's Budget. But it resurfaced in 1912 to begin a
two year circuit through parliament to overcome the Lords' veto. Cynics
suggested that this time it was not only intended to compensate
nonconformists for the lack of an education bill, but to reconcile them
to Irish home rule and a Catholic-dominated parliament in Dublin.

But the other great advantage of Welsh church disestablishment was
that it united nonconformists and Liberals in a way that the education
issue, for instance, did not. Committed nonconformists and Anglicans
throughout Britain could interpret it as another chapter in the struggle
of church and chapel. Indeed it would be unwise to underestimate the
issue's power to inflame these feelings and its significance in politics in
1912–14.[46] The Unionist party and the Anglican Church fought the bill
furiously, organising prolonged parliamentary obstruction and thousands
of mass meetings.[47] For many young Anglican Unionist MPs who were
destined to play a leading role in the party's future, like Edward Wood
and Samuel Hoare, it was quite as crucial an issue as Irish home rule.[48]
Nonconformist bodies were enthusiastic about the bill and the Liberation
Society underwent a revival on the back of its support for the measure.[49]
But Welsh disestablishment was also an issue about the recognition of
Welsh national identity and this made it much easier for the Liberal
party to unite behind, when it was already passing measures to recognise
the separate identity of Ireland and, to a lesser extent, Scotland. The
principle that the Welsh people should determine the nature of their
church establishment was able to produce a unanimous Liberal vote for
the bill's third reading in 1914. But it should be noted that Liberal

divisions did open up in debates over the specific details of how much of the Welsh state church's property should be given to the disestablished Church and how much should be retained by the state and used for secular purposes. Some Liberal Anglicans and members of the Church of Scotland (and some Wesleyans, too) wished for a generous settlement for the new Church and the government made some concessions in January 1913, much to the dismay of the bill's nonconformist supporters.[50] This showed once again the potential of denominational struggles to divide Liberalism and why such issues were so difficult for the party, but the bill struggled through parliament and was on the verge of becoming law in 1914 when war intervened.

It is, however, necessary to be cautious about interpreting Liberalism's involvement with the church versus chapel conflict in 1905–14 as evidence that this issue was becoming less significant in politics. The education issue was one of the major parliamentary topics of 1906–8, as was Welsh Church disestablishment in 1912–14. The former was still unresolved in 1914 and likely to cause more trouble in the future. Liberals were increasingly weary of the topic, though, not because it was irrelevant but precisely because they could not ignore it. The issue was so troublesome because the priorities and ideology of Liberalism, though they generally coincided with those of nonconformity, did not mesh exactly. Just as they had in 1870, the Liberals showed in 1906–8 that they cared more for popular accountability in education than the exclusion of denominational teaching. As in the 1870s this produced considerable frustration and disillusion on the part of active nonconformists. But it is a long way from this reaction, which was a fairly typical event in Liberal–nonconformist relations, to suggesting that religion was a declining force in politics.

The moral agenda

Moreover, the impact of religion on politics was not just a matter of the direct clashes between church and chapel on the battlefields of education and disestablishment. It seeped into many other areas of public life. One of the most obvious of these issues was the regulation of personal conduct, which was often cited as something that particularly obsessed nonconformists. Most significantly, this area included temperance, anti-gambling, sabbatarianism and the regulation of sexuality. In all these fields nonconformists were often prominent in pushing for more regulation in a 'puritan' direction. But these were also exceptionally complicated issues which produced a variety of political cross-currents and none should be viewed as merely a product of the political programme of nonconformity, or of Liberalism.

By far the most significant of these issues was that of temperance. But temperance above all was never exclusively a nonconformist issue, though forms of its expression in politics became closely associated with Liberalism. The question of how to reduce excessive drinking in the British population was hardly a new one in the late nineteenth century, but it was becoming increasingly controversial as the forces behind the temperance movement made themselves heard in national life. However, while temperance was a widespread feeling by the 1880s, it was also extraordinarily diverse. It could mean anything from personally abstaining from alcohol and arguing that the sale of drink should be prohibited, to looking for ways to gradually reduce or restrict the opportunities for alcohol consumption. Temperance could also be supported for a bewildering variety of reasons. It could be argued that working people had only themselves to blame for poverty, because this was entirely due to their dissolute drinking habits. John Burns suggested in 1907 that if the working class stopped spending £75 million every year on drink there would be much less hardship among the unemployed.[51] But, on the other hand, many figures in the trade unions and the early Labour party were temperance enthusiasts. Indeed the teetotal movement to encourage total abstention from alcohol was the creation of a group of working class radicals in the 1830s. It was certainly possible to argue that giving up drink increased a workman's self-respect and made it possible for him not only to improve himself, but to analyse the social system and how it should be changed. Beer was nothing but 'the opium of the masses', which reconciled the wretched worker to his lot. As Keir Hardie advised his fellow-workers 'drink less, read more and think more', while 'The Public house was the strongest ally on the side of the usurer, the sweater and the landlord.'[52] There was also a distinctive feminist angle to temperance.[53] Many women temperance workers argued that male wage earners spent far too much of their money on drink, thus depriving their wives and children of essentials and leading the way to domestic violence and the break-up of families.

Temperance could be supported by critics of working class culture, by trade unionists and socialists and by feminists. But in the 1870s and 1880s it made increasing headway in the Christian denominations under the impact of a wave of revivalist preaching, inspired by American examples, which fused temperance with the gospels and led over a million men to pledge themselves to abstinence from alcohol. Nonconformist ministers increasingly took to this policy and the

United Kingdom Alliance, which argued for the prohibition of alcohol sales, started to draw much of its support from among nonconformists.[54] This reflected an increasing self-confidence among nonconformists and a feeling that they should enter the mainstream of politics in order to combat sin and create a more godly society. But temperance was never just a nonconformist issue even when considering its religious support. It was quite possible to be an agnostic and an enthusiastic supporter of temperance, like the Countess of Carlisle, the President of the Women's Liberal Federation and of the National British Women's Temperance Association.[55] But the largest temperance organisation in Britain was the Church of England Temperance Society, which was eagerly supported by Randall Davidson, the Archbishop of Canterbury in 1903–28.[56] Many Anglicans were quite as worried as nonconformists were by the social problems caused by excessive drinking.

The disparate nature of the support for temperance meant it was not inevitable that it should become a matter for political partisanship. Initially, in the mid nineteenth century, temperance reformers had been a minority in both Liberal and Conservative parties. But, from the 1850s onwards, the United Kingdom Alliance started to press politicians on the issue of whether they would support a bill to allow local districts to vote on banning the issue of liquor licences in their area. This plan was known variously as the permissive bill, local option or the local veto. Many Liberals found it attractive, as it embodied Liberal ideals about giving communities the right to manage their own affairs and extending the operations of local democracy. It also, of course, sidestepped concerns that temperance legislation would interfere with personal liberty by emphasising its democratic credentials. But Conservatives disliked the policy, mainly because an attack on liquor licences could be interpreted as an attack on the licence-holder's property. It was the local option issue which drove a wedge between the two parties, rather than the promotion of temperance, which continued to have its supporters within Conservatism and Anglicanism.[57] This gap widened when Sir William Harcourt took up local option and introduced government bills on the subject in 1893 and 1895. It became one of the most controversial elements of the 1895 election, when it was endorsed by 72 per cent of Liberal candidates.[58] This controversy above all else identified the Liberals as the party of temperance and the Conservatives as its opponents.

Thus far, temperance bore some relationship to the Liberals' attitude to the education controversy. The central plank of both was Liberals' commitment to local democracy. But, in contrast to education, the Liberal party started to retreat from its local option commitment after the 1895 election. Undoubtedly this was partly tactical. The *Westminster Gazette* asked Liberal candidates what effect local option had on their campaigns and 134 of 157 losing candidates who responded suggested it had been a hindrance.[59] But if most people did not want the right to vote on whether to ban local liquor licences, this also meant that if they did receive this opportunity, most would vote against local prohibition of alcohol sales.[60] Local democracy was not a means of tackling intemperance.

This realisation altered the Liberal approach. They did not drop temperance. This would have been difficult given the number of committed supporters the idea had in the party. But this decision also reflected the ways in which temperance continued to connect with developing Liberal concerns. Liberals who were interested in tackling poverty could hardly ignore social surveys like those of Charles Booth and Seebohm Rowntree, which suggested that drinking did place an undue strain on many meagre working class budgets and was a real cause of hardship. Rowntree insisted that for the 18.5 per cent of York's population who were in 'secondary' poverty, which he defined as earning enough money to supply their basic needs, but unable to do so, the 'predominant factor' in their poverty was drink.[61] Intemperance was also being blamed for contributing to the nation's economic problems. It made workers inefficient and locked up spending power in alcohol that could have been used to stimulate other industries.[62] Temperance did not seem like an 'old' agenda to many Liberals in the 1900s, but one that was strikingly relevant. Increasingly, the party focused its attack on the alcohol industry itself as the main problem. It helped, of course, that 'the trade' had become closely aligned with Conservatism in order to defeat local option proposals.[63] Brewers and distillers came to take their place alongside landowners in Liberal demonology as a privileged group who benefited at the public's expense and whom Liberalism would be entirely justified in attacking. Once again this linked temperance together with Liberal ideology by making it a matter of a parasitic elite versus the people. This focus on the evils of 'the trade' also reduced the need to tackle the idea that temperance was infringing individual liberty. In fact, the twin appeals to democracy and anti-elitism ensured the libertarian criticism of temperance failed to surface within Liberalism, even among those Liberals, like Asquith, who were notorious for their fondness for alcohol. The only objections in the party came from those few Liberals who retained links with the brewing industry.[64]

A new means of attack on the brewers and distillers was outlined in 1899 in the minority report of a Royal Commission headed by Lord Peel on the drink trade.[65] It suggested taking advantage of the fact that liquor licences had to be renewed every year by local magistrates to require the justices to drastically reduce the number of pubs over a seven year period. In return, licensees would receive compensation for the loss of their licence, but only during this seven year period. Local option was postponed to the indefinite future, except in Wales and Scotland, where it was believed to have much more support. Campbell-Bannerman and Herbert Gladstone, his chief whip, orchestrated a retreat from local option to these proposals in time for the 1900 elections, despite howls of protest from convinced proponents of the veto policy, and they remained the core of the Liberals' approach in the Edwardian era.[66] The Licensing Bill of 1908 proposed to reduce licences by about one third over a period of 14 years (amended to 21 years in committee).[67] The local veto was retained as a very distant prospect at the end of that period and even then was combined with a scheme to tax licences according to the increased value that they imparted to a property (this was usually known as the monopoly value). The cabinet can have had no illusions that the Lords would agree to these two latter proposals. It is probable that the government was willing to jettison or modify these policies in order to persuade the Lords to agree to the scheme of licence reductions.[68] This was the central feature of the Liberal approach to temperance and what really mattered to the cabinet. But the refusal of the Lords to negotiate killed the whole bill in November 1908.

The Liberals were forced to turn to another route for securing the reduction in the number of licences they sought. Lloyd George's budget of 1909 not only increased taxes on the brewing and distilling industry, but steeply raised taxation on licences. The aim, as the chancellor made clear, was not only to raise revenue but to force a reduction in the number of licences by making it uneconomic to run the less profitable public houses.[69] The budget ultimately provided the Liberals with a route to enact what had been their temperance policy for the last ten years. In achieving this they received overwhelming support from the nonconformist denominations and undoubtedly Lloyd George hoped to arouse their fervour, which had been cooled by the lack of progress on educational grievances. But temperance could not have been such a popular policy within Liberalism if it had just been a 'nonconformist issue'. In fact it appealed to a wide span of Liberal interest groups and to a number of important elements in Liberal ideology.

The other items in what might be described as the 'moral agenda' of Edwardian nonconformity – sabbatarianism, anti-gambling and the regulation of sexuality – presented an even more complex picture when expressed in politics. Sabbatarianism, or the belief that Sunday should be reserved for worship rather than leisure or work, was widespread among nonconformists, but it was difficult to make into a political issue at national level.[70] There was already a battery of legislation outlawing activities on a Sunday, particularly the 1861 Lord's Day Observance Act. Enthusiasts for this measure tended to concentrate on enforcing the legislation through putting pressure on local authorities and police forces and this took much sabbatarian activity out of national politics. From the 1880s onwards sabbatarians were fighting a losing battle against the increasing availability of commercialised leisure on Sundays. But sabbatarianism did not just appeal to nonconformists. It was important to all Christians who emphasised the authority of the bible and many evangelical Anglicans were prominent in the movement. It appealed, therefore, to many who were Conservatives, as well as to Liberals, and this tended to remove the issue even further from straight-forward party controversy.

Anti-gambling sentiment developed in the late nineteenth century as a reaction against another form of commercialised leisure – the rise of off-course betting on horseracing by working class gamblers, once the electric telegraph made odds and results easily and rapidly available in newspapers.[71] Hostility to gambling mirrored the temperance movement in many ways. It could be motivated by a feeling that gambling was a disreputable expression of working class fecklessness, or by an analysis that suggested the bookmaker was a parasite, preying on the gullible workers and distracting them from the struggle for self-improvement and better conditions.[72] The Labour party remained generally hostile to gambling into the inter-war period.[73] Nonconformity was also opposed to gambling as indulgent, self-destructive and opposing chance to God's plan for the world.[74] But it also had plenty of opponents within Anglicanism, including prominent bishops.

However, anti-gambling differed from temperance in that it never became a partisan issue. Pro-temperance opinions existed in all parties, but the issue had divided Liberals and Conservatives because Liberals were determined to use the law against the property and interests of the drink trade. But off-course bookmakers who catered for working class customers were always regarded as shady figures whose legal status was dubious and they could not look to the Tory party for the kind of protection it was eager to extend to brewers and distillers. The only equivalents of 'the trade' in the sphere of gambling were those directly involved in horseracing – especially owners and trainers of horses and operators of racecourses. If the Liberal party had attacked the financial interests (and pleasures) of their sport by attempting to outlaw betting at racecourses then anti-gambling could have become a partisan issue, especially as racehorse owning was widely associated with landowners. But this did not happen. Instead, anti-gambling enthusiasts in all parties accepted a non-partisan approach to the issue and concentrated on outlawing off-course betting, which they could all agree to condemn.

The key legislation to outlaw cash betting away from the racecourse was the 1906 Street Betting Act. It was the outcome of a House of Lords select committee of 1901–2 that included prominent Liberals like the Earl of Aberdeen, the Bishop of Hereford and Lord Davey, but also Unionists like Lords Derby and Newton.[75] Legislation based on its recommendations passed the Lords in 1904 and 1905 before Herbert Gladstone, the Liberal Home Secretary, agreed to support the bill and ensure its passage through the Commons, where it received endorsement from MPs in all parties. Some Liberal MPs wished to push the measure further and outlaw betting at racecourses, arguing that the existing bill created a special exemption for the social elite.[76] But Gladstone refused to go down this route. A bill that banned on-course betting was 'a big question' which could never pass the Lords, while the 'smaller question' of tackling off-course gambling had wide support.[77] This was accepted by most of the bill's Liberal supporters and the 1906 act passed in its original form. When debating temperance, the Tory party would not accept any attack on the operations of the drink trade. At least, Liberals could console themselves, where gambling was concerned, Conservatives were offering to suppress some bookmakers' operations. Much of the controversy went out of the issue in 1906 and it was only after the First World War that the huge difficulties in implementing the measure started to be recognised.

The regulation of sexuality was even more difficult to relate directly to party politics. As with anti-gambling, nonconformists were prominent in campaigns to tighten up and enforce laws against activities that they regarded as sinful. But much of this meant working through pressure groups like the National Vigilance Association (NVA) to encourage local authorities or police forces to take action, in for instance, closing down brothels under the provisions of the 1885 Criminal Law Amendment Act.[78] This kept much 'purity' activity out of the national arena. The Liberal governments of 1905–15, like their Unionist predecessor, were happy with this situation and not keen to raise these issues in national legislation, regarding them as troublesome and distasteful. It was noticeable that a Royal Commission of 1906–8 on the Metropolitan police and street offences failed to produce any legislation.[79] These factors helped keep the regulation of sexuality away from party politics. This outcome was reinforced by the fact that nonconformists were not the only activists in this kind of cause. They were able to work with a wide variety of allies, including evangelical Anglicans like Bishop Winnington-Ingram of London, socialists like Ramsay MacDonald and Beatrice Webb, feminists like Millicent Fawcett and welfare pressure groups like the National Society for the Prevention of Cruelty to Children (NSPCC).[80] The condemnation of sexual transgressions and the protection of women and children from male exploiters were (at least theoretically) such widely agreed aims in society that they could not belong exclusively to any one group.

The combination of government reluctance to tackle these issues and the very disparate nature of support for action on them, meant that at the national level the rare appearances of the regulation of sexuality were not treated as a party issue. The 1908 Incest Act was the result of pressure from both the NVA and NSPCC, and was not treated as a controversial measure by the Unionist opposition.[81] The 1912 Criminal Law Amendment Act again tightened up the law on prostitution. While it was a government measure, the Home Office took over a private members bill introduced by two Unionist MPs. Again, it had overwhelming support and voting was not on party lines.[82] However, it was on this issue that some Liberal MPs started to have qualms about the infringements of personal liberty that might follow in the wake of even a widely-agreed moral agenda. F. H. Booth, in particular, objected to the act's provisions to increase police powers of arrest on suspicion of some offences, rather than as a result of a warrant.[83] But this was very much a minority position. There were too many other arguments in favour of the act which appealed strongly to Liberals – including religious injunctions, feminist arguments about the need to condemn transgressive male sexual behaviour and the perceived need to protect vulnerable women from male exploitation.

Thus, the idea that Liberalism pursued a moral agenda at the behest of nonconformity was very far from the truth. All of the main items in this agenda had widespread support in society and were not just, or even mainly, the enthusiasms of nonconformists. Sabbatarianism and sexual morality were not usually party political issues at the national level and indeed were rarely discussed there. The main anti-gambling legislation passed in this period had cross-party support. Only temperance was a partisan issue, or rather the attack on the drink industry aroused partisan feelings while temperance itself was a widespread sentiment. Even on this issue, Liberals supported temperance legislation for a variety of reasons, of which nonconformist pressure was only one. The Liberals were not a 'puritan' party, any more than they were just an expression of nonconformist interests. The real significance of nonconformity for the party lay elsewhere.

The religious context of Edwardian Liberalism

Nonconformity could not dictate a political programme to Liberalism – hence the difficulty of their relationship. However, the two movements were closely intertwined in the Edwardian period. Areas of the country where nonconformists were strong tended also to vote Liberal.[84] Some statistical work on the pre-1918 electorate suggests nonconformists all over England were disproportionately Liberal and the connection between nonconformity and Liberalism seems to have survived into the post-1945 period.[85] Religion and politics remained inextricably linked at the local level and many studies of local councils in the Edwardian period have confirmed that the main social division between Liberal and Conservative councillors was that Liberals tended to be disproportionately nonconformist, while Conservatives were mainly Anglicans.[86] In parliament the connection was less strong, but about 40 per cent of Liberal MPs were nonconformists, while only six or seven Unionists were Free Churchmen after 1906.

At cabinet level, there were few active nonconformists, reflecting their weakness in the professions and the landed class who made up most of the Liberal government's professional politicians. David Bebbington has suggested there were only four chapel-goers in the cabinet in 1914 and of them Lloyd George was not an orthodox Christian and Jack Pease was only a Quaker by inheritance, rather than belief.[87] That left Walter Runciman (a Wesleyan) and Thomas McKinnon Wood (a Congregationalist), whose numbers were matched by the cabinet's two agnostics, Morley and Burns.[88] However, a number of other important cabinet ministers came from nonconformist families or had been brought up as nonconformists, including Asquith, Birrell, McKenna, Haldane and Sir John Simon.[89] This meant that even at cabinet level, nonconformity provided a kind of social cement for Liberalism, based on shared backgrounds and, often, family ties. Asquith's first wife, for instance, was a second cousin of Campbell-Bannerman's brother's wife.[90] This effect was even more powerful in the Commons, which contained a number of extended Liberal nonconformist cousinhoods, like the Peases, Brights and McLarens, as well as MPs who shared a school, business links, a chapel or charitable endeavours.[91]

Nonconformity remained central to the social reality of Liberal identity in the Edwardian period. But it also continued to play an important role in Liberal ideology and policy in areas that did not seem to be explicitly religious. An important example of this was the battle against the House of Lords in 1909–11. Many nonconformist leaders insisted that historically the Commons had stood for the liberties of dissent, while the Lords had upheld the privileges of the Church. 'Our history, our principles, and our needs make us extremely tenacious of the privileges of the House of Commons' declared the Methodist minister John Scott Lidgett.[92] For some Baptist ministers, like John Shakespeare, modern Peers like Curzon were merely 'Strafford Redivivus' and 1909–11 was a revival of the English Civil War, which the descendants of seventeenth-century puritans had to win again to ensure English liberties in politics and religion. This reading of history and politics helped to bind many nonconformists into the Liberal viewpoint. But it also reinforced the majority view in Liberalism that the political struggle must involve the victory of the Commons over the Lords, rather than any democratic experiments like an elected second chamber or the referendum.

Another general nonconformist influence on Liberalism was over Irish home rule. Nonconformists were deeply ambivalent about this policy. Most could accept it in theory as an expression of liberty and local self-government – always elements that appealed to nonconformists as these were the whole *raison d'être* of religious dissent. But they also profoundly disliked the idea of setting up a Roman Catholic-dominated parliament in Dublin, which could govern the protestant minority in Ireland.[93] This idea played on the powerful hostility to Catholicism which always simmered beneath nonconformist attitudes. This ambivalence strengthened the position of Liberals who were doubtful about home rule. In particular, the fears of many nonconformists about the possible persecution of protestants in a home rule Ireland reinforced Liberal suspicions that Irish nationalism was not a liberal movement and would govern Ireland in an illiberal fashion. Nonconformists, particularly Wesleyans who had many members in southern Ireland, were an important element in making Liberalism wary of tackling the issue of home rule.[94]

But nonconformity was not just woven into Liberal attitudes to the constitution and the nation. It also played an important role in allowing the party to accept the new agenda of social reform that the leadership espoused in the Edwardian era. This was because the evangelical theology that dominated nonconformity was changing in the late nineteenth century to accommodate social reform.[95] Nonconformist ministers wished to ensure that their faith remained central to national life and one way of approaching that task was to emphasise the need for nonconformity to be involved in society's concerns. A range of theological arguments were used to emphasise the importance of social reform. Emphasis increasingly shifted from Christ's atoning death on the cross to his life as a moral guide and the need for the churches to perform good works after his example. Immanentist theology popularised the idea that God was in everyone and everything and Christians had a responsibility to care for all members of society. The concepts of the fatherhood of God and the kingdom of God were reinterpreted to outline the duty of Christians to look on all men as brothers and to build a realm of justice on earth. Leading nonconformist divines like John Clifford and Scott Lidgett took up these ideas and used them to emphasise the necessity for nonconformists to accept social reform as a natural outcome of their faith.

These developments meant that nonconformists did not have to see any incompatibility between religion and state action to help the poorest. This helped some wealthier and more socially conservative Liberals to go along with social reform and provided powerful reinforcement for New Liberal ideas which emphasised the need to extend interpretations of Liberalism to include welfare reform. In some cases there was a clear link between the involvement of Liberals with the 'new evangelicalism' and with New Liberalism. One of the most striking examples of this was the Quaker Rowntree family of York.[96] The head of the family confectionary firm was Joseph Rowntree and his eldest son, John Wilhelm Rowntree, was the leading exponent of the new thinking in late nineteenth-century Quakerism; Joseph's second son was Seebohm Rowntree, the renowned social investigator; and his nephew was Arnold Rowntree, Liberal MP for York 1910–18 and prominent advocate of social reform. For good measure, Arnold's brother-in-law, T. E. Harvey, was Liberal MP for West Leeds 1910–18 and another prominent advocate of the New Liberalism. Family ties, theology and political activism all came together to provide a bloc of Liberals who helped push Liberalism in Yorkshire and the North East towards accepting social reform.

The relationship between Liberalism and nonconformity was always fraught, but it was not necessarily becoming more distant in the Edwardian era. In 1906 the nonconformist denominations were unusually united behind the Liberals because of their opposition to Balfour's Education Act. The failure to produce any action on this subject produced a good deal of disillusion, but this was a normal feature of Liberal–nonconformist relations, which reflected the complex way in which nonconformist demands interacted with other aspects of Liberal ideology and priorities. There was still probably more nonconformist enthusiasm for the party in 1910 than there had been in, say, 1900. Liberalism and nonconformity remained closely entwined and many aspects of Liberal thought and policy were influenced by nonconformist views. Even the New Liberal agenda of social reform was buttressed by the changing theology of many evangelical nonconformists and its acceptance by Liberals was related to their ability to reconcile it with how nonconformity was interpreted. On this basis the separation of religion and politics still had a long way to go in 1914.

6
The Economy and Finance

Early twentieth-century Liberalism was exceptionally diverse. It contained those who felt there should be a distinctively Liberal foreign policy and those who denied such a thing existed; enthusiasts for Irish home rule and profound sceptics about this policy; passionate advocates and opponents of women's suffrage; and those who felt the party should be the political expression of religious nonconformity, together with those who had no interest in religion at all. In some ways, Liberalism was the illogical amalgam famously identified by George Dangerfield in *The Strange Death of Liberal England*.[1] But if anything united all Liberals it was their adherence to free trade. This was the one policy on which there was no room for disagreement within Liberalism's many mansions. Historians have not always looked on this commitment favourably, though, seeing it as an essentially negative and conservative defence of the status quo, especially against exciting Conservative plans to modernize the economy through tariff reform and more far-reaching ideas for state intervention emanating from Labour.[2] But free trade did not carry the same meaning for Edwardian Liberals that it did for Liberals in the 1840s. Its role was constantly redefined and updated and it provided one of the most powerful weapons in the political arsenal of Edwardian Liberalism as well as acting as the centrepiece of the party's whole approach to the economy and finance.

The meaning of free trade

In the first half of the nineteenth century, both Conservatives and Liberals had shared in the task of removing duties from goods imported into Britain. But the Conservatives' repudiation of their own prime minister, Sir Robert Peel, when he capped this policy by abolishing the

121

Corn Laws in 1846, allowed the Liberals to firmly associate themselves with free trade.[3] The idea that removing government intervention in the nation's trade must lead to prosperity seemed to be established beyond doubt by the long boom in the 1850s and 1860s that followed Peel's actions. Liberals, and especially Gladstone, who was chancellor of the exchequer in 1852–5 and 1859–66, were happy to take the credit for this. But free trade became such an established orthodoxy that the Conservatives, too, embraced it. Until the early 1900s there was no difference between the two parties in their policies on trade.

But this consensus was always fragile. Many Conservatives continued to dislike free trade, especially when increased foreign competition in the later nineteenth century affected the prosperity of interests like agriculture which were central to the party. The huge cost of the Boer war of 1899–1902 led to renewed interest among Tories in tariffs on foreign imports as a source of revenue.[4] Then, in 1903, Joseph Chamberlain shattered the Edwardian political framework by declaring in favour of a policy of 'tariff reform'. His abandonment of free trade proved immensely popular among Conservatives and in 1903–6 he won over all but a small, but distinguished, rump of Unionist free traders to his cause. Chamberlain's tariff policy was meant to be a comprehensive answer to Tory political concerns in the early twentieth century. It promised a new source of revenue to pay for armaments and, possibly, social reforms. Tariffs would, Chamberlain claimed, protect domestic industries from foreign competition, thus securing the jobs of British workmen. They would also bind together the British empire into a great trading and political bloc, by allowing empire goods to enter Britain at a preferential rate. This would secure the country's future as a world power. All of this was wrapped up in the Union Jack as a great patriotic policy which would make foreign manufacturers, like 'Herr Dumper', the unscrupulous German exporter portrayed in party propaganda, pay to secure British power and prosperity.

Tariff reform represented a comprehensive challenge to free trade on every level, from sophisticated economic argument to the crudest propaganda. But it was also an unsuccessful challenge. It was decisively rejected by the electorate in 1906 and, more narrowly, twice in 1910. This was at least partly because tariff reform united Liberals around the banner of free trade and forced them to present their policy in the form of a series of compelling and coherent arguments. Liberal unity on free trade was not, in fact, total, but it was as near as possible to this goal in a heterogeneous party. A handful of Liberal Imperialists, like the Duke of Sutherland, Sir Edward Reed, MP for Cardiff, the businessmen

Sir Charles Tennant and T. A. Brassey, and the geographer and ex-Liberal candidate, Halford Mackinder, came out in support of tariffs, especially because of their role in promoting imperial unity.[5] Only one or two very exceptional cases, like Samuel Storey, ex-MP for Sunderland, were recruited to tariff reform from other strands of Liberalism. Significantly, all became Unionists, thus accepting the identity of Liberalism with free trade. All of the leading Liberal Imperialists, including Rosebery and his acolytes, remained free traders, despite their enthusiasm for the 'clean slate' in Liberal policy, imperialism and efficiency.

This impressive show of unity rested on the intersection of free trade with many of the central pillars of Liberal identity and the ability of Liberals to convincingly project these arguments to the electorate. First, for most Liberals, free trade was closely equated with the interests of the many against the few. It was, in fact, a kind of economic twin of democracy. This reflected the confident belief of Liberals that Britain's successful industrialization and the rise in working class living standards in the nineteenth century was the result of free trade. Particular attention was paid to emphasising the idea of the 'hungry (18)40s' – the period before free trade, characterised by poverty, unemployment and high prices.[6] The clear message was that tariff reform would plunge Britain back into this abyss and undo the gains of sixty years of working class prosperity. Its immediate impact would certainly be to raise the price of everyday, essential items in the working class budget – a theme that was dramatised in the notion of the 'Big Loaf' that workers could buy under free trade and the 'Little Loaf' they would be forced to settle for under tariff reform.[7] In January 1910 no fewer than 75 per cent of Liberal candidates' election addresses stated that tariff reform would increase the price of food.[8]

Naturally, this left Liberals open to the charge that there was still a great deal of poverty under the free trade system. But this could be countered in two ways. Firstly, by asserting that tariff reform would only make this worse. It would hinder the movement of capital and labour to the most productive and thus high wage areas of the economy. For instance, British industry under free trade benefited from cheap imports of raw materials and this allowed the consumer sector to expand. This was essential as Britain's future as a skilled, high wage economy lay in the consumer and service sectors.[9] Some trades might be threatened by competition, but it could be argued these were the low wage, 'sweated' sectors that Britain would be better off without.[10] Tariff reform would also bring catastrophe to those crucial sectors of the economy that relied on exports, like textiles, coal and shipping, by provoking foreign countries to raise tariffs against British goods. But Liberals could also argue that poverty could be tackled without attacking free trade. The state could help industrial growth by investing in technical and scientific education, diplomatic support of commerce and the country's infrastructure.[11] It could also help eradicate poverty more directly by promoting social reforms like minimum wages, land reform, social insurance and pensions.[12] Thus Liberals who held a range of divergent views on the state's role could all unite in defending free trade as a principle.

Liberals believed that free trade protected the interests of the people as a whole, just as democracy did. But just as democracy had powerful and sinister antagonists who sought to manipulate the political process for their own ends, so free trade was confronted by the 'interests' hoping to benefit from tariff reform at the expense of the public.[13] An obvious link was provided by the great landowners. They had consistently opposed the widening of political participation and sought to concentrate power in their own hands. Similarly with tariff reform they were trying to protect British agriculture from foreign competition in order to increase their rent rolls but raise the price of food for ordinary people. Liberals argued that businessmen who sought tariffs on imports were trying to make a similar imposition on the public, who, as consumers, benefited from cheap prices. Tariffs would inevitably corrupt British public life as different economic interests attempted to influence parliament to protect their own profits, while free trade allowed the people's representatives to concentrate on the general good.[14] Thus democracy and free trade were natural allies in the popular cause.

But free trade was not just a domestic policy. It also deeply informed Liberal attitudes to foreign policy and the empire. In the 1840s Cobden had argued that free trade would ultimately lead to a peaceful world, in which countries were united by trade. In the Edwardian era this looked a utopian ideal, especially as most countries had introduced tariff barriers. But Liberals clung to the idea that tariffs were an essentially aggressive weapon, which would needlessly increase friction with other countries and lead to a build-up of armaments.[15] As Lloyd George put it in a speech of 21 April 1908, free trade was 'a great pacificator'.[16] This did not mean that all Liberals were relentlessly international, let alone pacifist, in their outlook. In fact free trade could be defended as a peculiarly British policy that suited Britain's needs, while tariffs were 'foreign'.[17] But hostility to tariffs was closely linked to Liberal suspicion of the Tories as a party wedded to an adventurous and expensive foreign policy.

However, the sharpest disagreement between Liberals and Conservatives was over trade policy and the empire. Some Liberals were sceptical of the economic value of the empire and had opposed its expansion, especially during the Boer war. They pointed to the simple fact that most British trade was with Europe and the Americas and that it was naïve to suppose that the empire could ever match these markets in importance.[18] Tariff reform and imperial preference would benefit only a minority of the British economy. This attitude had been developed into a sophisticated critique by J. A. Hobson, in response to the Boer war.[19] He argued that the war was provoked by a small group of financiers and speculators who could not find a high return on their investments at home. Increasingly, they would seek to press the nation into imperial preference to protect their interests, supported by the 'kept press' and jingoistic crowds at home. But none of this benefited the mass of the British people, whose interests would be better served by reform at home.

But even Liberal Imperialists who had supported the Boer war refused to accept the necessity for imperial preference. They argued it was simply not compatible with the British imperial situation.[20] British firms were only keen to remove or reduce the tariffs imposed by the self-governing colonies. In turn, the colonies of settlement were willing to lower tariffs on British imports, but not to such a level whereby they could effectively compete with their own fledgling industries. Canada and Australia had no interest in remaining as primary producers in order to foster imperial unity. It could also be argued that tariff reform was a policy that seemed only to consider the colonies of settlement. But Britain's most important imperial trading partner was India and it was much more difficult to frame a policy of imperial preference that would be likely to bind India closer to the empire. Should India have to put duties on non-empire imports, this might only inflame opinion on the sub-continent. The only tariffs likely to be popular or in India's interests would be on British goods. Above all, Liberals just did not accept the need to fundamentally reappraise the relationship between the colonies and the mother country. In their view, the empire worked well and the existing ties of sentiment and self-interest should not be disrupted.

The state and the economy

Thus the Liberal case for free trade embraced every section of the party and tapped into fundamental Liberal ideas about popular rule, resisting the pretensions of privileged elites and the need for a 'sane' foreign and imperial policy. In 1906 it was arguably the most important factor in the Liberal election victory, mentioned by 98 per cent of candidates.[21] In the 1910 elections it was only outstripped by the House of Lords as an issue in election addresses.[22] Its centrality to Liberal thinking and Liberal identity was incontestable and this had important consequences for the ways in which Liberals viewed the entire field of the state's relationship with the economy. Generally, just as Liberals favoured the free play of economic forces in trade, so they believed the best method of ensuring growth and prosperity was to allow the market to guide domestic production. State activity always ran the risk of the same sort of favouritism and inefficiency that Liberals believed blighted tariff reform. But this did not mean that no state action at all could be justified. This was especially true where there was no real possibility of competition and there was an effective monopoly provider of an essential service. In these cases it might be necessary to intervene to protect the public from exploitation by the same kind of 'interest' who was trying to impose on the public with tariff reform. Thus many Liberals had no trouble supporting the municipal ownership of local utilities like gas, water, electricity and tramways in order to ensure these services were run in the interest of local people who had little alternative but to use them.[23] More controversially, some Liberals supported state ownership of the railways on the grounds that the regional companies were local monopolies licensed by the state. It was argued that the state already controlled many aspects of their activities and that public ownership would stop the railway companies taking advantage of their position to overcharge rail users, especially for freight carriage, and this would in turn benefit business activity. The Railway Nationalisation Society had the support of a significant number of Liberal businessmen as well as the main rail union.[24]

But the most difficult field where state intervention in the economy was urged in the Edwardian era was in order to relieve unemployment – a subject that was particularly pressing in the Liberals' first years in office. Unemployment among registered trade unionists was pushing 9 per cent by October 1908.[25] This was both a pressing social issue and a major political embarrassment. The Conservatives were not slow to blame free trade for this situation and to embrace the slogan 'tariff reform means work for all'. Labour, too, were able to develop a distinctive position with their Right to Work Bill, which was introduced for the first time in 1907.[26] It advocated the principle that local authorities should have to provide either work or maintenance for all genuinely unemployed men. Both of these positions entailed drastic interventions in the workings of the economy in very different ways. But the Liberal response involved much less government direction of the economy.

It had been accepted since 1886 that local authorities could speed up necessary public works in order to soak up local unemployment and in 1905 the Conservatives' Unemployed Workmen's Act had set up local distress committees, which could make use of charitable funds and government loans to dispense some sorts of relief and provide work for the unemployed.[27] But this work had to be a 'public utility', which was required by the local community. It could not just be a job creation scheme. This reflected the Tory government's position that it was not the state's concern, or within its powers, to provide employment for those out of work. The Liberal leaders discussed the issue of unemployment at some length in late 1904 and early 1905 and Campbell-Bannerman did not advance beyond this position, insisting that any relief works be profitable and useful to the community and not created solely to manufacture work.[28] The rest of the leadership agreed, in particular refusing to countenance anything which would 'start competition with existing industries'.[29] This would only be counter-productive and create further unemployment. The only sort of work the state could helpfully undertake was in areas that private enterprise would not tackle. Asquith suggested 'The most practical plan has for some time seemed to me to be a large and well thought out scheme of afforestation.'[30]

In effect, the Liberal response to unemployment differed from that of the Conservatives over the relative merits of free trade and tariff reform, but not over the efficacy of state-sponsored public works.[31] In office, the Liberals were as cautious as their predecessors. They appointed a Royal Commission to look into developing the canal system, though this did not come to anything.[32] In July 1906 the government supplemented the Tories' 1905 act with a government grant of £200,000, but only to finance emigration schemes and possibly labour colonies. In 1908 the grant was increased to £400,000.[33] But the cabinet refused to accept Labour's right to work principle, even when it was supported by 54 Liberals in an amendment to the address on 13 March 1908.[34] As Asquith said, this would involve admitting 'the complete and ultimate control by the state of the full machinery of production' and this could not be tolerated by Liberals, who believed in the efficiency of the market in allocating the factors of production.[35] P. W. Wilson, the Liberal who moved the right to work motion, seemed to acknowledge this, and the Liberal rebellion was more than anything a plea for the government to take the issue seriously.[36] Even the most advanced thinkers in the Liberal camp retained their doubts about using public works as a solution to unemployment and J. A. Hobson, for instance, always insisted they should not compete with industry or provide pay that was equivalent to that in the private sector.[37]

When the government did manage to produce a more effective response in 1908–9, it revealed that the cabinet had remained firm in its rejection of further state intervention to produce work for the unemployed. Instead, Churchill at the Board of Trade promoted state-run labour exchanges – something that had already been experimented with under the 1905 unemployment act.[38] Together with Lloyd George he also produced the idea for a limited scheme of unemployment insurance (finally introduced in 1913) and concentrated in industries particularly prone to bouts of short-term unemployment. Both these measures were designed to help workmen cope with unemployment and to find work more easily. Neither involved any state intervention in the process of production, or any encouragement of particular areas of the economy. Finally, as elements of his 'People's Budget' of 1909, Lloyd George produced plans for a Development Commission and Road Board.[39] Both were nationally-funded bodies empowered to make grants towards necessary public works in areas where private enterprise was unlikely to intervene. The Development Commission, for instance, was intended to develop areas like afforestation and land reclamation. Both institutions were modestly funded and dependent on initiatives from local bodies. In effect, they were no more than a national application of the principles that lay behind the circular of 1886 to local authorities on public works. Some members of the government, like Churchill, wished to go further and to try and co-ordinate the government's entire expenditure in such a way as to counter-act the cyclical nature of unemployment in the economy, but this was rejected as impossible to implement.[40] However, even Churchill was not necessarily suggesting that the government spend any more money, or direct it to particular areas of the economy, merely that already planned expenditure might be timed to alleviate unemployment – just as local authorities could arrange their affairs.

The Liberals were fortunate that the crisis in unemployment eased after 1908, for on this issue they were vulnerable to the populist panaceas of the Tories and Labour. But the Liberals' caution in using the state to intervene in the economy and tackle unemployment was a complement to their defence of free trade. It was difficult for Liberals to argue that the nation's trade should proceed without government interference, but that the state should undertake vast programmes of public works, or direct or take over sections of industry in order to provide work for the unemployed. This would produce just the kind of opportunities to distort the free, and thus most efficient, allocation of resources as would occur under tariff reform. The state's role had to be confined to those areas where there was a monopoly of provision or where there was no realistic possibility of private initiative. Indeed, experience of municipal works for the unemployed in 1905–8 only helped convince most ministers that this method was both hugely expensive and unable to provide the unemployed with any long term help. The government was left with the conclusion that the only real solution to unemployment was economic recovery and there was little state intervention could do to provide this. It was lucky for them that the last great boom of the pre-First World War era started to make itself felt after 1908.

National taxation

For nineteenth-century Liberals free trade was not only complemented by a desire to remove the state from the economy, but by a determination to reduce government expenditure and thus taxation – a process that was often referred to as retrenchment. If taxation of imports was economically harmful, then it seemed logical to assume that any taxation was and the government should leave the people's wealth in their own pockets, as far as possible. This would allow the most productive use of income and investment, which the government would only waste. One of the central features of Gladstone's famous budgets of the 1850s and 1860s was the simple aim to reduce taxation as much as possible.[41]

But given that some taxation was essential, Gladstone worked on the theory of proportionate contributions from the different sectors of society. While most goods entered the country free of charge, small tariffs were retained, for revenue rather than protective purposes, on a handful of everyday items like tea, coffee and cocoa, together with taxes on the twin 'luxuries' of alcohol and tobacco. These indirect taxes were paid by most working class consumers when they bought these products and made up about two thirds of all government revenue (though the proportion had declined to about a half by the end of the century). The rest came from direct taxes on the wealthier sections of society, mainly from income tax and a variety of duties levied on inherited wealth. Gladstone believed this created a system where the entire country had an interest in keeping government expenditure down and which everyone could accept as fair because they all contributed a modest and fairly similar percentage of their income.

Gladstone's great scheme was, however, steadily undermined by the gradual and inexorable rise in government expenditure, especially on defence, in the late nineteenth century under Tory and Liberal governments. Both parties were worried by the public's reaction to rising taxes and the Conservatives paid for 70 per cent of the Boer war through loans, despite raising income tax from 8d to 1s 3d and reintroducing taxes on sugar, corn and coal exports.[42] It was this fiscal dilemma that helped push Chamberlain and the Tories into support for tariff reform. While their arguments about the benefits that would accrue from closer imperial union and industrial protection made a decisive break from the mid-Victorian economic consensus, their case for tariffs as a form of taxation referred to some central themes of Gladstonian taxation theory. They argued that tariffs would spread the burden of new taxation widely, thus avoiding any section of society being penalised. It would also avoid rises in direct taxation which would be economically harmful, by reducing the amount of capital available to invest in the economy.[43] Conservatives suggested there was no other way of coping with increasing expenditure.

The Liberals' commitment to free trade meant they could not accept tariffs as a solution to the crisis in government revenue. In opposition in 1895–1905 they regularly protested at Tory extravagance and raised the old cry of retrenchment, especially in military expenditure, which, with debt repayments inflated by wartime borrowing, accounted for 63 per cent of government expenditure in 1905.[44] In 1906 54 per cent of Liberal candidates demanded retrenchment in their election addresses.[45] But Liberals were not reduced to playing the role of Canute, vainly protesting at the incoming tide of rising expenditure. Instead, the Liberals increasingly concentrated on their own solution of raising direct taxation. In doing so, they broke decisively with their Gladstonian legacy and the commitment to minimal government interference that guided their approach to the state's role in other features of the economy. This was possible because Liberals increasingly redefined what was equitable in direct taxation. To Gladstone this had meant a system where all those over a certain threshold paid a similar percentage of their income, with some abatements at the lower end.[46] But by the time of Gladstone's last government in 1892–4, many Liberals had come to believe this was no longer just when overall rates of taxation were rising and beginning to be felt more acutely by those on relatively modest incomes. In January 1894 Harcourt received a memorandum from 94 Liberal MPs, complaining 'the weight of taxation, which is really felt as a severe burden, by persons of small means, ought to be diminished by a much heavier assessment upon persons of fortune who do not at present feel the burden at all, and whose share of taxation might be greatly increased without even then imposing upon them any substantial sacrifice'.[47] In other words, the key test of fairness was 'ability to bear' taxation, rather than a uniform rate. The wealthy would not miss a few more pennies on direct taxation, but the struggling clerk or tradesman might be forced to do without some of the necessities of life.

This redefinition of equity in taxation provided a strong moral reasoning for graduating taxes and charging a higher rate on upper levels of wealth. Harcourt unreservedly accepted this principle when preparing his 1894 budget and only practical difficulties prevented him introducing it into the income tax.[48] But he did introduce it into the new scheme of death duties in the budget and this established the principle of graduation for subsequent Liberal administrations to develop.[49] This initiative was also less open to the idea that graduation was destructive of trade or industry, because it did not affect income earned during a taxpayer's life. Harcourt's increase in death duties was also combined with an extension in the abatements at the lowest level of income tax and this implied a further refinement of Liberal principles of equity in taxation.[50] Inheritance of a large estate provided the legatee with a secured income for life, without any exertion on his part. But small income tax payers were usually dependent on their own earnings, which would die with them. They were, therefore, obliged to save out of their income to provide for dependents, pensions, life assurance and a host of other matters. Income tax was a particularly heavy burden for them and it was merely creating a fairer balance to tax their income at a lower rate, while taking a higher percentage in death duties from large estates. This was the effective origin of the practice of taxing incomes differentially, on the basis of whether they were 'earned' or 'unearned'.

Graduation and differentiation of direct taxation provided the Liberals with an answer to the question of how free trade could be made compatible with increasing government expenditure. It also provided a powerful political weapon because it allowed the Liberals to relieve taxation for the mass of the population at the expense of the very wealthy. Finally, by arguing in terms of a fair balance of taxation throughout the population, it could at least make some sort of claim to the language of Gladstonian taxation. All of these factors made it possible for most Liberals to accept at least the principle of this strategy, even if the very wealthy among them may have felt some qualms. In 1902 the whole parliamentary leadership rallied behind a motion to graduate the income tax.[51] As soon as the party emerged from the 1906 election, Asquith, the new chancellor, appointed a select committee to look into reforming the income tax.[52] At the end of the year it reported favourably on a new supertax for the very richest and the differentiation of taxation. Asquith carried out a long argument with his Treasury officials in 1906–7 over the supertax before finally deciding not to include it in his budget.[53] But he did reduce income tax on 'earned' income under £2,000 p.a. to 9d, while maintaining it on 'unearned' income at 1s., thus enshrining the principle of differentiation in the income tax.[54] At the same time he reduced the revenue tariffs on tea in 1906 and sugar in 1908, to ensure that working class consumers, as well as lower level income tax payers, benefited from this rebalancing of the tax system.

The ground had, therefore, been thoroughly prepared for Lloyd George's 'People's Budget' of 1909, which had to meet an estimated deficit of over £16 million.[55] By raising income tax to 1s2d on earned incomes over £3,000 and unearned incomes over £2,000 and intro- ducing a 6d supertax on incomes over £5,000 Lloyd George was clearly following in Asquith's footsteps. The increases in death duties on estates over £5,000, with a top rate of 15 per cent on those over £1 million would have been recognisable to Sir William Harcourt. While Lloyd George's budget raised considerable misgivings in the cabinet, none of his colleagues challenged the principles of graduation and differentiation which underlay his changes to the income tax and death duties.[56] In fact, the amendments which the cabinet insisted on sharpened the application of these principles, by reducing tax rises at the lower end of the income scale, especially by keeping the existing rate of income tax on earned incomes up to £3,000 p.a.[57] Nobody, not even Loulou Harcourt, son of Sir William and the budget's most persistent critic, suggested reducing the proposed top rates of taxation. When the budget went to the Commons, discontent among cautious Liberal MPs focused on the land taxes, rather than the supertax.[58] This reaction suggests that Liberals found it relatively easy to unite around the ideas of graduation and differentiation and that the Liberal redefinition of equity in taxation in the 1890s had become deeply embedded. When defending the budget, the Liberals repeatedly emphasised that it repre- sented a 'fair' and equitable distribution of the burden of taxation.[59] In January 1910 the most common argument in favour of the budget by Liberal candidates was simply that it taxed those who could most afford to pay.[60]

However, the 1909 budget produced a far greater rise in taxation than anything seen in the 1890s and this forced Liberals to develop their ideas about taxation further. Above all, Liberals had to counter the Conservative argument, and their Gladstonian inheritance, which suggested that increased taxation was detrimental to the economy because it destroyed the capital needed for investment. Liberals continued to oppose government interference with trade and, generally, with production, so they had to find ways to suggest that raising direct taxation did not contradict these views. Often, Lloyd George sidestepped the problem by insisting that Britain was rich enough to afford the levels of taxation he proposed.[61] But, most importantly, he emphasised much more strongly than any of his Liberal predecessors the positive virtues of the expenditure provided for in the budget. Rather than just suggesting he was making an unpalatable burden as fair as possible he proclaimed 'This,... is a War Budget. It is for raising money to wage implacable warfare against poverty and squalidness.'[62] Lloyd George took care to list in his budget speech all the measures of social reform the budget would provide for, especially old age pensions and national insurance. It was, of course, also a budget to finance major new naval construction, but the chancellor gave this much less emphasis. Liberal candidates followed the chancellor's lead and in January 1910 some 50 per cent defended the budget as the cornerstone of social reform.[63]

The key to this approach was that Lloyd George would be hard pressed to present expenditure on the navy as anything else but wasteful within Liberal economic theory, however necessary it might be for national defence. But he intended to reassure the party and public that his social expenditure was of a different order. In fact there were a number of ways it could be justified within a Liberal economic framework. Perhaps the most developed came from J. A. Hobson, who believed that the economy was suffering from a crisis of 'underconsumption'.[64] The poor simply had too little disposable income to provide a market for British goods and redistributing more resources to them would stimulate economic activity. This was too heretical for most Liberals outside of the *Nation* circle, but some MPs were prepared to stress that the budget was not destroying capital, merely reallocating some of it to government use on behalf of the community.[65] Lloyd George, however, was keen to appropriate the language of business, suggesting that the Liberal social reforms meant investing in the nation's most important resource – its labour force.[66] Other Liberals were anxious to contest the Conservatives' description of Liberal expenditure as wasteful, by arguing that the real problem was the economy's wastage of human resources.[67] Liberal social reform would allow workmen to survive periods of illness and unemployment and pensions meant they would no longer become demoralised towards the end of their working lives. All these approaches suggested the budget was taxing the country in order to promote its productivity.

This represented the positive set of economic arguments in favour of the budget's increases in direct taxation. But the second major innovation in the budget was that its tax rises were defended not just in terms of their overall equity, but because the wealth taxed in the budget was not essential to the functioning of the economy. As the *Westminster Gazette* pointed out, the budget was 'taking toll of superfluity'.[68] The most direct way in which this could be justified was again in the work of J. A. Hobson who had popularised the concept of the 'unearned increment'.[69] This was essentially the idea that each component of the process of production was entitled to a return on its involvement in the form of interest, profits or wages. However, in situations when capital was dominant it could extract a return that was surplus to its needs. This piled up in great accumulations of wealth which could be safely taxed by the state as they were superfluous to the process of production.

However, sophisticated as these arguments were, they were not the main thrust of Liberal rhetoric on the unearned increment, as developed by Lloyd George. The chancellor instead used a prodigious sleight of hand to distract attention away from the rises in income tax and death duty and to focus the spotlight of debate onto his land taxes. Lloyd George had originally proposed a simple 1d/£ tax on all land, to be paid by the occupier, but deducted from the rent.[70] Cabinet objections to the effects of this on agricultural land and small property owners, as well as its proposal to break existing contracts where occupiers of land agreed to pay all rates and taxes, transformed the tax into three cumbersome and involved duties on increments in land values, the reversion value of leases and undeveloped land.[71] They were accompanied by a mineral rights duty, which was not strictly a land tax. Together, all of these taxes were predicted to raise no more than £500,000 per annum, while necessitating a huge and complex land valuation. The new death duties and income taxes in contrast were expected to raise £6.35 million and this sum was expected to grow substantially in the future.

In terms of their fiscal utility the land taxes were of little significance. But Lloyd George deliberately drew attention to them. They were taken first in the Commons, where they occupied no less than 22 days of debate and Lloyd George made them the focus of his famous (or notorious) orations at Limehouse on 30 July and Newcastle on 9 October 1909.[72] This strategy was meant to reassure Liberals that the budget was an attack on an interest which they felt had determinedly opposed them since the 1880s. When the landlord-dominated House of Lords rejected the budget in November 1909 this only confirmed its status as an assault on landownership. But this emphasis also deliberately created the misleading impression among Liberals, and the public at large, that most of the taxes on wealth were actually taxes on land. This was extremely useful in narrowing the front of the Liberal assault and reassuring wealthy Liberals. But it was also much easier to present the land taxes as a raid on 'unearned increment' that would not harm the economy, than it was to make this point about all accumulations of capital and large earnings.[73] Lloyd George repeatedly insisted that the whole purpose of the land taxes was to tap wealth that landowners did not earn themselves, but which they gained from the efforts of the community. As for the landlord; 'His sole function, his chief pride, is stately consumption of wealth produced by others.'[74] Lloyd George illustrated this point by referring to individual cases where urban landlords had leased their land to tenants and then appropriated the fruits of their hard work at the end of the lease – a scenario in which the unfortunate London businessman, Mr Gorringe, and the owner of the ground lease on his premises, the Duke of Westminster, loomed large.

The other great benefit of concentrating on the land taxes was that Liberals had already developed a range of arguments to justify taxing landlords for the benefit of local government. In the 1880s Liberals, especially in London, had pointed to the way in which great landowners like the Dukes of Bedford and Westminster had seen the value of their urban properties soar, while they avoided contributing to the growing burden of local rates, because local taxation was usually paid by the occupiers of land or buildings, rather than the ultimate landowner.[75] The NLF endorsed the taxation of ground rents in 1888 and London Liberals began to press the matter in the Commons. This movement was reinforced by the nostrums of Henry George, an American whose book, *Progress and Poverty*, was a best-seller in Britain in the 1880s. George contended that the continuance of poverty amongst advanced industrial nations was the result of the appropriation of national income by landowners in the form of rent. His plan to replace all taxation with a tax on land values (the 'single tax') seemed bizarre to most contemporaries, but the controversy around his book helped concentrate attention on land taxation and created a band of enthusiasts in the Liberal party who raised the issue at every opportunity.

But the key to the popularity of taxing 'the land' among Liberals lay in the late 1890s and early 1900s, when an increasing number of Liberals in urban Britain were drawn to the idea of using land taxation as a supplement to, or even a complete replacement for, the local rates.[76] This scheme was usually referred to as site value rating. Its advocates claimed it had two great advantages. First, it would stimulate house building by taxing vacant land at its capital rather than its use value, thus encouraging landowners to sell land for development, rather than withholding it from the housing market. Secondly, site value rating would provide another form of income for local authorities, who had seen rates rise by 141 per cent in 1875–1900. Liberals were worried by this development, partly because high rates were seen as a disincentive to local business. But rates also violated the ideas Liberals were developing about equity in taxation. Rate increases were highest in the poorest local authorities, which had the greatest needs, but the lowest property values. Rates were also the only direct tax that most working or lower middle class people paid (though it was often compounded with their rent). Moreover, they were a regressive tax that tended to take a higher percentage of the income of the poorest rate-payers than of the richest. Site value rating, its advocates claimed, would redress this situation by forcing landowners to contribute to the cost of the local services from which they benefited. C. P. Trevelyan claimed a modest 1d/£ levy on the capital value of land would produce £15.6 million a year. These arguments ensured that 52 per cent of Liberal candidates at the 1906 election endorsed land taxation.

Thus by concentrating on land taxation, Lloyd George was drawing on an idea that was already popular among Liberals and one which most of them believed would stimulate the economy, rather than over-load it with taxation. Moreover, he often yoked the land taxes with his new duties on licences to suggest the budget was an attack on intemper-ance as much as on landowners. By steeply increasing taxes on licences, Lloyd George expected to raise a further £2.6 million towards the budget deficit.[77] Again, this appealed to Liberals as an assault on a tradi-tional enemy and helped to range temperance enthusiasts behind the bill. But these taxes could also be justified, in line with developing Liberal views on temperance, as duties that did not interfere with the economy, because the drink industry itself inhibited production, by making workers less efficient and diverting spending from more useful outlets.[78] Like landowners, the drink trade was classified as essentially parasitical to industry and production, rather than as important components of the economy. This was a development of the Liberal idea that a distinction, or 'differentiation', could be drawn between certain types of property and income for taxation purposes and helped to further blur the fact that the Liberals were taxing all wealth more severely. This definition of some forms of property as more susceptible to taxation because they were economically harmful or superfluous was vigorously rejected by the Conservatives. When Balfour replied to Lloyd George's budget speech he claimed the Liberals 'have apparently made it your principle to distinguish arbitrarily between one kind of property and another.'[79] For Conservatives all property was threatened by the Liberals' proposals and the budget had opened up a fundamental division between the parties.

Much of the rest of Lloyd George's deficit in 1909 was met by tinkering in a fairly traditional way – especially by raising £3.5 million by raiding the sinking fund.[80] However, one important way in which the Liberals kept in touch with their Gladstonian past was by rejecting the Tory path of papering over deficits by borrowing. Virtually all of the expansion in expenditure in 1905–14 was paid for out of taxation and £41 million of the national debt was actually reduced under Asquith's chancellorship.[81] This was partly because the low price of government stock made loans a difficult route, but it also expressed the Liberals' unwillingness to abandon all claims to fiscal prudence. This also influenced their attitude to the final important source of revenue in 1909 – the £3.5 million raised from tobacco and spirits taxes.[82] These taxes were a useful source of revenue and a standby of hard-pressed chancellors. But they also meant that the Liberals were able to retain the Gladstonian idea that every member of the community should contribute to taxation – a concept that Lloyd George endorsed in his budget speech on 29 April 1909.[83] In fact the rises in spirits and tobacco duties were so steep that a working class family that smoked and drank was probably paying a similar percentage of its income in taxation in 1913–14, as it had been before the Liberals came to power.[84] But Lloyd George did not reverse Asquith's reductions of the tea and sugar duties, nor did he raise any of the other revenue tariffs. This meant that the indirect taxation paid by non-income tax payers had decisively shifted away from foodstuffs and towards 'luxuries', or purchases that detracted from the efficiency of workers, rather than providing them with essential nourishment (though clearly not all workers would agree with this definition).

Thus, while the 1909 budget did clearly break with previous Liberal notions of what a budget should contain, it also appealed strongly to powerful elements in Liberal ideology, especially through its attack on landowners and the drink trade. The budget also retained some contact with Gladstonian notions of finance and presented a case that its increases in taxation would help rather than harm industry and production. Only such a multi-sided budget could possibly have persuaded the Liberal party to abandon its commitment to retrenchment and endorse a huge new package of expenditure. As it was, after seventeen difficult meetings, Lloyd George was able to unite the cabinet behind the budget and drive it through the Commons.[85] A threatened cave of Liberal MPs against the budget collapsed, with rebels able to raise no more than 20 or 30 votes against some of the budget's details, especially on the land taxes. The Lords' rejection of the budget solidified its appeal in Liberal eyes and identified its proposals with the defence of the rights of the Commons. By the time of the January 1910 election it was not possible to remain a Liberal and to reject the budget's strategy. About 20 to 30 Liberal MPs chose not to stand again, because of doubts about the budget, but they could organise no opposition within the party, so successfully had Lloyd Georgian finance captured the meaning of Liberalism.

1909 was clearly a watershed for Liberal finance, but it was followed by a number of important innovations. The first was contained in Lloyd George's national insurance legislation of 1911.[86] This measure of social reform also introduced an important new principle. Those who received sickness benefit under its provisions were required to contribute the largest share of its costs. All those in employment earning under £160 a year (the income tax threshold) paid 4d per week into the new national insurance fund, while employers contributed 3d and the state only 2d. This principle was extended to the experiments in unemployment insurance introduced in 1913. Lloyd George's prime motivation was fiscal necessity. He felt that the pensions scheme of 1908 had been so expensive that it had required the extraordinary measures of the 'People's Budget' to provide for its costs. If the Liberals were not to abandon further major social reform, they had to find a way for paying for it that would not entail a permanent financial ferment. The insurance principle represented the way out of this dilemma. By creating a self-financing fund separate from general taxation and utilising the word 'insurance' it was arguable that the state was not taxing people at all, but enrolling them in a scheme of self-help. Indeed, the whole concept of national insurance was meant to resonate with existing traditions of contributions to the friendly societies and insurance companies which were enrolled to administer the scheme. Lloyd George often implied that all he was doing was allowing these bodies to offer extended benefits to a wider section of the population.[87] But national insurance was also an undeniably regressive system, under which the poorest were making compulsory contributions to national government out of their income for the first time. This was what underlay the scheme's initial unpopularity. But it also represented a principle that was enshrined in the 'People's Budget' that everyone was required to contribute to the costs of national expenditure. All that was new under national insurance, was that the poor were paying direct as well as indirect taxes to central government.

However, the regressive nature of national insurance was balanced by Lloyd George's 1914 budget. The new taxes in the 'People's Budget' proved remarkably successful in raising revenue and covering rising expenditure. By 1913–14 they were contributing £27.2 million towards a total expenditure of £198.2 million.[88] It was only in 1914 that increased naval expenditure forced Lloyd George into making further tax rises. Unwilling to produce a budget that merely paid for more dreadnoughts, he hastily prepared a scheme to increase state grants to local authorities by £11 million in 1915–16.[89] This would allow for improvements in educational provision in particular, and, so the chancellor claimed, would also reduce the average borough's rates bill by 9d/£. Thus, while Lloyd George had imposed a form of direct national taxation on non-income tax payers in 1911, he proposed in 1914 to give them some compensation by reducing the rates, the other form of regressive direct taxation which they paid.

This rates relief was entirely paid for out of impositions on the upper levels of direct taxation. The top rate of income tax was increased to 1s 3d, the supertax was graduated and death duties on estates over £60,000 were raised. There were no increases in indirect taxes paid by ordinary consumers. This strategy obviously developed the approach of 1909 by taxing the wealthiest to pay for social reform. Lloyd George was unapologetic about this in 1914. 'Why should men who have much not contribute something to those who have too little? Providence has been very good to them. Let them share their luck' he proclaimed.[90] But it also went further towards enshrining Liberal ideas of equity in taxation by dealing with local and national taxation as part of one scheme and using graduated national taxation to help correct the perceived unfairnesses of a regressive local tax. The 1914 budget shared another feature with 1909: it obscured its general assault on accumulations of wealth with a controversial attack on landowners. Liberals had long disliked increasing central grants to reduce the rate burden, because they believed that landowners would benefit from this, by raising their tenants' rent on the grounds that tenants had less to pay in rates.[91] Lloyd George dealt with this problem by proposing that the land valuation started in 1910, to collect the national land taxes, should be adapted to provide local councils with separate valuations of land and of the improvements on land. In the future, they would levy both a composite rate on land and improvements and a site value rate on land alone, but they would only be empowered to reduce the composite rate. Thus none of the new grants would help landowners and Liberal councils would in the future be able to pile rate increases on landowners. The First World War foiled this scheme, but its general thrust represented another attempt to focus Liberal energies on fighting landownership and to appeal to the party's longstanding identification with land taxation as equitable and helpful to the economy.

The 1914 budget also ran into trouble in the Commons. Lloyd George's attempt to tie the distribution of some central grants in 1914–15 to his scheme for reforming local taxation failed for lack of parliamentary time – a miscalculation which delayed the scheme until 1915–16, rather than wrecking it entirely.[92] Moreover, a motley collection of backbench MPs showed considerable disquiet at the new budget and abstained on a guillotine motion on the finance bill on 7 July. However, this should not be seen as an indication that the party had reached the limit of its toleration of Lloyd Georgian finance. Though some of the Liberal rebels, like the leader of the 'cave', Richard Holt, were generally sceptical about this strategy, this was not representative of the group as a whole. Many saw the revolt as a continuation of the protests earlier in the year against increased naval expenditure. Others were horrified at the prospect of another autumn session to pass the legislation needed to reform the rating system, were seeking to protest at the failure to arrest Sir Edward Carson, or were alienated from the government for a variety of personal reasons. This collection of tired and crotchety MPs was not a serious threat to the budget or Lloyd George's general strategy. When the First World War broke out the chancellor's ingenious conduct of his office remained one of the central elements in Liberal policy.

Liberal attitudes to finance and the economy were Janus-faced. They remained committed above all to their tradition of free trade. But this policy was increasingly defended as a means of protecting working class living standards, rather than as part of a laissez-faire economic theory. While Liberals remained suspicious of attempts to direct the economy, increasing government expenditure meant they could only preserve free trade's credibility by abandoning their commitment to minimal taxation. As a solution, they embraced the graduation and differentia-tion of direct taxation – a solution that proved more popular than the Tory policy of tariff reform. The Liberals succeeded in ensuring that the burden of increased expenditure fell on the very wealthiest members of society, particularly those earning more than £5,000 per annum, while lower rate income tax payers paid less in taxation in 1914 than they had done in 1905. The tax system also shifted towards much greater reliance on direct, rather than indirect, taxation. But, at the same time, Liberalism was distracted from these simple facts by an attempt to fiscally persecute landowners and the drink trade and it ensured that the poorest members of society continued to make some contribution towards national expenditure. This allowed the party to reject charges that it was engaged in a war against all wealth, to continue to connect itself with Liberal traditions and to claim it spoke for all the community against the vested interests that, while they were superfluous to the economy, threatened to use government for their own ends.

7
Social Reform and Labour Relations

If any area of pre-1914 Liberalism can claim to have been thoroughly investigated it is the party's role in promoting social reform.[1] This is partly because it seemed to later twentieth-century eyes to be the most obvious way in which Edwardian Liberal governments created a lasting political legacy. It was relatively easy to portray these administrations' achievements in the field of pensions and national insurance as precursors of the welfare state, while their struggles with the House of Lords, Irish home rule or nonconformist grievances seemed to belong to history's dead ends and long-forgotten controversies. But Liberalism's commitment, or lack of it, to social reform is also essential to arguments about whether Liberalism was already doomed to obsolescence before 1914, or had been able to renew its vitality and create a programme that could appeal to working class voters and stave off the rise of the infant Labour party.[2] These controversies have generated a huge literature, but they are necessarily inconclusive and leave the nature of the Liberal social reforms of 1905–14 open to a variety of interpretations.

Social reform

Mid-nineteenth-century Britain had witnessed the triumph of the idea of the minimal state, embodied in the concepts of low taxation and as little governmental interference in society and the economy as possible.[3] This idea had been particularly associated with the Liberal party, but it was also widely shared throughout Victorian society. Necessarily, it precluded any important role for the state in promoting its citizens' social welfare. It had always been a theory, though, rather than an exact description of the state's role and there had been numerous exceptions to the principle of non-intervention, particularly at the local level. In the late nineteenth century the concept of the minimal state effectively broke down. Not only did it no longer describe the relations of state and society, but it was becoming increasingly clear that government non-intervention had not solved and could not solve pressing political issues, including the persistence of poverty in what was, in historical terms, a very wealthy society. Conservatives turned to tariffs and imperialism to promote flagging economic growth. Labour and socialist leaders started to argue for new measures like the compulsory eight-hour day as the solutions to unemployment and poverty. This general trend towards collectivism was reflected in many areas of thought, including sociology, philosophy and theology, and was a widely-recognised feature of the political landscape. It was scarcely surprising that it was also a feature of Liberal thought.

Many mid nineteenth-century Liberals were hostile to the state's role in society because they believed the state was controlled by a narrow clique, who did not act in the interests of the general public. But when the state came increasingly under popular control in the later nineteenth century, it became possible for Liberals to think of it as a liberating influence, which could act to protect the people against powerful 'interests' in society, rather than furthering the ends of sinister elites. Once this essential pre-condition was met, Liberals could begin to think of the state as an instrument to promote the people's welfare. The best-known Liberal thinkers who argued for the re-orientation of Liberalism towards social reform were the duo of L. T. Hobhouse and J. A. Hobson.[4] Neither was a politician, but they both wrote widely for the Liberal Press, especially the *Manchester Guardian, Daily News* and the weekly *Nation*, as well as distilling their thoughts in books like Hobhouse's *Liberalism* (1911) and Hobson's *The Crisis of Liberalism* (1909). Both men regarded themselves as writing from within the Liberal tradition and eagerly upheld many elements of the traditional Liberal approach. Hobhouse served as secretary of the Free Trade Union and Hobson was a noted critic of imperialism. For both of them, social reform was merely an extension of existing Liberal precepts and they had a great deal of success in showing how Liberal language and ideas were not incompatible with social reform.

Hobhouse in particular tackled the idea that a free society depended on upholding freedom of contract between parties, including between employers and employees, and excluding the state from regulating working conditions. Hobhouse argued that in reality 'true freedom postulates substantial equality between the parties. In proportion as one party is in a position of vantage, he is able to dictate terms. In proportion as the other party is in a weak position, he must accept unfavourable terms.'[5] The state was, therefore, justified in intervening to secure better conditions of work for employees, because this merely created the conditions for a free and equal bargain that represented true freedom of contract. 'True consent is free consent, and full freedom of consent implies equality of both parties to the bargain' as Hobhouse put it.[6] This sort of activity necessarily restrained the freedom of employers. But, Hobhouse argued, 'The function of State coercion is to override individual coercion...' and this was necessary to secure liberty for employees at work, just as it was to maintain all other civil liberties when these were threatened by powerful groups.[7] Thus, Hobhouse reached the conclusion that 'in many directions, increased control is essential to liberty – e.g. in matters of industrial contracts. There is, for me, no antithesis between liberty and public control'.[8]

Similarly, Hobson suggested that if the aim of Liberalism was to spread liberty then this could best be interpreted as a question, 'What are the equal opportunities which every Englishman requires to-day in order to secure real liberty of self-development?'[9] Liberty meant not just freedom from restraint, but freedom to develop the individual's personality and gifts – a definition that could be traced back to John Stuart Mill, the patron saint of mid-nineteenth-century Liberalism. Hobhouse's formula was that 'it was the function of the State to secure the conditions upon which mind and character may develop themselves'.[10] This involved a much more organic view of the relationship between the individual and society and their mutual responsibilities. In particular, Hobhouse suggested that while the state could expect the individual to do everything in their power to support themselves, the individual could expect 'the means of maintaining a civilized standard of life' as this was a prerequisite for any real sense of liberty or opportunity for self-realisation.[11] Thus, both Hobson and Hobhouse strongly supported Liberal legislation for guaranteed minimum conditions of welfare in the form of pensions, insurance and trade boards as essential to the vision of a liberal society. This redefinition, or rather extension, of Liberalism came to be known as the New Liberalism.[12] After the 1906 election there were a number of devotees of the cause amongst the ranks of younger Liberal MPs, most prominently C. F. G. Masterman, a journalist who, like many other New Liberals, had spent some time in social investigation and settlement work and regarded himself as an expert on social reform.[13] A number of avowed New Liberals formed a 'collectivist' group of backbench MPs to press their views.[14] According to some analyses of Liberal MPs' voting records there was a core of 25–30 MPs prepared to vote consistently against the government in order to push it further along the path of social reform.[15] There were, of course, those like Rosebery, who complained 'The new Liberalism is in reality directed largely against liberty; the old Liberalism was meant to promote it.'[16] But Rosebery, feeling the tide was running against him, had largely severed his connections with the Liberal party by 1907.

However, the fairly abstract arguments of men like Hobhouse and Hobson did not necessarily commit Liberal governments to any particular course of action. Instead they showed that Liberalism was not incompatible with social reform and provided a *mélange* of arguments to justify action by Liberal governments in the field of welfare. New Liberal principles could be found embedded in most Liberal social legislation of 1906–14. But they only determined the context, rather than the form or timing of the government's actions. In fact, there were three distinct waves of cabinet initiatives on social reform in 1905–14, together with a number of *ad hoc* responses to particular situations. This complex pattern of movement took the Liberals a long way towards defining one of their identities as being 'the party of social reform', though this did not necessarily supersede the party's others enthusiasms. Rather it co-existed with and melted into other ways of thinking about Liberalism.

The first wave of Liberal social reforms was largely a response to the political agenda that had built up in the previous decade. While historically the Liberals had little claim to be more enthusiastic social reformers than their Tory rivals, the party had started to show itself to be malleable on this issue in the last years of the nineteenth century. This was partly because the defections by cautious Liberals over the home rule issue in 1886 left the trade union lobby, which had largely stayed loyal to Gladstone, in a position of increased influence within the party. The 1892–5 administration had attempted to legislate on employers' liability for industrial accidents, introduced machinery that could be used to limit railway workers' hours of labour and began to institute shorter hours and 'trade union rates' for government employees.[17] But, just as importantly, Joseph Chamberlain associated the Unionists with the policy of appealing to working class voters with material inducements.[18] The outcomes of this strategy were fairly meagre, apart from the 1897 Workmen's Compensation Act. But by taking up the issue of old age pensions in 1891, Chamberlain pushed social reform into the forefront of national politics for the first time. This was confirmed by his espousal of pensions in the 1895 general election.[19] Liberals were only too willing to criticise Chamberlain for failing to deliver on this policy, but in doing so they had to be prepared to take the idea up themselves. In the

1906 election no fewer than 59 per cent of Liberal candidates endorsed the need for pensions.[20]

This development provided the centrepiece for the first wave of Liberal welfare reforms. While Asquith, the new chancellor, remained cautious in public about the existence of the necessary finance for pensions, he started collecting information on the subject in 1906. In 1907 he announced in the budget speech that £1.5 million of the government's surplus would be set aside for old age pensions.[21] The whole matter was reviewed by a cabinet committee in 1907 and the foundations were laid for the plan unveiled on 7 May 1908.[22] This provided for a pension of 5s. per week for all citizens over 70, whose annual income was under £31 10s. A raft of disqualifications hedged the measure around, including anyone who had received poor relief in the last two years and those guilty of 'habitual failure to work', but these proved difficult to implement and lapsed.[23] The motive seems to have been concern at the cost of the measure, rather than an obsession with maintaining incentives for the elderly to be thrifty. Indeed, Asquith had underestimated the costs involved by some £2 million per annum, even at the initiation of the scheme and pensions were an important contributory factor in the financial crisis of 1908–9.[24]

The Old Age Pensions Act was undoubtedly expected by the Liberals to be immensely popular and the available evidence suggests they were right in this expectation.[25] They had also fulfilled an idea that had been circulating in politics for over fifteen years. For both these reasons, pensions were not, officially, a matter of party contention. The Tories did not oppose them in the Commons or the Lords and seemed anxious to extend their scope – though cynics suggested this was in the hope that the scheme would prove unworkable.[26] But they could not disguise the fact that while Conservatives had talked about pensions, the Liberals had introduced them. Moreover, the pensions act contained a host of new principles. Most importantly, it separated welfare provision from the poor law. Pensions were given to the elderly as a right, rather than as grudging and humiliating relief to paupers. As critics of the measure complained, 'A phrase constantly used in the matter was that old-age pensions were to be given as a right, and not as charity, as a recompense for previous services to the State.'[27] This dovetailed neatly with New Liberal thinking on the mutual rights and responsibilities of the individual and society.

Pensions were widely and enthusiastically welcomed throughout the party and their handful of opponents dismissed as eccentrics. Lloyd George dubbed such people 'the new anarchist party ... frankly and ruthlessly individualist'.[28] This rhetorical strategy marked an important break from Liberalism's past, because it made it clear to the party that the supremacy of the individual's liberty, which had been so celebrated by nineteenth-century Liberals, was no longer to be considered Liberalism at all, but 'anarchism'. Anyone who rejected old age pensions was placed in the same category as those who wanted to deny the state any role at all in society. Edwardian Liberals were undoubtedly helped to accept this analysis by the perceived popularity of pensions and their usefulness in the party battle with the Tories. But once they acclaimed the idea of pensions, Liberals could start to think of themselves as a party that was particularly associated with social reform. This process was hurried forward once pensions became entwined with the 'People's Budget' of 1909, that raised much of the finance for Liberal social reform, and the constitutional struggle between the Lords and the Commons which followed. 75 per cent of Liberal candidates dwelt on pensions in their election addresses in January 1910, making it one of the central Liberal themes of the election.[29] For most Liberals, social reform began to be inextricably linked with other items in the Liberal agenda, especially graduated taxation and the achievement of democracy.

Pensions were not alone amongst the Liberals' achievements in the field of social reform in 1906–8, but they were by far the most eminent and the only measure that caught the imagination of the party. Most of the other legislation was smaller-scale and did not make much public impact, even though it did sometimes embrace some important new principles. It was also the product of a bewildering variety of impulses. The Workmen's Compensation Act of 1906, for instance, extended existing legislation to more groups and allowed workers to be compensated for some industrial diseases, as well as injuries.[30] It was widely seen as a concession to the trade union lobby for their assistance in the 1906 election. The case for organising and extending existing provision for school meals had been broadly accepted in the previous parliament, passing the Commons easily in 1905.[31] It had strong support from the Labour party, active feminists, the medical and educational fraternities and even within Toryism, which was susceptible to arguments about the need to ensure the next generation were fit for their imperial duties. It was treated as a non-controversial measure when reintroduced by the government in 1906, though crucially the Liberals removed the scheme from any connection with the poor law. Though some Liberals grumbled about the state assuming a parent's responsibilities, the vast majority of the party were happy to see it as a minor application of the principle that the state should give the poorest children the opportunity to learn, and so develop their potential, in similar circumstances to less impoverished children.

These two measures were very much 'unfinished business' from the previous parliament and did not create much of a stir. It helped that neither directly tackled the subject of state regulation of the economy, which caused Liberals far more qualms than social reform did in itself. However, the 1909 Trade Boards Act violated a long-standing tenet of political economy by, very cautiously, introducing minimum wages in four areas of production.[32] This was a major new development, that was to have important repercussions for the development of Liberal social policy. But this first step in wage regulation was justified by accepting the case of campaigners against low wages that the regulated trades were 'sweated' industries. This implied that not only did they pay exceptionally low rates of pay to home-workers, but that these trades were 'degraded' or 'parasitic'.[33] Wages could only be so low because most of those employed were women, whose income was supplemented by charity or poor relief – giving their employers an unfair advantage over 'healthy' trades. Moreover, conditions were so bad in the sweated industries that they spawned slums and unhealthy future generations. They undermined Britain's industrial vigour and the economy would not lose, even if they disappeared. In fact, the sweated industries lay outside of the parameters of Britain's normal economy and could safely be subjected to the experiment of wage regulation. This allowed the case that was being made by a broad coalition of reformers within and outside the Liberal party to be accepted by the government.[34] Indeed, the measure could be portrayed as an extension of existing factory legislation, or even as an attack on prostitution and infant mortality – both of which were alleged to be endemic among poorly-paid outworkers. The National Anti-Sweating League, which was set up in 1906, did such a good job of making this case that the Trade Boards Act was not opposed by the Conservatives and secured an easy passage through the Commons in 1909.

Much more difficult was the miners' eight-hour day legislation of 1908. The coal industry was central to the economy in a way that the 'sweated' trades were not and interfering with its operations would arguably reduce the competitiveness of a major British industry and, by raising coal prices, of many other industries too.[35] The result would inevitably be unemployment and a rising cost of living for ordinary consumers. This should have provided a watertight case against legislation by any Liberal government. Yet as far back as 1893 an eight hours bill had been endorsed by Liberal MPs by 185–33 and 9 per cent of Liberal candidates in 1906 had specifically included the legislation in their manifesto.[36] The only explanation for this behaviour was the powerful backing which the miners' unions gave to the bill. The miners were still largely within the Liberal fold and their union dominated a number of local Liberal parties. Several miners' leaders like Enoch Edwards, William Abraham and John Wadsworth sat as Liberal MPs and coal mining was a significant electoral factor in over 80 seats.[37] It simply could not be ignored by the party. The result was a head-on collision between the Liberal party's interests and some aspects of its economic ideology.

The Home Secretary, Herbert Gladstone, wriggled his way to a compromise.[38] He introduced a bill which limited miners' hours to eight hours, but excluded some of the time spent reaching the coal face. This provided a more modest reduction in hours than the union had campaigned for, and so was just about acceptable to most Liberal MPs – though ten voted against the principle of the bill. The party at large was notably dubious about this measure, if local press reaction is anything to go by. However, it is clear that the arguments about the bill concentrated on its wider impact on the economy. This was what really worried the committee Gladstone appointed to look into the matter in July 1906 and the Coal Consumers' Defence League which he covertly encouraged to campaign against the miners' version of the bill. But this objection could be toned down by making the actual reduction in hours fairly modest. The bill could only pass, though, because most Liberals were prepared to accept that it was justifiable in principle for the state to intervene in freely negotiated contracts between employers and employees. This eminently New Liberal idea was only opposed by a handful of MPs, particularly Harold Cox, who left the party in 1909. Outside of parliament there was much grumbling from some Liberal businessmen who feared their costs would go up and from miners in the north-east, who already worked less than an eight hour shift. But the party survived the crisis intact, thus revealing how far it was prepared to go, when pushed, in the direction of state intervention in working practices.

Thus by 1908 the government could boast a considerable record in social welfare, but old age pensions was its only really major measure. However, this was only the Liberals' first wave of reforms. A second phase set in during 1908, which took the government much further. While the initiatives of 1906–8 stemmed from issues that had been circulating in politics for some time and were dealt with by a variety of cabinet ministers, the new departures of 1908 represented a fresh agenda and were largely the work of two ministers – Lloyd George and Churchill. Between them, they ensured that the cabinet's impetus towards social reform did not fizzle out and that the new edifice of national insurance was erected alongside that of old age pensions.

The origins of the whole idea of national insurance seem to lie with Lloyd George's involvement with piloting the old age pensions legislation through the Commons in 1908.[39] The popularity and scale of the proposals convinced him that social legislation represented the key to the party's future success and that pensions should be used as a precedent for further state benefits. This gave Lloyd George the idea of a vast new scheme to provide sickness benefits and payments for widows and orphans, thus tackling some of the crucial remaining areas where people might be thrown into destitution by an unavoidable inability to work.[40] But Lloyd George was also convinced that any scheme could not be financed out of general taxation and devised the national insurance system as a way of spreading payments between employers and employees and the state.[41] This would also make use of the insurance principle that was already familiar to millions of people and of the expertise of the friendly societies who would administer the scheme. In some ways, all Lloyd George proposed to do was to set up a state system which would extend and subsidise existing forms of insurance provision. But to be successful, it would have to be compulsory and it would enact another huge advance in the state's role in welfare. The poor law dealt with many of these issues already, but national insurance was a very different scheme, because, even more so than with pensions, it rested on rights and entitlements to relief. People would receive benefits on the grounds that they were part of, and had contributed to, an insurance scheme. It represented a practical expression of the New Liberal doctrine of the organic nature of the relationship between the state and the individual.

Lloyd George may have been building on existing voluntary foundations, but such a scheme had not previously been widely canvassed. Most political debate had not looked much beyond the provision of pensions and even Labour and socialist politicians had been more concerned with issues like the eight hour day and 'right to work' legislation.[42] Thus Liberals had little preparation for the national insurance proposals that started to leak out in 1908 and 1909.[43] But the party accepted them willingly. There was virtually no opposition to the idea of national insurance while the legislation wound its way through the Commons in 1911. As Lloyd George said when replying to the Second Reading debate, 'I do not think there has been any challenge to the main principle of the Bill.'[44] Indeed, the Tories were so worried by the precedent of pensions that even they did not oppose the legislation.[45] Instead, most of the obstruction came from interest groups. The doctors, for instance, nearly wrecked the whole plan by delaying registering to operate its provisions. Liberal disquiet only surfaced when the scheme came into operation and it became clear that many workmen and small employers objected to the bureaucracy and regressive nature of insurance contributions. Rather than proving an electoral asset as Lloyd George had hoped, national insurance was increasingly blamed for the party's poor performance at by elections in 1912–13.[46] Masterman reflected gloomily 'I doubt if the scheme will ever be popular.'[47] Nevertheless, the Liberals pressed ahead with implementing the second part of the national insurance scheme, which Churchill had devised at the Board of Trade and presented to the cabinet in 1909.[48] This created an experimental system of unemployment insurance for 2.5 million workers in trades where cyclical and seasonal unemployment was common. Benefits were modest at 7s per week for 15 weeks of the year, but the scheme was obviously capable of future expansion.

Whether that expansion was imminent was dubious, though. National insurance was the government's great achievement of 1910–11 in the field of welfare, but the unease its initial operations caused seemed to mark out the limits of the government's programme. Once it was clear that social reform could be unpopular, the political imperative that drove the process of reform suddenly became less compelling. Moreover, if future welfare measures had to depend on the regressive taxation embodied in national insurance, it was difficult to see a way out of this impasse, however easily Liberals could accept further social reform as a genuine expression of Liberalism. The second great wave of Liberal welfare measures was in real danger of petering out in early 1912, especially as the government's parliamentary timetable in 1912–14 was mortgaged to Irish home rule and Welsh Church disestablishment. In addition, Churchill, one of the architects of national insurance, had moved to the Admiralty in 1911, removing him from domestic policy-making.

The third wave of Liberal proposals in the field of social reform was sparked off by the unforeseen industrial crisis launched by the national miners' strike in support of a minimum wage in March 1912.[49] As industrial production and transport were faced with a slow-down and eventually a total cessation, demands for the government to 'do some-thing' to remedy the situation were insistent. One Liberal MP noted 'The empty wagons in the sidings, the crowds cutting trees and turning old waste heaps in search of coal prove how trade is paralysed &

suffering has reached the poor.'[50] The cabinet attempted a compromise between the union and the employers. But this still meant the drastic step of emergency legislation to set up boards in each mining district to determine local minimum wages. This solution obviously built on the Trade Boards Act of 1909, but it had never been intended that minimum wages should be extended to other, 'normal' areas of the economy. Asquith was at pains to point out that the legislation of March 1912 was a response to a national emergency and should not be construed as setting a precedent.[51] But of course it had set just the precedent he denied. As Grey put it, 'a door had been opened with regard to the minimum wage which cannot be closed again'.[52] Moreover, this had happened in such a way that Liberals who were cautious about state regulation of the economy found difficult to oppose, because the government was acting as a conciliator in a crisis, rather than planning an agenda of state intervention. There was far more trouble for the government from the 50 or so Liberals who wished to support the union's contention that specific minimum wage figures should be inserted in the bill, than from Liberals who objected to a massive and unforeseen extension of state intervention in the economy.[53]

This development convinced Lloyd George that state regulation of wages was a practical policy which most Liberals would accept and made him its foremost advocate in the cabinet.[54] But from this starting point he developed his plans in a startling new direction by insisting in an interview with the *Daily News* of 13 May 1912 that 'It is the agricultural labourer on whom we must concentrate attention' and suggesting a minimum wage for farm workers. This tangent was based on Lloyd George's conviction that low agricultural pay led to migration to the towns, swelling the number of unemployed and lowering wages. Employers could fix low wage rates by reference to the prevailing rate for agricultural labourers. Thus a minimum wage in the countryside 'would be much the most effective way of improving the minimum wage in other industries.'[55]

This rather crude analysis was not a personal foible of Lloyd George's. It reflected a widely-held feeling in the Liberal party that many industrial difficulties could ultimately be traced back to the need to reform the social structure of the countryside and in particular to attack the role of landowners who were held responsible for rural poverty.[56] Many Liberals in the nineteenth century had been suspicious of landowners as an elite who monopolised power for their own ends and this feeling had crystallised after the mass desertion of Liberal landowners to Unionism when the party declared in favour of Irish home rule in 1886. Many Liberals eagerly seized on the idea that the party was only so weak in rural England after 1886 because the landowners were exerting a policy of 'feudal' political and economic pressure to enforce Tory dominance. In the late 1880s and early 1890s Liberal social investigators and propagandists painted a relentlessly bleak portrait of rural society in which not only was political intimidation rife, but labourers were paid starvation wages and forced to live in miserable hovels.

This picture of the English countryside as a place characterised by landed tyrants and oppressed serfs had become deeply ingrained in Liberal thinking by 1912. It was seen as a standing affront to the kind of open, democratic society that Liberalism stood for and, therefore, drastic measures of state intervention could be justified in order to extend liberty to agricultural districts. It was the obvious place where the state's authority was required to override the coercion of society by a powerful caste. These assumptions lay behind the party's persistent interest in land reform as an assault on the basis of landowners' dominance. But a number of other factors bolstered this concern.[57] Land reform could be offered as a panacea for the depression which had blighted British agriculture since the late 1870s. It also drew on various strands of nineteenth-century working class radicalism that saw the land as the heritage of all the people, rather than being the exclusive possession of landowners. These ideas could be traced back to Thomas Spence, Tom Paine, Robert Owen and the Chartists and reflected ideas that the land was either God's or belonged to all the people and had been stolen at some distant point in history, either when the 'Norman Yoke' was imposed in 1066 or at the time of the enclosures. Many Liberals did not believe that land was merely another form of property, which should be protected from state interference in the name of liberty. Instead, it was a special case, in which the people were entitled to use the power of the state to promote the welfare of society as a whole.

That the state could intervene in landed society had been decisively demonstrated by the Irish and Scottish land legislation of the 1880s and 1890s.[58] The extension of the household franchise to the counties in 1884–5 gave the Liberals the incentive to produce policies that would appeal to agricultural labourers and free them from 'feudal' domination. Chamberlain's proposal for 'three acres and a cow', or state-supplied allotments, in 1885, and the party's establishment of parish councils with powers to purchase land in 1894 were outcomes of this desire to appeal to the labourers and establish their economic, and thus political, independence.[59] The Liberals had returned to this issue with their 1907 Smallholdings Act, which allowed county councils to acquire land, compulsorily if necessary, to meet local demand for small farms.[60] The whole thrust of this policy was to break landowners' dominance of the countryside through state intervention in the rural economy. The difficulty for the Liberals was that the legislation of 1907 did not prove very successful and in 1910 the party had suffered a 'debacle' in English rural seats.[61] Lloyd George's kite of May 1912 was intended to combine the need for a new rural policy with taking the party down the line of least resistance in extending minimum wages, because Liberals already had a long history of supporting state intervention in rural areas. Lloyd George could feel that by focusing on a minimum wage in agriculture, he was folding social reform into more traditional Liberal concerns, in the same way that the crisis of 1909–10 had focused on both progressive taxation and constitutional reform. In a sense, social reform was being given a particular Liberal twist by becoming part of the war on 'feudalism'.

However, given the government's crowded legislative programme, there was no real possibility of Lloyd George translating his plans into law before the next election. Instead, he decided to set up a detailed investigation of the land issue, effectively directed by Seebohm Rowntree, who was already famous for his report on poverty in York.[62] In October 1913 the Land Enquiry produced an elaborate rural report, advocating not only minimum wages for agricultural labourers, but rent courts for farmers, state-built cottages and more smallholdings legislation.[63] The key was that farmers would be able to claim back their increased wage costs through a rent reduction. Ultimately it would be the landowners who paid the price of Liberal social reform, rather than the taxpayer, as with national insurance. The cabinet had little trouble accepting this programme in October 1913 and the party launched a Land Campaign in 1913–14 to explain its proposals.[64] This provoked a good deal of enthusiasm throughout the party. New Liberals rallied to another programme of social reform, while more cautious party members could interpret the Land Campaign as merely an extension of the events of 1909–10. The proposals were undoubtedly intended to play the leading role in the Liberals' plans for the next election.

However, once Lloyd George launched his land enquiry in 1912 it soon became clear that it would not just cover rural issues. There had to be some question as to whether urban Britain was interested in agricultural reform – Chamberlain had certainly failed to win over the towns with his allotments proposals in 1885.[65] Moreover, there were already a number of important manifestations of an urban land issue by 1912 and these could scarcely be ignored in any wide-ranging enquiry into land problems. Almost from its beginning the Land Enquiry determined to bring out a separate urban report to accompany its rural findings, thus considerably expanding Lloyd George's original vision.[66] The urban land issue was a complex of problems and controversies surrounding the role of landowners in the towns. Its most prominent component in the Edwardian era was obviously land taxation, which Lloyd George had thrust to the fore in his 1909 budget. This policy had proved its political usefulness in 1909–10 and was heartily supported by the majority of Liberals.[67] For a few, like Josiah Wedgwood and half a dozen other followers of Henry George among the Liberal MPs, it was their sole reason for being in politics.[68]

But land taxation had not been a success in practice. It had collected very little in the way of revenue and its introduction had coincided with a downturn in the building industry, leaving it open to the charge that it had caused a slump rather than a boom in house building.[69] Moreover, a core of Liberal MPs had always been sceptical about the policy.[70] Lloyd George's enquiry took the opportunity to downgrade the significance of the issue, recommending only a minor dose of site value rating in the future.[71] Instead it concentrated on outlining a huge plan to stimulate house building in the suburbs. Local authorities would be empowered to draw up preliminary town plans, buy up land and lease it to developers and promote new public transport to these areas. This would ensure the creation of higher-standard housing for working class families. Effectively, the enquiry was proposing that the Liberals should make housing the centrepiece of their next election campaign, though, intriguingly, it also suggested the need for an urban minimum wage to ensure the very poorest could afford the new housing. These proposals were linked into the battle against the landlords because the enquiry insisted it was necessary for local authorities to have the powers to acquire land compulsorily and at its use value from landowners in order for new housing to be built at a reasonable price.

The urban report was not published until April 1914 and its policies were only gradually being considered by the cabinet in the period up until the declaration of war in August 1914.[72] But it is very likely that the urban proposals would have joined their rural counterparts in the Liberal programme for the next election – Asquith promised his support for the idea of an urban minimum wage in June 1914.[73] This meant that the Liberals' interest in social reform was far from flagging and was about to take a new and interesting turn. Pensions and national insurance legislation had shown what all New Liberals had argued – that Liberalism was not incompatible with social reform. But with his land proposals

Lloyd George had demonstrated the flexibility of traditional Liberal concepts and how they could be expanded and reinterpreted to accommodate major measures of social reform. The land issue was redefined to make it possible for the party to combine its assault on 'feudalism' with minimum wages and housing reform, and marked out a particularly Liberal solution to the problem of how to develop the party's social reform agenda. In effect, social reform seemed to be in the process of becoming more, not less, integrated within Liberalism as the government's programme developed.

Labour relations

However, Liberalism's increasing involvement with social reform was only one aspect of its relationship with the working class. Just as important was its involvement with the forces of organised labour. This was a longstanding saga, matched for complexity only by the party's dealings with Irish nationalism. Traditionally, trade unions had looked to the Liberals as the party most likely to produce legislation to benefit the working class – particularly the extension of the franchise, religious equality and free trade.[74] Most trade union activists and officials from the 1860s onwards had supported the Liberals, though there had always been some support for independent political action. From 1874 onwards there were a few working class trade unionists sitting as Liberal MPs, most importantly the miners' representatives.[75] Liberals also took care to appoint trade unionists as JPs and to absorb some of them into the civil service, particularly into the Board of Trade and the new national insurance machinery created in 1911.[76] This meant that trade unionism could function as one of the many interest groups within Liberalism. But this situation had been confused by the emergence of the separate Labour party in 1900 and the merger of most of the miners' MPs into this group in 1909.[77] After this date, most trade union officials operated within a non-Liberal party, but one which had an informal and partial electoral agreement with the Liberals under the terms of the MacDonald-Gladstone pact of 1903.[78] Moreover, Labour MPs sat on the same side of the Commons as the Liberals after 1910 and invariably supported the government in crucial votes.

Thus, by the Edwardian era organised labour was gradually becoming an external pressure group with links to Liberalism, rather than a section of the Liberal party. This in itself was something that Liberals regretted as a matter of ideology as well as practical politics.[79] It implied that trade unionism, and by extension the working class, had interests which were separate from those of society as a whole. This idea was profoundly antipathetic to Liberalism, which insisted on the basic identity of interests of the people, against the threat from powerful groups which sought to manipulate power for their own ends and to infringe the citizens' liberties. In this vision, it was the duty of trade unions to co-operate with their employers in raising the living standards of their members and with other 'progressive' forces in society in furthering the interests of all workers. Employers and workers were essentially engaged in a common enterprise to increase the nation's wealth and needed to work together. Separate political organisation was superfluous and divisive. Moreover, Liberals believed that their party and ideology represented the real interests of the working class and that trade unionism could not be allowed to monopolise the representation of the workers. Indeed, it was possible, if unions became too powerful, that they could act against the interests of the working class as a whole, or some of their own members, in the pursuit of their own narrow and particular aims.[80] This would make them little different to those forces like the Church and the House of Lords with which the Liberals had been doing battle for the previous hundred years.

However, Liberals were not antipathetic to trade unions as such. It was, after all, an essential liberty that workers should be able to organise themselves to bargain with their employers. After the Taff Vale judgement by the House of Lords in 1901 put trade unions in danger of expensive law suits if they called strikes, Liberals had to decide how far they were prepared to go in reversing this judicial decision through legislation.[81] Most Liberals thought something had to be done and at the 1906 election 59 per cent of Liberal candidates called for a reform of trade union law.[82] But what this reform should be presented something of a dilemma. Much legal opinion favoured the principle of the Taff Vale judgement on the grounds that it was only reasonable and consistent with developments in the law that unions should be able to be sued for actionable activities by their representatives during strikes. To allow unions to escape this risk altogether would be to put them in an anomalous and privileged position 'above the law'.[83] This argument appealed to a fundamental tenet of Liberalism that the rule of law should be applied equally to everyone without exception. A number of Liberal lawyers, especially Haldane and Asquith, started to draw up elaborate plans which would allow the principle of a union's liability to be preserved, while giving the unions much more freedom to organise strikes without fear of prosecution as long as they behaved lawfully.[84]

The result was the government's initial Trade Disputes Bill of 1906, which bore some resemblance to the recommendations of the royal commission appointed by the previous Tory government.[85] It proposed that only acts committed by a union's executive committee, or its regular agents acting on its instructions, should be liable. However, the attorney-general's speech when introducing the bill admitted of a certain amount of ambiguity and suggested that the final form of the bill was a matter for the Commons. This recognised the fact that many Liberal MPs were committed to a total repeal of the Taff Vale decision. They believed that without this certainty, unions would be unable to call strikes without the threat of bankruptcy. This represented an attack on the very existence of unions – and one inspired by the House of Lords which had overturned the accepted legal position for the previous thirty years. Two days after the government's bill was introduced Campbell-Bannerman indicated it would be ditched in favour of a total reversal of Taff Vale.[86] But he was only able to take such drastic action because this position was widely held to be an authentic Liberal response to the situation, rather than just a capitulation to the unions' position. As New Liberalism argued, the only free bargain between employers and workers was one based on equality and the Taff Vale judgement had given employers an unfair advantage because they knew unions would be unwilling to call strikes. Campbell-Bannerman insisted all he was doing by completely reversing Taff Vale was to 'place the two rival powers of capital and labour on an equality'.[87] However, this decision effectively meant that Liberals had accepted the unions' position and what they argued was even-handedness could be interpreted by employers as a victory for trade unions.

The government claimed that once Taff Vale was reversed it was up to unions and employers to settle industrial disputes. It was certainly not the task of Liberals to intervene to support one side or the other. All strikes were regrettable and represented a failure of normal relations between the two sides of industry. This remained the official position of Liberalism down to 1914 and distinguished the party from Labour's instinctive sympathy with the trade union position.[88] However, it was increasingly obvious in the Edwardian era that Liberalism could not just stand aside from industrial disputes, as some of these threatened to provoke national economic crises. The government's usual model was to make *ad hoc* use of Sir George Askwith, its chief industrial relations expert at the Board of Trade, and to try and encourage conciliation procedures.[89] Occasionally, when the situation was especially threatening, intervention was more direct, as in the 1912 miners' strike and

Lloyd George's famous meetings to settle the railway disputes in 1907 and 1911.

In all these conflicts the government presented itself as the 'honest broker', attempting an agreed settlement and acting in the interests of the nation as a whole. Liberals were happy with this approach, for it chimed well with their idea of themselves as the party of all the people, rising above sectional interests. However, it also allowed Liberals to reconcile pressures that pulled them in opposite directions. Some Liberals were prone to blame trade unions for initiating strikes and to accuse them of putting the welfare of the rest of the people at risk. This reaction was especially apparent in the 1912 miners' strike and railway disputes which threatened to deprive ordinary people of fuel and to throw millions out of work.[90] On the other hand, as the reversal of the Taff Vale judgement showed, many Liberals regarded unions as organisations that were genuinely struggling to improve the welfare of millions of their members and strikes as a regrettable, but occasionally necessary, weapon.

It was noticeable, though, that in practice Liberal industrial policy tilted matters in favour of the trade unions, though not to the extent which they wished. Lloyd George's actions in the railway strikes of 1907 and 1911 produced compromises, but ones which eventually forced the companies to concede the principle that they would meet trade union representatives – something they had always insisted was incompatible with the efficiency and safety of the railway network.[91] In 1912 the miners obtained the principle of a minimum wage from the Liberal government, when it was far from certain that they could have forced this from all the employers (especially those in Scotland and South Wales) in their strike.[92] Armed force was not used to break strikes, even though unions protested at its use in situations where local commanders perceived public order had broken down.[93] Indeed, even Winston Churchill, when he was Home Secretary in 1910–11, was not usually anxious to provoke confrontations with strikers, despite his taste for extravagant rhetoric.[94] Government-inspired prosecutions of strike leaders were very rare and produced huge embarrassment and eventual retreat, as in the 'Don't Shoot' case of 1912 and Larkin's imprisonment over the Dublin transport strike.[95] Liberals instinctively believed this sort of action was contrary to the party's commitment to liberties of speech and publication.

Above all, the cabinet refused to go down the path of compulsory arbitration of industrial disputes. As Sydney Buxton told the cabinet in April 1912 it would not be practicable to gaol millions of men for disobeying injunctions to delay a strike.[96] Liberals continued to believe that free and open discussions between both sides in industry was the only solution. To Liberals this meant they were merely producing a level playing field for unions and employers. But to many large employers this claim rang hollow.[97] They felt that their position had substantially deteriorated since the halcyon days of the early 1900s when the Taff Vale judgement had been in force. The cabinet seemed only too willing to twist their arms to secure a settlement, while refusing to back up the employers with the resources of the state. For most of the nineteenth century trade unions had been arguing for the creation of a neutral state in the field of industrial relations. By 1914 many employers felt that it was they who needed to make this case.

If, in retrospect, the Liberal party's relationship with social reform and industrial relations has seemed one of its most interesting and problematic features, this was not always apparent to contemporaries. Social reform was never the dominating issue of political debate, certainly when compared with free trade or home rule. Moreover, Liberals were not divided about social reform in the same way as they were about home rule or women's suffrage. To most of them it was clearly compatible with Liberalism and under Lloyd George's direction it was becoming more, not less, closely integrated with Liberal ideology. Labour relations were always much more of a minefield for the party and the idea of government neutrality was increasingly strained by the necessity to intervene in high-profile disputes. Liberalism had no answer to the problem of strikes and was threatened by any polarization of class opinion which industrial disputes could provoke. By 1914 the party was just hoping that these issues would quieten down.

8
Epilogue: A Liberal War?

Edwardian Liberals had been confused and divided about defence and foreign policy. But they had been united in thinking about the prospect of British participation in a European conflict with trepidation. Some regarded it as inevitable if the continental powers went to war, while others saw it as something to be avoided at all costs. But few, if any, welcomed it as the kind of spiritual purging, Darwinian struggle or good fun that appealed to elements in Tory thinking.[1] The Liberals were a long way from being a pacifist party, but they lacked Conservatism's close identification with the armed forces and the more visceral forms of patriotism that were displayed in policies like tariff reform.[2] Some of the party's traditions, like free trade, offered a peaceful solution to European disputes and many Liberals remained suspicious of foreign 'entanglements' and the threat that war posed to long-cherished Liberal values.[3] But despite all these doubts, Asquith was able to lead a relatively united party and cabinet into the First World War on 4 August 1914 and to ensure that the first nine months of the conflict were largely directed by Liberal politicians, until the last Liberal government succumbed to a coalition in May 1915. This coda to the Edwardian Liberal era produced immense strains within the party and some historians have been eager to discern signs of Liberalism's inability to cope with the stresses of a 'modern' war.[4] But the party showed remarkable tenacity and its ideology caused it far fewer difficulties than might have been expected in fighting a prolonged war that required an unprecedented mobilisation of the nation's resources.

The decision for war

The question of whether Britain would intervene on the side of France if war broke out with Germany was still tantalisingly unresolved in July 1914. Nobody in Britain would support an unprovoked French action against Germany, but it was widely held in diplomatic and military circles that Britain could not allow Germany to invade and defeat France. This would leave Germany dominant in Europe while Britain was friendless and alone after deserting its partner in the entente cordiale. Leading figures in the Conservative opposition like Arthur Balfour had moved to the position that the entente should be converted into a formal defensive alliance between Britain and France against any German attack.[5] But the Liberal cabinet had rejected this option, with only Churchill a decided advocate. Even Grey had been unwilling to make so momentous a step, because he held that Britain would retain more influence to prevent an outbreak of war if she remained free from any formal alliance.[6] But the intense cabinet disagreements of 1911–12 on defence strategy had made it plain that most of the leading figures in the cabinet, including Asquith, Grey, Haldane, Churchill and Lloyd George, all believed that Britain must make preparations to intervene on the side of France. Henry Wilson, the head of military planning, had been allowed to draw up a detailed schedule to assemble the BEF at Maubeuge on the French army's left flank, in order to help repel a German invasion. Whether the order for the army to move to France would be given was left an open question, for the cabinet to decide should war break out between France and Germany.

The assassination of the Archduke Franz Ferdinand in Sarajevo on 28 June 1914 did not initially seem likely to bring this hypothetical war any closer. It was only in late July 1914 that most Liberals became aware that a war between Austria and Serbia was probable and also likely to involve Germany and Russia. This seemed like a classic example of a continental struggle that did not involve Britain and the Liberal Press and Liberal MPs were united in calling for restraint from all sides but also for British non-intervention. When Lloyd George told C. P. Scott on 27 July that 'there could be no question of our taking part in any war *in the first instance*. [He] Knew of no Minister who would be in favour of it', he was accurately reporting the cabinet's views on a central European conflict.[7] It was only when Germany and Russia were on the very brink of going to war at the end of July that the focus of public and political interest started to shift to the possibility of a German invasion of Russia's ally, France.

It was clear from the beginning of the crisis that Grey believed that if Germany attacked France then Britain must stand by the entente, or abdicate its position as a world power. If the cabinet refused to support his interpretation he would have no option but to resign, as his entire policy since 1905 would have been repudiated.[8] But Grey had no wish to recklessly endanger the cabinet's unity after nine years of service together. He wished to bring his colleagues with him. So he did not bombard the cabinet with threats of resignation, though he refused to bind himself not to resign. Instead, he reported on his, entirely genuine, efforts to avert the looming conflict by, for instance, proposing an ambassadorial conference in London.[9] This helped convince many in the cabinet that Grey faced the prospect of war as unwillingly as they did and that he was driven by considerations of Britain's honour and interests, rather than acting as a warmonger.[10]

But Grey also knew he could still rely on the backing of the group of ministers who had supported the military conversations with France in 1911–12. Most crucially, Asquith would do almost anything to avoid Grey's resignation.[11] As far as the public and most Liberals were concerned the most likely leader of an anti-war faction was Lloyd George. But he, too, had not blanched at the prospect of war with Germany in 1911 and he had long ceased to hold anti-intervention views on foreign affairs. By remaining largely silent and inactive in the crucial week of 29 July–4 August 1914 he deprived the doubters of their most formidable potential leader.[12] The task of the pro-intervention ministers thus remained the same throughout the crisis. They had to limit the number of potential resignations from anti-war ministers to as small a number as possible to ensure the cabinet and the party could remain intact and in government.

Grey and his allies never suggested that intervention could be justified on specifically Liberal grounds, like the defence of treaties or the independence of small nations. When the possibility that Germany would invade Belgium was discussed on 29 July the whole cabinet accepted that their attitude would be decided by considerations of 'policy rather than of legal obligation'.[13] But the pro-interventionists also did not press the case that Britain was committed to help France because of the previous military discussions. They knew this was not something most of the cabinet could accept and indeed the discussions had only been able to continue on the understanding that they were not binding.[14] In fact, Asquith did not press matters at all, relying on delay and the movements of the German armed forces to achieve unity. Matters did not come to a head until the two crucial cabinets of Sunday,

2 August were faced with two contingencies where Grey argued that British intervention was necessary: if German warships entered the Channel; and if German troops invaded Belgium.[15] The key to both was that they could be represented as posing a direct threat to Britain, by allowing a potentially hostile power to command a future invasion route to the British Isles. In two tense meetings lasting from 11am to nearly 2pm and again from 6:30pm to 8pm, the cabinet was gradually brought to accept that these actions represented a sufficient threat to warrant intervention on the side of France, should either occur. As the German war plan necessitated the invasion of Belgium the cabinet had committed itself to the war that was declared on 4 August.

In the end only Burns and Morley resigned from the cabinet in protest at these decisions.[16] C. P. Trevelyan was the only minister outside the cabinet to leave his post, though the Quaker, T. E. Harvey, also resigned as an unpaid parliamentary private secretary. Both Burns and Morley were at the end of their careers and neither attempted to persuade any of their colleagues to follow them, or even to explain their views.[17] The rest of the cabinet fell in behind Asquith and Grey, with Simon and Beauchamp hastily retracting their proffered resignations on 4 August.[18] Effectively, the cabinet had accepted the force of the case that national security was endangered and this must override every other factor. If anybody could claim to have organised the anti-war point of view in the cabinet it was probably Harcourt and even he admitted there were 'overwhelming British interests which I could not abandon'.[19] In this sense, the cabinet were under no illusion that they were fighting a specifically Liberal war for Liberal aims. They were doing what any British cabinet would do in their situation.

However, by the time Grey explained the international situation to the Commons on 3 August, Liberals had already started to find reasons why the war should be regarded as compatible with Liberalism as well as with the country's national interests. This was crucial in ensuring that the party as well as the cabinet overwhelmingly backed the decision to go to war. In his speech Grey presented the coming war in terms of the country's security from the German threat, but he also dwelt at some length on the treaty of 1839 in which both Britain and Prussia had guaranteed Belgium's neutrality – even citing Gladstone's views on the matter from the Franco-Prussian war of 1870–1.[20] This proved the kernel of the idea that the war was necessary to uphold international law, an essential plank of the 'Gladstonian' Liberal view of foreign policy. This factor became increasingly vivid in Liberal minds with some rapidity. The Liberal backbencher, R. D. Holt, had opposed the war up until 2 August. But, a week later, he wrote 'when Germany decided on an unprovoked attack upon Belgium, whose neutrality Germany equally with ourselves had guaranteed, it seemed impossible for us to stand by. Germany has acted with great brutality and haste and is, in my judgement, the party mainly responsible for the war'.[21] By upholding international law, Liberals could also believe they were defending the rights of smaller nations, like Belgium, to their independence against the demands of greedy powers, like Germany. As Asquith said in the Commons on 6 August 1914, Britain was 'fighting to vindicate the principle that small nationalities are not to be crushed in defiance of international good faith by the arbitrary will of a strong and overmastering power'.[22]

The idea of the conflict as a war to uphold international law was soon joined by the concept of a war for democracy, in which the aim was to free Belgium and Europe from 'Prussian militarism'. There had been some Liberal criticism of Germany's constitution before 1914 and the importance it gave to the monarchy and the army.[23] But the Liberals' bugbear among European systems of government had always been Russia rather than Germany.[24] The idea that Germany was an especially brutal military dictatorship was essentially an outcome of the war. As early as 4 August both Simon and Masterman told the Liberal newspaperman, C. P. Scott, that the war had been provoked by the 'German military camarilla', who had seized control of policy.[25] Later, Liberals accepted that the German armed forces had perpetrated a series of atrocities, including the massacre of civilians in Belgium, the use of poison gas, unrestricted U-boat sinkings of civilian shipping and the execution of nurse Edith Cavell.[26] It was noticeable that the commission to investigate German actions in Belgium was headed by the eminent Liberal elder statesman, Lord Bryce, and failed to scotch even some of the wildest rumours.[27] Some Tories were happy to attribute German war crimes to the bestial, 'Hunnish' nature of the German people. But this explanation made most Liberals uneasy as it savoured of racial determinism. They preferred to blame Germany's unelected rulers and the absence of real democracy, which had led to the dominance of 'militarism'. By March 1915 Asquith was insisting that Britain's war aims should include the destruction of this system and the creation of a liberal state in Germany.[28]

Moreover, many Liberals hoped for the creation of some sort of post-war international system which would prevent any more European conflicts. As the backbencher, Alexander MacCallum Scott wrote in his diary on 3 August 1914, the war was a struggle between 'blood & iron alone or the policy of enforcing international obligations', so 'may we not use this calamity to set up an international court of arbitration in Europe'.[29] In a speech in Dublin Asquith called for the creation of 'a real European partnership based on the recognition of equal right, and established and enforced by a common will'.[30] This was rather vague, to say the least, and in early May 1915 the decision was taken to set up a 'League of Nations Society', with two Liberal backbenchers, Willoughby Dickinson and Aneurin Williams, as chairman and treasurer.[31] The society aimed to put flesh on the bones of Liberal aspirations by producing concrete proposals for the organisation of international relations and the prevention of war in the post-war world.

Thus, whatever the cabinet's motives were, one of the most important reasons it was possible for most Liberals to rally behind the government was that they could claim the war as a Liberal enterprise that matched 'Gladstonian' aspirations in foreign policy. But there was remarkably little substance to be found to this idea in the cabinet's thinking. Asquith was unwilling to formulate precise war aims as this might complicate relations with France and Russia. Most of the ideas he did have, like an insistence that Germany evacuate all occupied territory, indemnify its opponents and, possibly, surrender its navy, were centred on securing British interests after the war, rather than enunciating Liberal principles.[32] The cabinet certainly showed little interest in widening out the demand for the restoration of Belgium's independence into a general principle of self-determination for small nations. Instead, Britain's interests and those of its allies remained paramount. The cabinet had few qualms about agreeing to Italian claims in Dalmatia in order to secure Italy's adherence to the allies in May 1915, or about accepting Russia's demand for Constantinople and the Straits.[33] Although Asquith accepted that the Ottoman empire would not survive if it was defeated, the cabinet did not show much interest in the fate of its various national groupings.[34] Samuel and Lloyd George were sympathetic to Zionism, while Asquith was sceptical, as he was about the need to permanently occupy Mesopotamia.[35] Perhaps the most that can be said was that some Liberal ministers were less obsessed with the need to expand the empire in the near and middle east after the war than most Conservatives.

But as long as it proved possible to construe the war as a 'Gladstonian' conflict, even if only at the level of general principles, it was extremely difficult to rally Liberal opinion against the cabinet's decision to intervene. Only a small section of about 20 MPs remained sceptical after Grey's explanation of the situation to the House of Commons on 3 August.

On 6 August they formed a group, for mutual support more than anything.[36] Tellingly, they never gave themselves a precise aim, other than to 'watch' the government's conduct of the war. The proposal to issue a public statement on the causes of the war was dropped and the group became inactive after September 1914, disbanding early in the following year.[37] This dispiriting ending partly reflected the difficulty of protesting against the start of a war which had already begun and the pressure for party and national unity in wartime. But it also pointed to the problem of forming a coherent criticism of the war which could find any ideological purchase within Liberalism. The Cobdenite position to which Burns and Morley had clung in August 1914, that the war was not Britain's business, seemed incredible when Germany appeared determined to dominate Europe and threaten Britain by occupying Belgium. As Arnold Rowntree lamented, 'the action of Germany makes it much more difficult to keep even men of goodwill straight'.[38] Some MPs, like Arthur Ponsonby, remained pathologically suspicious of Grey's conduct of foreign policy, but this was an argument for reforming the post-war world, rather than a plan to end Britain's participation in the war.[39] Even those who were personally pacifists on religious grounds, like the Quakers T. E. Harvey and Arnold Rowntree, accepted the need to undertake a form of service, like ambulance or relief work, equivalent to the sacrifice being made by Britain's troops, rather than try to publicly criticise the war.[40] Those few Liberals who could not accept the decision of 4 August increasingly began to look to organisations outside of the party, like the Union of Democratic Control set up in September 1914, to express their views. By 1918 many of them had severed their connection with Liberalism, or been drummed out by their constituency associations if they were MPs, like C. P. Trevelyan and Arthur Ponsonby.[41] Supporting the Liberals' war rapidly became a definition of who was a Liberal.

Strategy and the economy

But this necessarily raised the question that if the war of 1914 was a Liberal war, could it be fought in a Liberal way? This involved questions of military strategy and of domestic policy that had not been closely considered before the outbreak of the conflict. However, there was an incipient division in the cabinet about military strategy. The key members of the pro-intervention group in July–August 1914, including Grey, Asquith, Churchill, Haldane and Lloyd George, had, by supporting the pre-war military discussions with France, all identified themselves with the idea of sending the BEF to support the French army.[42] The precise meaning of this action was never satisfactorily resolved.[43] As Britain had at most 6 divisions to send, while France could deploy 66 and Germany 84 against each other, it could be argued that the despatch of the BEF was merely a gesture of solidarity with France, which would make little difference to the outcome of the fighting. But Henry Wilson had convinced himself, and possibly some of the politicians, that they might tip the balance in the allies' favour. If the BEF went to France it certainly raised the prospect that the British war effort would focus on using its army to try and defeat Germany on the continent.

However, the arguments over defence strategy in 1911–12 had revealed another option was popular in the cabinet, especially with McKenna, Harcourt and Runciman.[44] They supported the naval leaders in arguing for a strategy based on a blockade of Germany. This would allow the British economy to function with minimum disruption and, hopefully, to grow stronger by capturing Germany's trade and colonies. This in turn would enable Britain to finance its continental allies through loans and enable them to turn their economies to war production and supporting their armies. This disagreement had seemingly been resolved in 1911 when Asquith had removed McKenna from the Admiralty, but he and his allies had never accepted this verdict as final. Both Runciman and McKenna had continued to oppose any planning for a war which seemed to contradict their views. In particular, they offered prolonged resistance to the idea that the government should fix prices or that the Treasury should underwrite marine insurance in wartime, as they feared this would disrupt the normal flow of trade.[45] They argued the government should trust in the entrepreneurial instincts of British businessmen and the royal navy to keep Britain supplied. David French, who has analysed these pre-war debates thoroughly, has dubbed this strategy an attempt to maintain 'business as usual'.

Herein lay the seeds of a major disagreement over how to conduct a war, which involved not just military strategy but the organisation of the economy. To a certain extent it reflected wider views about Liberalism. McKenna, Runciman and Harcourt all came from different strands of Liberalism – Runciman had been associated with Liberal Imperialism, Harcourt had been critical of the Boer war and McKenna had sided with neither position.[46] But none were enthusiastic social reformers and all were committed to the idea that Liberalism should allow the economy to operate as freely as possible.[47] Those who favoured a continental strategy were all ex-Liberal Imperialists, apart from Lloyd George, but they were much more committed to social reform and a positive role for the state.[48] McKenna and his allies regarded their viewpoint as more authentically Liberal, but by the Edwardian era it was no more than one interpretation of Liberalism, as well as referring to other traditions, especially constructions of how Britain had defeated France in the wars of 1793–1815.[49] It may also have been attractive to some Liberals because it seemed to offer a kind of compromise between the need to defend British interests and lingering Cobdenite dislike of continental entanglements.

Asquith had papered over these differences by his assurance to the cabinet of 1 August that the BEF would not be sent to France 'at this moment'.[50] In other words, the decision would not be taken until after war was declared. But once Britain was at war, the decision proved remarkably easy. On 5 August Asquith assembled a War Council of his allies Grey, Haldane and Churchill, together with a smattering of army and navy figures. Not surprisingly, they agreed the BEF must go to France and armed with this authority, Asquith persuaded the cabinet to endorse this decision the next day 'with much less demur than I expected.'[51] This appeared to be a decisive victory for the continentalists, but McKenna and Runciman were probably prepared to go along with this decision because they believed their strategy was effectively running in tandem with that of sending the BEF to France. At the same cabinet plans were enthusiastically discussed to seize Germany's colonies, drive her shipping from the seas and institute a blockade of the German coast. McKenna and his allies hoped this would prove to be the more effective strategy as the war progressed, as it offered the opportunity for Britain's economy to take advantage of the war and prove it would be most efficient to keep state planning to a minimum. As Pease put it on 28 August, 'we could win through by holding the sea, maintaining our credit, keeping our people employed and our industries going – by economic pressure, destroying Germany's trade, cutting off her supplies we could gradually secure victory'.[52]

But almost from the start of the war, there were signs that these hopes would be proved false. McKenna and those who thought like him had always been happy for the government to take overall control of the railway system on the outbreak of war. But the marine insurance scheme that Runciman had resisted so strongly was also introduced on 3 August in the face of desperate appeals from the shipping industry and Lloyd George intervened to shore up the financial system from collapse, introducing a moratorium on debts and a new paper currency.

The Bank of England was soon underwriting the majority of foreign trade to ensure it continued. Without any planning the government seemed to be drawn increasingly into managing the economy in order to ensure it functioned with a semblance of normality.[53]

Moreover, the hopes invested in 'business as usual' as a means of defeating Germany rapidly faded in the first months of the war. The loans that the allies asked for were far more than had been expected – the Russians requested £100 million in December 1914.[54] At the same time, Britain was gaining little from the war to finance such bills. While most of Germany's colonies were easily occupied (with the exception of Tanganyika), they were worth very little in economic terms. The drive to capture Germany's overseas trade was a conspicuous failure, with manufacturing exports being £7 million less in April 1915 than they had been a year earlier. The blockade showed no signs of bringing Germany to its knees. Germany could still import materials across its continental land borders and the naval blockade proved extremely difficult to enforce, especially in the face of American protests that could not be ignored, given the scale of Britain's reliance on American loans and imports. Runciman and McKenna continued to fight a rearguard action, ensuring, for instance, that all merchant shipping was not placed under state control in February 1915. But their strategy seemed increasingly unrealistic.

Moreover, the cabinet had received some astonishing news at its 6 August 1914 meeting which effectively doomed the 'business as usual' strategy in the long term. Asquith was in the curious situation at the beginning of the war of being both prime minister and Secretary of State for War, as he had taken over the latter post to steady the ship of state after J. E. Seely had been forced to resign over his role in the 'Curragh mutiny' in March 1914. It was impossible for one man to do both jobs in wartime and Asquith appointed the eminent general and proconsul Lord Kitchener to the war office on 5 August.[55] This stilled a press campaign in his favour, gave the public confidence that military affairs were in expert hands and made it much more difficult for the opposition to criticise decisions at the war office. But Kitchener was not a Liberal (or a Conservative) and he had no inclination to take on board the nuances of Liberal ideology when deciding his policies. Moreover, once he was appointed the cabinet had to go along with his strategy. In any disagreement between the general and the politicians the opposition and the public would be sure to support Kitchener.

The cabinet had, therefore, no option but to agree when Kitchener informed them on 6 August that he would be raising a vast new army, drawn from members of the public who chose to volunteer.[56] Nobody on the Liberal side had anticipated this development. It had been universally assumed that any war between the great powers would be short and therefore there would be no time or need to increase the size of the army once war was declared. But Kitchener informed his new colleagues the war would last two to three years and that the only way to defeat Germany was to raise a vast British army to fight on the continent. Some ministers clung to the belief that the war would be over before these men were ever called on to fight. But if it was not, 'business as usual' would be unsustainable.

Even before the new armies took the field, though, it was becoming increasingly clear that just recruiting these men was putting the economy under intolerable strain and invalidating much of the idea that the economy could continue without significant government intervention.[57] By December 1914 over one million men had enlisted and the economy was becoming seriously distorted as the munitions industry expanded and other sections of the economy ran down as they were starved of manpower and imported raw materials. Prices had risen 40 per cent by May 1915 as shortages appeared in some areas. The cabinet was increasingly drawn into managing and expanding the munitions and engineering industries in an attempt to maintain supplies even to the existing army at the front. In March 1915 the Treasury Agreements both limited wartime profits in these areas and suspended normal trade union activities.

Thus, by the time the government fell in May 1915 it was fairly clear that 'business as usual' could not survive as a major strand in government thinking. It was being driven back by its own manifest failings, the government's unplanned and chaotic interventions in the economy and Kitchener's recruitment drive. But this did not mean that the cabinet was abandoning its Liberalism, only one possible interpretation of Liberal attitudes to fighting the war. The key advocate of a more planned economy was Lloyd George. He presented his attitude to the cabinet, as in his memorandum of 22 February 1915, as the outcome of dire necessity and the need to win the war above all else, rather than as a particularly Liberal approach.[58] But Lloyd George's views were not incompatible with Liberalism. While Liberals had generally wished to maintain the operations of a free market before 1914, they had made significant exceptions to this policy in the field of social reform and direct taxation. Arguably it was only an extension of these developments to suggest increased government controls of production and trade in wartime, especially as a temporary expedient. After all, Lloyd

George's argument with McKenna was a matter of degrees, as the latter had willingly accepted far more intervention than he would have believed conceivable before August 1914. Moreover, while no Liberal had foreseen the need for the kind of army that Kitchener was raising, the party rapidly accepted that this was a matter for military judgement in wartime and threw itself into supporting the recruitment campaign.[59]

The only areas of this dispute where it can convincingly be argued that Liberal principles really were at stake were free trade and conscription and neither matter was brought to a crisis before May 1915. It was important for Liberals that in the technical sense, they could claim they had preserved free trade because the government had not introduced taxes on imports. This disguised the fact that inevitably the war had led to restrictions on trade, including government controls of capital exports and of dealings with the enemy.[60] Liberals could also congratulate themselves that Kitchener had not suggested his new army should be raised through conscription. As he told the cabinet in August 1914 this was simply not necessary as so many men had volunteered.[61] This relieved the cabinet from confronting a potentially explosive issue. Thus when Churchill raised the matter on 25 August, it could be brushed aside.[62] Lloyd George insisted the country would not hear of it and Asquith that Liberal MPs could not be brought to endorse such a measure. But it was not definitively ruled out for the future, nor does any minister seem to have opposed the measure as a matter of Liberal principle. Several important cabinet ministers, including Churchill and Lloyd George, had privately supported conscription before the war and by November 1914 Lloyd George had probably joined Churchill in being converted to its necessity in wartime.[63] By the time the government fell in May 1915 voices were also being raised in its favour on the Liberal backbenches.[64] Increasingly, it seemed conscription was the only way both to continue to raise men for the army and to prevent recruiting denuding crucial home industries of workers. Conscription would bring to a head Lloyd George's argument in the cabinet with the proponents of 'business as usual', as it was the antithesis of that strategy. But it would also combine such a conflict with a clash with those Liberal MPs who felt that conscription was incompatible with liberty of conscience and a free society. Fortunately for the last Liberal government this argument was postponed until after it fell, because it had the potential to divide the cabinet and the parliamentary party in a way that no conflict over the organisation of the economy could.

Preserving Liberalism

But the question of whether the cabinet could conduct a 'Liberal' war was far wider than that of the McKenna–Lloyd George argument. In some areas the cabinet seem to have had no qualms at all about infringing what were in peacetime essential Liberal principles. In 1914 a CID sub-committee had looked into the need for a Defence of the Realm Act, which allowed the army to requisition any property they required, order citizens to leave their homes, arrest spies, control the movement of aliens and censor the press. The Liberal law officers were only concerned that such powers might not be sweeping enough.[65] The government had already passed the Official Secrets Act of 1911, making the divulging of virtually any information held by the state a potential crime, and set up a secret register of German and Austrian aliens in Britain.[66] The cabinet view was that in wartime many civil liberties would have to be suspended temporarily in order to secure victory over German militarism. Defeat might ensure they would be lost for good.[67]

But the way in which these regulations were enforced suggested that Liberals retained a much less cavalier attitude towards civil liberties than their Tory opponents would have liked. While news from the front was rigorously censored, those opposed to the war continued to be free to voice their opinions in print, as in socialist newspapers like the *Labour Leader*.[68] Most controversially, the cabinet refused to take seriously agitated calls from the opposition benches to deal with the 'menace' of alien spies and saboteurs. This reflected the Liberals' long-established tolerance towards immigrants and the much lower levels of xenophobia in the party, compared to the Tories.[69] The Aliens Restriction Act of 5 August 1914 empowered the home office to order the arrest of all Germans and Austrians of military age, but at the end of September probably only a third had been interned, on the grounds that the rest were no threat and internment was a waste of scarce resources. The opposition rained criticism down on McKenna's head and called for all naturalised Germans to have their citizenship revoked and the repatriation of all aliens.[70] Asquith declared himself 'entirely unconvinced' there was a problem.[71] His own actions bore this out. At the outbreak of war he had helped the German fiancé of his children's governess return home, even though he was a reserve officer.[72] He even continued to socialise with the financier, Sir Edgar Speyer, after well-founded doubts about his loyalty to Britain became widespread.[73] This relative tolerance was politically unwise in wartime, but it was an essential component of Liberals' dislike of persecuting individuals and minorities.

Liberalism also reasserted itself in other controversial areas of nationality. The outbreak of the war raised the thorny issue of what to do about the Irish Home Rule bill and Welsh Church disestablishment bill, which were just about to become law under the 1911 Parliament Act, though the government intended the home rule bill to be accompanied by an amending bill excluding at least part of Ulster from home rule for some time. Partisan strife was supposed to be suspended for the duration of the war, but the Irish issue in particular was difficult to cast in such a way that both parties could accept the government's actions as fair and judicious. Asquith wished for a genuine compromise. But Nationalists and Unionists were still in no mood for agreement.[74] He then toyed with the suggestion that home rule should be enacted but a six county Ulster should be excluded for three years, after which each county could vote on inclusion or permanent exclusion.[75] In this he initially had the backing of Churchill and Lloyd George, who had argued for Ulster exclusion in 1912–14.[76] This might have been acceptable to Carson and the Tories, but Redmond would not hear of permanent exclusion. He insisted that home rule must be enacted immediately and the search for a solution of the Ulster question postponed. His speech of 3 August 1914, pledging support for the war, put him in a commanding position, as the government needed Irish nationalist acquiescence in the war, both to recruit Irish troops and to ensure no major garrison was needed in Ireland.[77] But Asquith's idea also ran into solid Liberal opposition. McKenna assured Asquith on 26 August that most Liberal MPs would back Redmond as 'they look upon Nationalist Ireland & its cause & claims as a second Belgium'.[78] In other words, even if the cabinet was reluctant to extend the principle of national self-determination beyond Belgium, most Liberals believed there was an analogy and a 'Liberal' war meant supporting Irish home rule. This Nationalist–Liberal coalition proved victorious and ensured the cabinet decided to enact home rule and suspend its operation rather than freeze the parliamentary situation on 4 August. This solution clearly favoured Redmond and the Tories walked out of the Commons on 15 September in a bitter protest at what they alleged was Asquith's chicanery. In a less controversial version of these events, the government was forced by its supporters in 1915 to withdraw a bill to suspend the procedure for implementing Welsh disestablishment until six months after the war's end.[79]

If anything, then, the war reinforced the Liberal party's determination to be the party of national distinctiveness within the United Kingdom, even when the Liberal leaders sought to make compromises with the opposition for the sake of wartime political unity. As in their attitude to enemy aliens, Liberals refused to accept a narrowly Anglo-centric definition of patriotism. This outlook was carried over into arrangements for fighting the war. Lloyd George eagerly re-emphasised the point with respect to Wales in his Queen's Hall speech of 19 September 1914, arguing that the defence of Belgium was equivalent to defending the rights of the 'little five-foot-two nations' like Wales.[80] He fought successful battles against Kitchener to secure the 38th Division of the new army as a distinctively Welsh formation, the appointment of nonconformist chaplains and the use of Welsh by the troops.[81] The promotion of Irish nationalist causes was less successful, though the 16th Division was eventually designated as an Irish Division and Redmond was consulted by army commanders in Ireland, if not very effectually. The Nationalists, though, wanted much more, including a Home Defence Force for Ireland made up of Redmond's Volunteers, and were bitter at what they perceived to be the privileged treatment that the Ulster Volunteer Force received from the war office.[82] However, these episodes made it clear that Liberals did not feel that partisan issues had been buried by the war. Rather, they hoped the war would favour many of the causes they cherished, especially if it could be argued that they furthered victory.

An obvious example of this feeling was temperance. Prohibitionists were encouraged by wartime regulations that allowed chief constables to limit opening hours and close public houses if requested to do so by military authorities.[83] They hastened to assert that drink was a major obstacle to Britain's success in the war, listing instances where alcohol had led to dire military consequences. This theme was taken up and expanded by Lloyd George in a speech at Bangor on 28 February 1915, when he touched on the loss of production caused by drinking among munitions workers.[84] This was undoubtedly part of his drive to drastically raise supplies of armaments to the troops, which was to lead to the Treasury Agreements of March 1915. But it was also an analysis that was distinctively partisan. The government was not being inundated by calls from munitions firms to restrict drinking and investigations of production levels had not hitherto stressed this factor. Lloyd George had to generate this support in the weeks following his speech in order to back up his analysis.[85] Rather, the chancellor's analysis reflected preconceived notions common in Liberalism about the harmful nature of excessive drinking to national life and the importance of government action to tackle the issue. Most Tories simply did not share this analysis.[86]

However, before 1914 Liberals had concentrated on reducing the number of public houses (as suggested in the 1908 Licensing Bill) and on increased taxation (as in the 1909 budget) as a way to reduce intemperance. Lloyd George, though, initially focused on a huge scheme for state purchase of the entire drink interest, including all pubs, breweries and distilleries.[87] This matched his plans to increase state control elsewhere in the economy, but perhaps more crucially, it offered some chance of an agreed settlement of the issue. Without the support of the Unionist opposition and the drink trade it would be impossible to carry legislation on a subject like temperance which had roused such fierce partisan passions before 1914. State purchase might suit Lloyd George's needs as the brewers, the most powerful component of the drink trade, indicated they might be prepared to accept a proposal that was sufficiently generous. The Unionist leadership were dubious but not uniformly hostile, with Bonar Law hoping the proposals would free his party of 'the Trade incubus'.[88]

Lloyd George suspected his real problem would lie within the Liberal party and he was right. Asquith was sceptical of the whole idea, claiming it would 'wd. ruin our finances & create a vast engine of possible corruption'.[89] But the real problem for Lloyd George was that he was attempting to overturn the existing consensus in the Liberal party on temperance. Increased taxation of alcohol and licences and reduction of the number of pubs were policies that had entrenched friends in the cabinet (including the prime minister). Attempting to supersede them with a policy of purchase only opened up old arguments about other great temperance schemes, including forms of prohibition, and showed why the party had been happy to settle for more modest proposals.[90] After a lengthy cabinet meeting on 19 April, Lloyd George was forced to produce a simpler scheme for higher taxation of beers and spirits and special measures, including possibly state purchase, in areas producing munitions.[91] This accorded much more closely with agreed Liberal views on temperance. Not surprisingly, the Unionists, the Irish Nationalists and 'the Trade' refused to accept the new taxes and only the proposals on munitions areas were enacted in May 1915.[92] This was a modest outcome of Lloyd George's plans, but it was probably still more than a Unionist government would have been prepared to countenance and showed the limits of inter-party consensus on topics of pre-war controversy. Temperance was one area where, as with Irish home rule, Liberals would not give up their ideology and insisted on its application in wartime.

The end

The Liberal government was certainly not without its critics by May 1915. Some in the Unionist leadership, like Walter Long, regarded Liberal ministers with contempt and did not hesitate to express their opinions in private correspondence.[93] The opposition Press and many backbenchers were restive at the failure to bring what was expected to be a short war to a victorious conclusion.[94] These feelings manifested themselves in an obsessive hunt for aliens and spies, sniping against ministers like Haldane and McKenna who were regarded as insufficiently super-patriotic, and a generalised demand for a more 'thorough' conduct of the war.[95] But the Unionists were trapped by parliamentary arithmetic. As long as the Liberals retained the support of Labour and the Irish Nationalists they had a clear parliamentary majority – one that was enhanced by the absence of so many Unionist MPs in the army. Moreover, if they went into open opposition to the government they risked the charge of unpatriotic behaviour. The only way the government could be replaced in the short term seemed to be through internal collapse. Conservatives had hoped for this eventuality since 1905, but it had stubbornly refused to happen. The cabinet had survived the crisis of August 1914 and though there were plenty of arguments in the cabinet in May 1915 it was not apparent to political observers that any of these was more insoluble than some of the problems that the government had surmounted in the past.

The cabinet's fall was therefore both sudden and unpredicted.[96] On 14 May 1915 *The Times* reported that British troops in France were being severely hampered by shell shortages. The following day Lord Fisher, the First Sea Lord, resigned after a series of disagreements with Churchill over the Dardanelles expedition. On 17 May Bonar Law called on Lloyd George to confirm the latter event.[97] In their conversation, the idea of a coalition arose and Asquith seized on the suggestion. That afternoon he asked Bonar Law to come to 10 Downing Street and in a fifteen-minute discussion the demise of the last Liberal government was agreed. Most Liberals were stunned by these events and saw no need to dissolve the cabinet that had run Britain for nearly ten years and let their old foe back into government. Asquith had to use all his powers of persuasion to swing the MPs behind him in an emotional speech to a party meeting on 19 May.[98]

The suddenness of these events, the small number of actors and the paucity of records have left an air of mystery over these proceedings and produced a variety of explanations. But one possible approach has been to suggest that the crisis of May 1915 was essentially a crisis of Liberal ideology.[99] Liberals had proved unable to adapt their beliefs to the demands of twentieth-century warfare and in particular to produce the national mobilisation and organisation required for victory. The coalition was an attempt to solve this problem by enabling Liberal ideology to be bypassed. This is a compelling explanation and has proved influential, particularly because it provides a larger backdrop to the dramatic events of May 1915. But it does not easily fit the events. The 'business as usual' strategy favoured by McKenna and Runciman was already on the wane by the time of the cabinet crisis. The most significant argument over the economy in the spring of 1915 was that between Kitchener and Lloyd George over how to organise munitions production and Lloyd George may well have been motivated to support a coalition as a way of removing Kitchener from the war office.[100] When Asquith saw Bonar Law on the afternoon of 17 May, 'He and Lloyd George both stated that it was absolutely necessary to get rid of Kitchener.'[101] But this was a disagreement about how to expand the war economy, not about whether this was needed.

Bonar Law and the Tory leadership undoubtedly favoured industrial and military conscription to organise manpower, but they did not press this as a matter of immediate concern in May 1915. Indeed, Bonar Law's only demands were about personnel, not policy.[102] He seems to have been largely concerned to avoid a breakdown of the party truce and an avalanche of Unionist backbench criticism of the government, which would have also destabilised his own leadership.[103] Asquith's motives have remained the most impenetrable. He may have already been considering the desirability of a coalition – he certainly claimed this was the case.[104] But most probably he reacted to the immediate political crisis caused by the shells scandal and Fisher's resignation. He believed a Commons debate on the issues would 'have had the most disastrous effect on the general political and strategic situation:'[105] In other words not only would the world see that the British political truce had collapsed, but the Liberal government would have suffered a major loss of prestige and probably faced the opening of a sustained campaign of criticism. As military victory was nowhere in sight Asquith may well have calculated that a slide in the cabinet's authority and the Liberal party's popularity was unavoidable. A coalition would defuse the shells and Fisher resignation issues and force the Tories to share responsibility (and unpopularity) for the problems facing the government. In these circumstances, Asquith needed to make a deal as soon as possible, while he still retained maximum credibility as a war leader, and certainly before any uncomfortable Commons debate. Hence his snap decision when faced with Bonar Law and Lloyd George's proposal and the lack of preparation of Liberal party opinion.

In the long run, a coalition was a highly probable outcome the longer the war continued. But its creation in May 1915 was the result of fine calculations of party and personal advantage, rather than any deep-seated issue. The government was not dissolved because it was tortured by Liberal principles, but because of an unforeseen political crisis. This may stand as an indication of the relationship between Liberalism and the war. The Liberal party had proved capable of uniting around the decision to declare war in August 1914 and of conducting the first nine months of the struggle. The cabinet was plagued by disagreements about the extension of state control, but this was a debate in all parties and Tories were certainly not immune from scruples over issues like raising taxes on the drink trade or, later in the war, controlling agriculture.[106] In these senses it is difficult to argue that the war was fatal to Liberalism or that the party could not adapt to fighting a modern, total war.

However, while this was true, war was in some ways uncomfortable for the party. The only member of the cabinet who felt any elation on 4 August 1914 was probably Churchill.[107] Everyone else emphasised the difficulty of the decision with which they were faced and the heavy responsibilities that lay ahead. The simple and aggressive assertion of patriotism and the supremacy of national interests that came so naturally to Toryism was absent. Instead, Lloyd George described to his friend Riddell the gloomy scene as he, Asquith, Grey and McKenna waited for the expiry of the British ultimatum to Germany. 'As eleven struck we felt it was the stroke of doom. . . . The terrible sense of responsibility; the necessity of taking a step the consequences of which it was impossible to foretell; a step which might wreck the world and might wreck civilization.'[108] Liberals could support the war, but many of them needed to convince themselves it served a higher purpose, hence their emphasis on the causes of international law, democracy, the rights of small nations and future international organisations to prevent warfare. For Conservatives matters were much simpler and they found it easy to berate the government for insufficient patriotism and vigour in prosecuting the war. Together with the simple failure to deliver victory this probably meant that the government's popularity had ebbed considerably by May 1915 and in any wartime election it would have suffered defeat. If Liberals were more demoralised in May 1915 than in July 1914 this was probably the reason.

But the party had not split and it did not do so, even when free trade was formally abrogated in September 1915 and conscription introduced in January 1916. The bonds of party proved strong enough, if only just, to stand the slaughtering of even the most sacred Liberal cows. What finished the Liberal party was Lloyd George's challenge to Asquith in December 1916. Given the strength of the leader's position as long as he retained the confidence of the Liberal cabinet members, it was no surprise that Asquith was not displaced as party leader. But the existence of a coalition government allowed Lloyd George to use support from the Tory and Labour parties to become prime minister and set up an alternative Liberal power base. This meant the party had suffered what it had studiously avoided in 1905–15 – a split at the highest leadership level. This led directly to disaster at the 1918 general election, when the Asquith faction were reduced to about 28 MPs, while Lloyd George's 133 followers owed their strength to an alliance with the old Tory enemy. War was fatal to Liberalism because it allowed a situation to develop where such a split could take place, rather than because Liberalism could not adapt to the twentieth century.

Notes

Introduction

1. P. Clarke, *Lancashire and the New Liberalism* (Cambridge: Cambridge University Press, 1971); P. Clarke, *Liberals and Social Democrats* (Cambridge: Cambridge University Press, 1978); S. Collini, *Liberalism and Sociology: L. T. Hobhouse and Political Argument in England, 1880–1914* (Cambridge: Cambridge University Press, 1979); M. Freeden, *The New Liberalism: An Ideology of Social Reform* (Oxford: Clarendon Press, 1978).
2. E. H. H. Green, *The Crisis of Conservatism: the Politics, Economics and Ideology of the British Conservative Party, 1880–1914* (London: Routledge, 1995); M. Fforde, *Conservatism and Collectivism, 1886–1914* (Edinburgh: Edinburgh University Press, 1990); D. Tanner, 'Ideological Debate in Edwardian Labour Politics: Radicalism, Revisionism and Socialism' in E. Biagini and A. J. Reid eds, *Currents of Radicalism: Popular Radicalism, Organised Labour and Party Politics in Britain, 1850–1914* (Cambridge: Cambridge University Press, 1991) pp. 271–93; F. Trentmann, 'The Strange Death of Free Trade: the Erosion of "Liberal Consensus" in Great Britain, c. 1903–32' in E. Biagini ed., *Citizenship and Community: Liberals, Radicals and Collective Identities in the British Isles, 1865–1931* (Cambridge: Cambridge University Press, 1996) pp. 219–50.
3. E. H. H. Green, *Ideologies of Conservatism: Conservative Political Ideas in the Twentieth Century* (Oxford: Oxford University Press, 2002) p. 3.
4. J. Parry, *The Rise and Fall of Liberal Government in Victorian Britain* (New Haven, Ct.: Yale University Press, 1993); E. Biagini, *Liberty, Retrenchment and Reform: Popular Liberalism in the Age of Gladstone, 1860–80* (Cambridge: Cambridge University Press, 1992).
5. A view best expressed in R. McKibbin, *The Evolution of the Labour Party, 1910–24* (Oxford: Clarendon Press, 1974).
6. P. Rowland, *The Last Liberal Governments*, 2 vols (London: Barrie & Jenkins, Barrie & Cresset, 1968–71).
7. H. C. G. Matthew, *The Liberal Imperialists: the Ideas and Politics of a Post-Gladstonian Elite* (Oxford: Oxford University Press, 1973).
8. N. Blewett, *The Peers, the Parties and the People: the British General Elections of 1910* (London: Macmillan, 1972) p. 344.

1   Government and Party

1. M. Diamond, 'Political Heroes of the Victorian Music Hall', *History Today*, 40 (January 1990) 33–9.
2. See J. Wilson, *CB: a Life of Sir Henry Campbell-Bannerman* (London: Purnell Book Services, 1973) pp. 279–96; P. Stansky, *Ambitions and Strategies: the Struggle for the Leadership of the Liberal Party in the 1890s* (Oxford: Clarendon Press, 1964) pp. 275–94.

 3. Stansky, *Ambitions and Strategies*, pp. 57–96.
 4. P. Gordon ed., *The Red Earl: the Papers of the Fifth Earl Spencer, 1835–1910*, 2 vols (Northampton: Northamptonshire Record Society, 1981–6) vol. 2, pp. 47–60.
 5. Wilson, *CB*, pp. 438, 446–8; G. H. Cassar, *Asquith as War Leader* (London: Hambledon Press, 1994) pp. 38–46.
 6. Consulting people who had not held office before could be seen as virtually a promise of a place in a future Liberal government and was thus avoided if possible, British Library, Add MS 45988, fos 132–3, Herbert Gladstone papers, Campbell-Bannerman to Herbert Gladstone, 5 December 1904.
 7. C. Hazlehurst and C. Woodland eds, *A Liberal Chronicle: Journals and Papers of J. A. Pease, 1st Lord Gainford, 1908–10* (London: Historians Press, 1994) pp. 122–5, Pease diary, 23 June to 12 July 1909 for the complex factors behind a minor ministerial reshuffle in the summer of 1909.
 8. G. Searle, *Corruption in British Politics, 1895–1930* (Oxford: Clarendon Press, 1987) pp. 103–5. Exceptions were made for honorary directorships, charities and private companies.
 9. Classifying the social background of MPs is a fraught process. For the best examination of Liberal MPs in this period, see G. Searle, 'The Edwardian Liberal Party and Business', *English Historical Review*, 98 (1983) 28–60.
10. See Searle, 'Edwardian Liberal Party', 37–9.
11. Hazlehurst and Woodland eds, *Liberal Chronicle*, pp. 94–5, Pease diary, 8 December 1908.
12. M. and E. Brock eds, *H. H. Asquith: Letters to Venetia Stanley* (Oxford: Oxford University Press, 1985) pp. 451–2, Asquith to V. Stanley, 26 February 1915.
13. R. Jenkins, *Asquith* (London: Collins, 1964) pp. 269–71 on the Asquith-Montagu friendship.
14. S. McKenna, *Reginald McKenna, 1863–1943: a Memoir* (London: Eyre & Spottiswoode, 1948) pp. 23, 43–4, 100–115.
15. E. David ed., *Inside Asquith's Cabinet: from the Diaries of Charles Hobhouse* (London: John Murray, 1977) pp. 158–60, Hobhouse diary, 27–9 January 1914.
16. Wilson, *CB*, pp. 451–6.
17. B. Gilbert, 'David Lloyd George and the Great Marconi Scandal', *Historical Research*, 62 (1989) 295–317.
18. Ripon and Wolverhampton were 80 and Carrington 68 when they left office. Tweedmouth was declared by Asquith to be a 'raving lunatic', Hazlehurst and Woodland eds, *Liberal Chronicle*, p. 25, Pease diary, 25 May 1908. Isaacs was a central figure in the Marconi scandal of 1912–13 and Seely as Secretary of State for War severely mishandled the Curragh 'mutiny' of March 1914.
19. C. Hazlehurst, 'Asquith as Prime Minister, 1908–16', *English Historical Review*, 85 (1970) 516–17.
20. M. Ostrogorski, *Democracy and the Organisation of Political Parties*, 2 vols (London: Macmillan, 1902) vol. 1, pp. 607–8; S. Low, *The Governance of England*, 2nd edn (London: Fisher Unwin, 1914) pp. 155–63.
21. Poor estimates of both men's energies in public office were common. Augustine Birrell claimed of Campbell-Bannerman, 'I have more than once seen him asleep during meetings of the Cabinet', A. Birrell, *Things Past Redress* (London: Faber and Faber, 1937) pp. 245–6; Lord Balcarres reported persistent rumours of Asquith's laziness and 'over-indulgence', including

a demand for whisky and soda before breakfast, J. Vincent ed., *The Crawford Papers: the Journals and Letters of David Lindsay, twenty-seventh Earl of Crawford and tenth Earl of Balcarres, 1871–1940* (Manchester: Manchester University Press, 1984) p. 149, Balcarres to Lady Wantage, 25 March 1910.

22. See Chapters 7, 2, 4.
23. See Chapters 6, 2.
24. Hazlehurst, 'Asquith as Prime Minister', 510.
25. See Chapter 2.
26. Lloyd George was a witness at Churchill's wedding. Churchill was one of the very few people to call Lloyd George 'David', R. Churchill, *Winston S. Churchill* (London: Heinemann, 1967) vol. 2, pp. 273–4, 306. Grey and Haldane had been friends since the 1880s. During the crisis of July-August 1914 Grey was staying at 28 Queen Anne's Gate, Haldane's London house, R. Haldane, *Autobiography* (London: Hodder & Stoughton, 1929) pp. 270–5.
27. G. Riddell, *More Pages from my Diary, 1908–14* (London: Country Life Ltd, 1934) p. 171, Riddell diary, 19 July 1913; House of Lords Record Office, Lloyd George papers C/4/17/3, 'Notes of interview with Haldane', 23 July 1913; National Archives, Cabinet papers 37/116/56, 'Land', 21 August 1913.
28. David ed., *Inside Asquith's Cabinet*, pp. 146–8, Hobhouse diary, 17 October 1913.
29. See Chapters 2, 4.
30. Grey backed Lloyd George strongly during the Marconi affair, K. Robbins, *Sir Edward Grey: a Biography of Lord Grey of Fallodon* (London: Cassell, 1971) p. 279. In return, Lloyd George called Grey, 'a kind fellow, the only man I would serve under except Asquith.', Riddell, *More Pages*, p. 171, Riddell diary, 19 July 1913.
31. See Chapters 2, 6, 7.
32. See Haldane, *Autobiography*, pp. 216–18 for a scathing analysis of the cabinet as 'a meeting of delegates' in which 'The Prime Minister knew too little of the details of what had to be got through to be able to apportion the time required for discussion'.
33. Hazlehurst, 'Asquith as Prime Minister', 508–10.
34. P. Jalland, *The Liberals and Ireland: the Ulster Question in British Politics to 1914* (Hassocks: Harvester Press, 1980) pp. 37–49.
35. In 1880 41% of the House of Lords were Liberals; by 1887 the figure was 7%, A. Adonis, *Making Aristocracy Work: the Peerage and the Political System in Britain, 1884–1914* (Oxford: Clarendon Press, 1993) p. 20, table 2.2.
36. A. Hawkins and J. Powell eds, *The Journal of John Wodehouse, First Earl of Kimberley for 1862–1902* (Cambridge: Cambridge University Press/Royal Historical Society, 1997) p. 462, Kimberley diary, 18 August 1898. Kimberley regarded his position as the leader of such a small group as 'almost ridiculous'.
37. It was widely rumoured that the Earl of Granard owed his position as a whip in the Lords to Campbell-Bannerman's amused response to a joke telegram the young peer received from his fellow-officers in the Scots Guards, pretending to offer him a post in the government, Wilson, *CB*, pp. 463–4. The Duke of Manchester, Captain of the Yeomen of the Guard, 1905–7 was a rakish figure who confessed 'sport has appealed to me more strongly than brain work', quoted in D. Cannadine, *The Decline and Fall of the British Aristocracy* (New Haven, Ct: Yale University Press, 1990) p. 403.

38. Adonis, *Making Aristocracy Work*, pp. 20–1; Searle, *Corruption*, pp. 145–56.
39. Cannadine, *Decline and Fall*, pp. 213, 393 for the financial problems of the Acton and Granville families.
40. Lincolnshire Archives, Misc. Dep. 96/1, Lincoln Liberal Association minutes, 8 November 1910 for the request to the Earl of Liverpool to become President of the Lincoln Liberals. The second Lord Airedale followed in his father's footsteps as President of both the Yorkshire Liberal Federation and the Leeds Liberal Federation, West Yorkshire Archive Service, Yorkshire Liberal Federation minutes, 11 July 1912, Leeds Liberal Federation minutes, 6 June 1913.
41. Hampshire Record Office, Portsmouth papers 15M84/5/9/3/10, W. Crook to Earl of Portsmouth, 15 December 1905, describing the Earl as 'the leader of Hampshire Liberalism', despite his recent conversion from Liberal Unionism. Correspondence in this archive certainly suggests he was the most generous donor to party funds in the area.
42. Searle, 'Liberal Party and Business', 32–4; G. Bernstein, *Liberalism and Liberal Politics in Edwardian England* (London: Allen & Unwin, 1986) pp. 13–17.
43. G. I. T. Machin, *Politics and the Churches in Great Britain, 1869 to 1921* (Oxford: Clarendon Press, 1987) pp. 278, 303.
44. J. Ramsden, *The Age of Balfour and Baldwin, 1902–40* (London: Longman, 1978) pp. 97–9.
45. M. Rush, *The Role of the Member of Parliament since 1868: from Gentlemen to Players* (Oxford: Oxford University Press, 2001) pp. 155–6 shows that government backbenchers participated in a mean number of 7.5 debates in the 1913 session and asked 14.3 questions.
46. J. Ridley, 'The Unionist Opposition and the House of Lords, 1906–10', *Parliamentary History*, 11 (1992) 252. 107 Bills were passed in 1902–5, but 158 in 1906–9.
47. W. P. Jolly, *Lord Leverhulme: a Biography* (London: Constable, 1976) pp. 68–70.
48. D. Young, *Member for Mexico: a Biography of Weetman Pearson, first Viscount Cowdray* (London, Cassell, 1966) pp. 244–6 relates one extreme case of how Pearson was unable to continue combining his oil interests in Mexico with being Liberal MP for Colchester.
49. R. E. Wilson, *Two Hundred Precious Metal Years: a History of the Sheffield Smelting Co. Ltd, 1760–1960* (London: Ernest Benn, 1960) pp. 170–1for H. J. Wilson, Liberal MP for Holmfirth 1885–1912, and his role in the family firm. Wilson took no active part in the business while he was an MP, but he refused to allow the firm to expand, fearing this would endanger his capital.
50. Gloucestershire Record Office, W. H. Dickinson papers D6 F175/12, Dickinson diary, 20 December 1907–12 January 1908.
51. I. Packer, 'The Liberal Cave and the 1914 Budget', *English Historical Review*, 111 (1996) 620–35.
52. National Library of Wales, E. W. Davies papers A/7, Davies diary, 31 December 1911, 31 December 1913 for one backbencher's rueful reflections.
53. Hazlehurst and Woodland eds, *Liberal Chronicle*, p. 20, Pease diary, 14 April 1908 for the chief whip's view of Masterman's appointment, 'a most unpractical politician, he was an idealist who let loose below the gangway could do & had done mischief, but I was glad his tongue was tied & that he might see the difficulties of putting into practice his theories at the Local Govmt Board.' I. Packer ed., *The Letters of Arnold Stephenson Rowntree to Mary*

Katherine Rowntree, 1910–18 (Cambridge: Cambridge University Press/Royal Historical Society, 2002), p. 60, A. S. to M. K. Rowntree, 7 August 1911 for the impact of Griffith's speech.

54. W. H. Dickinson never recovered his confidence after his speech moving the address in 1906, recording 'It was a hideous failure. I did not get the mind of the House at all', W. H. Dickinson papers D6 F175/12, Dickinson diary, 19 February 1906.

55. Even his opponents had to give Elibank grudging praise for his work as chief whip in 1910–12, see Vincent ed., *Crawford Papers*, p. 168, Balcarres diary, 17 November 1910.

56. Hazlehurst, 'Asquith as Prime Minister', 521–2.

57. H. Berrington, 'Partisanship and Dissidence in the Nineteenth-Century House of Commons', *Parliamentary Affairs*, 21 (1968) 338–74.

58. *Hansard*, 5th series, 1914, lxiv, 1820.

59. See H. V. Emy, *Liberals, Radicals and Social Politics, 1892–1914* (Cambridge: Cambridge University Press, 1973) pp. 184–8, 253–62, 270–2, 279–80.

60. See Chapter 2.

61. See Chapter 7.

62. See Chapter 3.

63. Emy, *Liberals, Radicals and Social Politics*, pp. 184–8, 279–80.

64. R. A. Jones, *Arthur Ponsonby: the Politics of Life* (Bromley: Christopher Helm, 1989) pp. 67–89.

65. G. Hosking and A. King, 'Radicals and Whigs in the British Liberal Party, 1906–14' in W. Aydelotte ed., *The History of Parliamentary Behaviour* (Princeton, NJ: Princeton University Press, 1977) pp. 136–58; I. Packer, *Lloyd George, Liberalism and the Land: the Land Issue and Party Politics in England, 1906–1914* (Woodbridge: Boydell & Brewer/Royal Historical Society, 2001) pp. 40–1, 44.

66. See voting statistics for Liberal MPs in Jalland, *Liberals and Ireland*, pp. 269–72.

67. A. Sykes, *Tariff Reform in British Politics, 1903–13* (Oxford: Clarendon Press, 1979) pp. 185–91.

68. Packer, 'Liberal Cave and the 1914 Budget'.

69. See Ramsden, *Age of Balfour and Baldwin*, pp. 98–9 on Tory MPs as 'a single integrated elite still drawing heavily on the most exclusive sources'.

70. M. H. Port, ' "The Best Club in the World"? The House of Commons, c. 1860–1915', *Parliamentary History*, 21 (2002) 166–99.

71. Emy, *Liberals, Radicals and Social Politics*, pp. 96–7.

72. Bodleian Library, Oxford, Asquith papers 11, fos 139–40, G. Whiteley to Asquith, 29 May 1908.

73. Searle, *Corruption*, pp. 149–51.

74. M. Pinto-Duschinsky, *British Political Finance, 1830–1980* (Washington, DC: American Enterprise Institute for Public Policy Research, 1981) p. 47.

75. National Liberal Federation, *Annual Report*, 1910, (London: Liberal Publication Department, 1911) p. 17, *Annual Report*, 1911, (London: Liberal Publication Department, 1912) p. 21.

76. Blewett, *Peers, the Parties and the People*, p. 332.

77. See B. Murray, *The People's Budget 1909/10: Lloyd George and Liberal Politics* (Oxford: Clarendon Press, 1980) pp. 188–90, 202–4; Packer, *Lloyd George, Liberalism and the Land*, p. 124.

78. J. W. Hancock, 'The Anatomy of the British Liberal Party, 1908–18: a Study of its Character and Disintegration' (University of Cambridge PhD, 1992) is the best study of the 1908 reorganisation.

79. Sir T. Barclay, *Thirty Years: Anglo-French Reminiscences, 1876–1906* (London: Constable, 1914) p. 318.

80. T. Lloyd, 'The Whip as Paymaster: Herbert Gladstone and Party Organization', *English Historical Review*, 89 (1974) 789–90.

81. *Brixton Free Press*, 20 February, 3, 10, 17 July 1914 on the situation in Lambeth, Brixton, which was usually a safe Tory seat.

82. University of Manchester, John Rylands Library, C. P. Scott papers, Sir F. Channing to C. P. Scott, 28 February 1909 [10?].

83. Though there is little evidence the whips deliberately tried to promote particular opinions within Liberalism, Lloyd, 'Whip as Paymaster'; 793–5.

84. D. A. Hamer, *Liberal Politics in the Age of Gladstone and Rosebery: a Study in Leadership and Policy* (Oxford: Clarendon Press, 1972) pp. 34–56.

85. S. Koss, *Sir John Brunner: Radical Plutocrat, 1842–1919* (Cambridge: Cambridge University Press, 1970) pp. 238–69.

86. Blewett, *Peers, the Parties and the People*, pp. 277–9.

87. Glasgow University Library, MacCallum Scott papers 1465/2, Scott diary, 16 March 1911.

88. Cabinet papers 37/97/10, 'Taxation of Land Values', 23 January 1909; Murray, *People's Budget*, pp. 151–4.

89. *The Times*, 12 January 1910; *Daily News*, 29 May 1914.

90. National Library of Scotland, Acc. 9491/1, Kinross Liberal Association, minutes, 26 November 1910.

91. Lincoln Liberal Association, minutes, 17 June 1910, 6 January, 21 October 1911, 17 September 1912, 1 October 1913, 27 January 1914.

92. K. Morgan, 'Cardiganshire Politics: the Liberal Ascendancy, 1885–1923', *Ceredigion*, 5 (1967) 311–45.

93. Cheshire and Chester Archives, CR159/3, Chester Liberal party minutes, 28 May 1906, 3 June 1908.

94. Lincoln Liberal Association, minutes, 19 October 1910. The local 'Four Hundred' and executive contained representatives of the Liberal Club, the WLA and the National League of Young Liberals.

95. National Library of Scotland, Acc. 9080/3, South Edinburgh Liberal Association, executive committee minutes, 22 September 1908.

96. Hancock, 'Anatomy of the British Liberal Party', 200.

97. *The Liberal Agent*, 16 (October 1913) 112–20 suggested 253 of 435 English Liberal associations were employing fully accredited and trained agents in 1912.

98. Leeds Liberal Federation, minutes, 15 October 1912, recording 690 Liberal gains to the register in North Leeds, while the Tories added 670 voters.

99. Blewett, *Peers, the Parties and the People*, p. 290, Table 14.1

100. In Lincoln, Charles Roberts, the MP, contributed over half of the Liberal Association's income, see Lincolnshire Archives, Hill/20, Lincoln Liberal Association subscription book 1910–35.

101. D. Tanner, *Political Change and the Labour Party, 1900–1918* (Cambridge: Cambridge), pp. 182, 257, 290.

102. Compare: National Library of Scotland, Acc. 11765/37, Dumbartonshire Liberal Association, minutes, 1899–1918, which are entirely devoid of political

discussion; with South Edinburgh Liberal Association, minutes, 22 September 1908, 9 February, 12 October 1909, 30 September 1910.

103. Chester Liberal party minutes, 21 May 1909, authorising a group of four members and the retiring MP to consult the chief whip on a candidate.

104. Leeds Liberal Federation, minutes of 'cabinet committee', 28 July 1913.

105. P. Lynch, *The Liberal Party in Rural England, 1885–1910: Radicalism and Community* (Oxford: Clarendon Press, 2003) pp. 63–72.

106. R. Gregory, *The Miners and British Politics, 1906–14* (Oxford: Oxford University Press, 1968) pp. 79–81, 165–7.

107. Packer ed. *Rowntree Letters*, pp. 12–14.

108. It is not even clear that NLF delegates represented the views of their local party. In Lincoln, the executive committee selected four delegates but any party member could attend the NLF conference if they wished to, Lincoln Liberal Association, minutes, 13 October 1910.

109. The nearest to such a thing was the well-publicised trickle of defections from the party over the People's Budget in 1909–10, see Blewett, *Peers, the Parties and the People*, p. 215.

110. See West Sussex County Record Office, Additional deposit 1191, Cobden papers, National Reform Union, minutes, 6 February 1914.

111. B. Porter, *Critics of Empire: British Radical Attitudes to Colonialism in Africa, 1895–1914* (London: Macmillan, 1968) pp. 50–5.

112. *Liberal Year Book, 1914*, (London: Liberal Publication Department, 1915) p. 20.

113. *Land Values*, January 1914 and *The Times*, 20 December 1913 for threats to put up candidates in Liberal seats in Scotland if the taxation of land values did not form a prominent part of the Land Campaign in Scotland.

114. Blewett, *Peers, the Parties and the People*, p. 310.

115. A. J. Lee, *The Origins of the Popular Press, 1855–1914* (London: Croom Helm, 1976) p. 166.

116. S. Koss, *Fleet Street Radical: A. G. Gardiner and the* Daily News (London: Allen Lane, 1973) pp. 129–34; H. A. Taylor, *Robert Donald* (London: Stanley Paul & Co., 1934) pp. 23–5, 77–84.

117. Lee, *Popular Press*, p. 287. The general manager of the *News of the World* was Lloyd George's confidante, Sir George Riddell.

118. Packer ed., *Rowntree Letters*, pp. 9–12.

119. The circulation of the *Daily News* increased from under 56,000 in 1899 to 320,000 in 1910, Koss, *Fleet Street Radical*, p. 36; Blewett, *Peers, the Parties and the People*, p. 301.

120. Blewett, *Peers, the Parties and the People*, pp. 303–4; National Library of Scotland, Elibank papers 8803, fos 25–8, R. Donald to Elibank, 12 March 1912 asking for more guidance from the cabinet on the *Daily Chronicle's* editorial policy.

2 Foreign, Defence and Colonial Policy

1. Wilson, *CB*, pp. 434–58 for this episode. Other candidates whose names were suggested to Campbell-Bannerman included Sir Edmund Monson (a career diplomat), Lord Crewe, Lord Edmond Fitzmaurice and Lord Burghclere.

2. *The Times*, 8 December 1905 focused its attempt to destroy the new ministry's credibility on reports that Grey would not take office.

3. Brock and Brock eds, *Asquith Letters*, p. 140, Asquith to V. Stanley, 1 August 1914. Even a critic of Grey like Lord Loreburn agreed with Asquith's assessment, 'the resignation of Grey would mean the break-up of the Cabinet', T. Wilson ed., *The Political Diaries of C. P. Scott, 1911–28* (London: Collins, 1970) p. 56, Scott diary, 1 December 1911.

4. Asquith described even Grey's speech to the Commons of 3 August 1914, which convinced many listeners of the need to declare war, as 'almost conversational in tone & with some of his usual ragged ends', Brock and Brock eds, *Asquith Letters*, p. 148, Asquith to V. Stanley, 3 August 1914.

5. See Robbins, *Grey*, pp. 55, 72, 102–4.

6. In the 1870s the Grey family owned under 3,000 acres in Northumberland, yielding about £4,000 p.a., J. Bateman, *The Great Landowners of Great Britain and Ireland* (Leicester: Leicester University Press, 1971) p. 195.

7. Cannadine, *Decline and Fall*, pp. 280–95.

8. Robbins, *Grey*, pp. 33, 72–3, 101–2.

9. A. G. Gardiner, *Prophets, Priests and Kings*, 2nd edn(London: J. M. Dent, 1914) p. 74.

10. See Chapters 3–4; *The Times*, 18 December 1911 for a robustly pro-suffrage speech by Grey to the Women's Liberal Federation; Nuffield College, Oxford, Gainford papers 39, Pease diary, 16 March 1912 for Grey's decisive cabinet intervention in favour of the principle of a legislative minimum wage to settle the miners' strike.

11. Grey uncritically accepted the Unionist government's case for war against the Boer Republics in 1899, see speeches in *The Times*, 26 October 1899, 6 November 1899, 21 March 1900.

12. A. Ponsonby, 'Some Members of the Liberal Government, Jan 1913', quoted in Jones, *Arthur Ponsonby*, p. 80; see *Hansard*, 5th series, 1912, xl, 2029–36 for Bonar Law's endorsement of Grey and his foreign policy at the height of party controversy over Irish home rule.

13. Grey intended the speech to establish that Liberal and Conservative attitudes to the entente with France were identical, British Library, Add MS 46389, J. A. Spender papers, Grey to Spender, 19 October 1905.

14. The doctrine of continuity was given a physical form by the fact that Grey's under-secretary at the Foreign Office, Lord Edmond Fitzmaurice, was the younger brother of Lord Lansdowne. Ironically, he disliked the ententes with France and Russia, Z. Steiner, *The Foreign Office and Foreign Policy, 1898–1914* (Cambridge: Cambridge University Press, 1969) p. 108.

15. G. Martel, *Imperial Diplomacy: Rosebery and the Failure of Foreign Policy* (London: Mansell, 1986) pp. 252–62.

16. Matthew, *Liberal Imperialists*, pp. 195–223.

17. P. Readman, 'The Conservative Party, Patriotism, and British Politics: the Case of the General Election of 1900', *Journal of British Studies*, 40 (2001) 141–5.

18. University of Birmingham Library, L. Add. 140, William Allard papers, Grey to W. Allard, 25 May 1904

19. *Manchester Guardian*, 24 July 1911.

20. Ibid, 11 April 1910.

21. See H. Weinroth, 'Norman Angell and The Great Illusion: an Episode in Pre-1914 Pacifism', *Historical Journal*, 17 (1974) 551–74; J. B. D. Miller, *Norman*

Angell and the Futility of War (Basingstoke: Macmillan, 1986). In 1913–14 Liberal MPs were regulars at meetings organised by the Garton Foundation to promote Angell's ideas, see Packer ed., *Rowntree Letters*, pp. 126–8, A. S. to M. K. Rowntree, 19–20 September 1913.

22. Matthew, *Liberal Imperialists*, pp. 198–200 for the friction this episode caused within the Liberal leadership.
23. *Nation*, 25 May 1909 for the significance of this concept.
24. *Manchester Guardian*, 24 July 1906.
25. Readman, 'Conservative Party', 142–3.
26. There is a plethora of accounts of this process, see for instance G. Monger, *The End of Isolation: British Foreign Policy, 1900–1907* (London: Nelson, 1963) pp. 104–46.
27. This commitment predated his period as Foreign Secretary, *Hansard*, 4th series, 1904, cxxxv, 516–24.
28. Add MS 46389, Spender papers, Grey to Spender, 19 October 1905.
29. B. Williams, 'Great Britain and Russia, 1905 to the 1907 Convention' in F. H. Hinsley ed. *British Foreign Policy under Sir Edward Grey* (Cambridge: Cambridge University Press, 1977) pp. 133–47.
30. *Nation*, 20 January 1912 for a comprehensive criticism of Grey on these lines. The phrase 'entangling alliances' was a motif of this point of view.
31. *Manchester Guardian*, 12 June 1907.
32. Russian intervention in Persia undoubtedly caused the greatest anger among Grey's critics, see D. McLean, 'English Radicals, Russia, and the fate of Persia 1907–13', *English Historical Review*, 93 (1978) 338–52.
33. D. Lloyd George, *War Memoirs*, 2nd edn, 2 vols (London: Odhams, 1938) vol. 1, pp. 27–31.
34. Gainford papers 39, Pease diary, 22, 30 October, 1, 6, 9, 11 November 1912.
35. Robbins, *Grey*, p. 233.
36. The workings of this grouping is analysed in K. M. Wilson, 'The Making and Putative Implementation of a British Foreign Policy of Gesture, December 1905 to August 1914: the Anglo-French Entente Revisited', *Canadian Journal of History*, 31 (1996) 228–55.
37. See particularly J. L Hammond in *The Speaker*, 13, 27 January, 21 April 1906.
38. *Nation*, 17, 24 October 1908; *Manchester Guardian*, 6–16 October 1908.
39. The Liberal Press was heavily lobbied to support the Cabinet's line, Wilson ed. *Scott Diaries*, pp. 46–51, Scott diary, 22, 25 July 1911.
40. Jones, *Arthur Ponsonby*, pp. 67–89.
41. See Grey's speech to the Commons, *Hansard*, 5th series, 1911, xxxii, 57–8.
42. E. B. Baker and P. J. Noel-Baker, *J. Allen Baker* (London: Swarthmore Press, 1927) pp. 173–9.
43. *Hansard*, 5th series, 1911, xxii, 1977–92 and the response of Arnold Rowntree, Packer ed. *Rowntree Letters*, p. 49, A. S. to M. K. Rowntree, 14 March 1911.
44. *Hansard*, 5th series, 1913, lvi, 2281–96.
45. Gainford papers 39, Pease diary, 8 March 1911; M. Kent, 'Constantinople and Asiatic Turkey, 1905–14' in Hinsley ed. *British Foreign Policy*, pp. 148–64; R. T. B. Langhorne, 'Anglo-German Negotiations concerning the Future of the Portuguese Colonies 1911–14, *Historical Journal*, 16 (1973) 361–87.

46. See the exchange of letters between Ponsonby and Pease in Hazlehurst and Woodland eds, *Liberal Chronicle*, pp. 34–6. 12 Liberal MPs voted against the government over Edward VII's visit.

47. *Hansard*, 4th series, 1908, cxc, 234–46. *Manchester Guardian*, 2 September 1907 for a positive view of the entente on these lines.

48. *Nation*, 23 January 1909.

49. C. Cline, *E. D. Morel, 1873–1924: the Strategies of Protest* (Belfast: Blackstaff Press, 1980) pp. 54–97. J. B. Osborne, 'Wilfred G. Thesiger, Sir Edward Grey and the British Campaign to Reform the Congo, 1905–9', *Journal of Imperial and Commonwealth History*, 27 (1999) 59–80 argues Grey did take a marginally stronger line on the Congo than Lansdowne.

50. R. K. Newman, 'India and the Anglo-Chinese Opium Agreements, 1907–14', *Modern Asian Studies*, 23 (1989) 525–60. This was a policy that the Conservatives did not oppose and they had initiated discussions with China while in office, but Grey pushed the matter forward when delay would have been possible.

51. B. Bond, *The Victorian Army and the Staff College, 1854–1918* (London: Eyre Methuen, 1972) pp. 220–3. Initially, Campbell-Bannerman had been suspicious the new CID would reduce the influence of elected politicians on defence policy, *Hansard*, 4th series, 1903, cxviii, 714.

52. Bodleian Library, Oxford, MS Eng. Hist. c.750, fos 241–2, Sandars papers, Baddeley to Sandars, 14 December 1905.

53. M. V. Brett and Vt Esher eds, *Journals and Letters of Reginald, Viscount Esher*, 4 vols (London: Ivor Nicholson & Watson, 1938) vol. 3, p. 246, Esher to Haldane, 1 June 1915; National Library of Scotland, Haldane papers 5973, fo. 33, Haldane to mother, 1 February 1905; Haldane, *Autobiography*, pp. 164–5.

54. This strategy is examined in R. Williams, *Defending the Empire: the Conservative Party and British Defence Policy, 1899–1915* (New Haven, Ct: Yale University Press, 1991).

55. Matthew, *Liberal Imperialists*, pp. 215–23.

56. Cobden Club, *The Burden of Armaments: a Plea for Retrenchment* (London: Fisher Unwin, 1905) makes these points and refers back extensively to the nineteenth-century context.

57. *Hansard*, 5th series, 1909, ii, 969–70 for Arnold Lupton on the dangers to 'our hard-earned liberties' from rising military expenditure.

58. D. Butler and A. Sloman eds, *British Political Facts, 1900–79* (London: Macmillan, 1980) p. 356.

59. Russell, *Liberal Landslide*, p. 65.

60. Haldane papers 5907, Haldane to Asquith, 28 December 1905. The army estimates were still only just over £28 million in 1913. Haldane's reforms have been widely described: see particularly E. M. Spiers, *Haldane: an Army Reformer* (Edinburgh: Edinburgh University Press, 1980).

61. This is made plain in Williams, *Defending the Empire*, pp. 106–19.

62. *Nation*, 13 April 1907 on 'the dangerous spirit lurking in these proposals'. Also *Hansard*, 4th series, 1907, clxxii, 1663–5 for Randal Cremer on 'the growth of militarism' in schools.

63. *The Times*, 20 January 1909.

64. These events have been often retold, see Monger, *End of Isolation*, pp. 236–56, but much remains unclear, especially the extent of British-French military discussions when the Liberal government took office.

65. British Library, Add MS 41218, Campbell-Bannerman papers, Grey to Campbell-Bannerman, 10 January 1906; Haldane, *Autobiography*, p. 190.
66. Wilson, *CB*, p. 530, suggests, probably correctly, that in 1906 only Campbell-Bannerman, Grey, Haldane, Asquith, Ripon and Fitzmaurice knew of the Anglo-French discussions.
67. Still best treated in S. R. Williamson, *The Politics of Grand Strategy: Britain and France Prepare for War, 1904–14* (Cambridge, Mass: Harvard University Press, 1969) pp. 167–204.
68. Brett and Esher eds, *Journals and Letters*, vol. 3, p. 74, Esher diary, 24 November 1911 on the 'packed Defence Committee'.
69. Gainford papers 39, Pease diary, 15 November 1911; David ed., *Inside Asquith's Cabinet*, pp. 107–8, Hobhouse diary, 16 November 1911.
70. Haldane papers 6011, Haldane to sister, 16 November 1911.
71. MS Eng. Hist. c.764, fos 56–9, Sandars papers, Balfour to Sandars, 21 September 1911.
72. Elibank papers 8814, A. C. Murray diary, 22 July, 27 November 1911.
73. Wilson ed., *Scott Diaries*, p. 56, Scott diary, 1 December 1911.
74. National Archives, F.O. 800/99, Grey papers, Loreburn to Grey, 26 August 1911.
75. Sir A. Fitzroy, *Memoirs*, 2 vols (London: Hutchinson & Co., 1925) vol. 2, p. 496, Fitzroy diary, 11 November 1911.
76. Wilson ed., *Scott Diaries*, p. 60, Scott diary, 7 January 1912 on McKenna's 'personal feeling' on the naval issue after his removal from the Admiralty. For a detailed exposition of the navy's case, Churchill College Library, Cambridge, McKenna papers 4/2, 'Memorandum of Asquith-McKenna conversation', 20 October 1911. His views were shared by Runciman and Harcourt, University of Newcastle Library, Runciman papers 63, Runciman to Harcourt, 24 August, 4 September 1911.
77. National Library of Scotland, Acc. 10047, Rosebery papers, Morley to Rosebery, 3 December 1908 on the futility of Britain's small army confronting a German invasion of the Low Countries; Add MS 46390, fos 176–80, Spender to Haldane, n.d., on fears that the ententes would lead to conscription.
78. David ed., *Inside Asquith's Cabinet*, p. 134, Hobhouse diary, 10 April 1913. Grey was conspicuously absent from the list of supporters of conscription. K. M. Wilson has argued he expected Russia to defeat Germany and so avoid the need for a huge British army, Wilson, 'Making and Putative Implementation', 250–5.
79. Churchill ed., *Churchill*, vol. 2, companion, part 3, p. 1500, Churchill to Lord Roberts, 23 January 1912.
80. Murray, *People's Budget*, p. 150.
81. See Chapters 6–7.
82. *Hansard*, 5th series, 1913, li, 1566 for Arnold Rowntree's opinion that conscription was 'a menace to English liberty'.
83. R. J. Q. Adams and P. Poirier, *The Conscription Controversy in Great Britain, 1900–18* (London: Macmillan, 1987) pp. 1–48.
84. This was something some Liberals recognised. As the backbencher, J. H. Whitehouse, pointed out, an enlarged army could be used for 'adventurous designs', *Hansard*, 5th series, 1913, li, 1533.
85. Williams, *Defending the Empire*, especially pp. 57–8, 147, 150.
86. Ibid., pp. 220–4.

87. A. Chamberlain, *Down the Years* (London: Cassell, 1935), p. 97 for Unionist attitudes.
88. These points are well-made in P. P. O'Brien, 'The Titan Refreshed: Imperial Overstretch and the British Navy before the First World War', *Past and Present*, 172 (2001) 146–69.
89. Williams, *Defending the Empire*, pp. 84–99.
90. G. H. S. Jordan, 'Pensions not Dreadnoughts: the Radicals and Naval Retrenchment' in A. J. A. Morris ed., *Edwardian Radicalism, 1900–1914* (London: Routledge & Kegan Paul, 1974) pp. 162–79.
91. *Hansard*, 4th series, 1908, clxxxv, 1336–8.
92. L. Masterman, *C. F. G. Masterman: a Biography* (London: Frank Cass, 1968) p. 123.
93. See A. J. A. Morris, *Radicalism against War, 1906–1905* (London: Longman, 1972) pp. 122–68.
94. Asquith papers 21, fos 76–7, Grey to Asquith 5 February 1909.
95. Bodleian Library, Oxford, MS Eng. c.6690, Margot Asquith papers, H. H. to Margot Asquith, 21 February 1909.
96. As Chancellor of the Exchequer in 1905–8 Asquith had done all he could to hold down naval expenditure, see Add MS 41210, Campbell-Bannerman papers, Asquith to Campbell-Bannerman, 30 December 1906.
97. The reductionist memorandum of 1907 is printed in Koss, *Brunner*, pp. 290–2; *Nation*, 22 February 1908.
98. See Morris, *Radicalism against War*, p. 142.
99. *The Times*, 22 January 1909.
100. For Richard Holt, MP for Hexham, as a representative of this school of thought, see D. J, Dutton ed., *Odyssey of an Edwardian Liberal: the Political Diary of Richard Durning Holt* (Gloucester: Alan Sutton, 1989), p. 31, Holt diary, 19 July 1914.
101. Churchill ed. *Churchill*, vol. 2, companion part 2, p. 938, Lloyd George to Churchill, 3 January 1909. Ibid, pp. 939–42 for Churchill's 11-point cabinet paper refuting the Admiralty's case.
102. C. Trebilcock, 'Radicalism and the Armaments Trust' in Morris ed., *Edwardian Radicalism*, pp. 180–202.
103. MS Eng. c.6690, Margot Asquith papers, H. H. to Margot Asquith, 25 February 1909 on the 'sudden curve' in the cabinet argument of which Asquith took advantage.
104. *Hansard*, 5th series, 1909, ii, 930–44.
105. Williams, *Defending the Empire*, pp. 156–79.
106. *Daily News*, 23 March 1909 for the need for Liberals to rally against the 'plague' of Tory demands for more dreadnoughts.
107. *Hansard*, 5th series, 1909, ii, 955–63.
108. H. Weinroth, 'Left-Wing Opposition to Naval Armaments in Britain before 1914', *Journal of Contemporary History*, 6 (1971) 111 for examples of Liberal MPs who changed their minds on this issue in March 1909.
109. *Nation*, 2 March 1907.
110. *Hansard*, 5th series, 1909, viii, 855–9.
111. Williams, *Defending the Empire*, pp. 160, 204–14.
112. Morris, *Radicalism against War*, p. 165, 330, 345.

113. Haldane, *Autobiography*, pp. 238–46; Morris, *Radicalism against War*, p. 332.
114. Murray, *People's Budget*, pp. 172–208.
115. Blewett, *Peers, the Parties and the People*, pp. 318, 326.
116. Bodleian Library, Oxford, MS Eng. hist. c.659, Ponsonby papers, Molteno and Harvey to Ponsonby, 19 December 1913.
117. Matthew, *Liberal Imperialists*, pp. 37–79.
118. Readman, 'Conservative Party' argues strongly that Liberal doubts about the Boer war were an electoral handicap and that this interpretation was widely accepted in the party.
119. Clarke, *Liberals and Social Democrats*, p. 69 for the solidarity under siege at the pro-Boer *Manchester Guardian*.
120. R. J. Hind, *Henry Labouchere and the Empire, 1880–1905* (London: Athlone Press, 1972).
121. J. A. Hobson, *Imperialism: a Study* (London: J. Nisbet, 1902).
122. Matthew, *Liberal Imperialists*, pp. 86–94.
123. Porter, *Critics of Empire*, pp. 291–7 for the development of a more imperial-minded attitude within Liberalism.
124. *Hansard*, 5th series, 1910, xvi, 1895–1902. Earlier, Campbell-Bannerman had claimed there was insufficient interest in the idea for it to be endorsed, ibid, 4th series, 1907, clxxiii, 288.
125. R. Hyam, 'The Colonial Office mind, 1900–14', *Journal of Imperial and Commonwealth History*, 8 (1979) 30–55.
126. This was especially true during the Boer war, when Asquith called for the nation to 'stand together with an unbroken front', *The Times*, 13 October 1899.
127. Wilson, *CB*, pp. 495–6, 502–4 for some of the political controversies around these measures.
128. R. Hyam, *Elgin and Churchill at the Colonial Office, 1905–8* (London: Macmillan, 1968) is still the best survey of these developments.
129. *Hansard*, 4th series, 1906, clv, 848.
130. *The Scotsman*, 6 April 1904.
131. British Library, Add MS 49698, fos 181–5, Balfour papers, 'Proposed Draft of a Circular Despatch to the Governors of the self-governing colonies', December 1904.
132. J. E. Kendle, *The Colonial and Imperial Conferences, 1887–1911* (London: Longmans, 1967) pp. 99–102.
133. D. C. Gordon, *The Dominion Partnership in Imperial Defence, 1870–1914* (Baltimore: Johns Hopkins Press, 1965) pp. 165–8, 182–3, 197–8.
134. Asquith's Reading speech, *The Times*, 11 June 1896.
135. There are a number of books on this issue: see S. A. Wolpert, *Morley and India, 1906–1910* (Berkeley, Calif.: University of California Press, 1967); S. E. Koss, *John Morley at the India Office, 1905–10* (New Haven, Ct: Yale University Press, 1969); M. N. Das, *India under Morley and Minto* (London: George Allen & Unwin, 1964); S. R. Wasti, *Lord Minto and the Indian Nationalist Movement, 1905–1910* (Oxford: Oxford University Press, 1964).
136. R. J. Moore, 'The Twilight of the Whigs and the Reform of the Indian Councils, 1886–1892', *Historical Journal*, 10 (1967) 400–14.
137. See Das, *India under Morley*, pp. 147–62.

138. Lord Morley, *Recollections*, 2 vols (London: Macmillan, 1917) vol. 2, pp. 180, 219, Morley to Minto, 27 July 1906, 7 June 1907; E. W. Davies papers A/6, Davies diary, 6 June 1907.

139. Morley, *Recollections*, vol. 2, p. 172, Morley to Minto, 6 June 1906. This did not mean that Liberals felt British institutions were inappropriate for all non-Europeans. There was considerable hope in 1911–12 that China would develop constitutional government, Elibank papers 8814, A. C. Murray diary, 9 November 1911.

140. Mary, Countess of Minto, *India, Minto and Morley, 1905–1910* (London: Macmillan, 1934) pp. 28–30, 110–11, Minto to Morley, 28 May 1906, 27 February 1907.

141. Morley, *Recollections*, vol. 2, pp. 297–8, Morley to Minto, 25 February 1909.

142. Ibid, vol. 2, p. 278, Morley to Minto, 7 October 1908 on one deportation as 'a monstrous outrage on common-sense.'

143. A. P. Kaminsky, *The India Office, 1880–1910* (London: Mansell, 1986) pp. 161–5. 75% of questions on India were asked by just 11 MPs, revealing the peripheral nature of the issue for most Liberals.

144. Morley, *Recollections*, vol. 2, p. 173, Morley to Minto, 6 June 1906.

145. A. L. al-Sayyid-Marsot, 'The British Occupation of Egypt from 1882' in A. Porter ed., *The Oxford History of the British Empire*, 5 vols (Oxford: Oxford University Press, 1999) vol. 3, pp. 651–64.

146. Porter, *Critics of Empire*, pp. 239–90.

147. Ibid, pp. 279–86.

148. Hyam, *Elgin and Churchill*, pp. 237–62.

3   Liberals and the United Kingdom

1. See Parry, *Liberal Government*, pp. 186–91 for a succinct overview of Liberals and foreign policy in the mid-nineteenth-century.

2. *Hansard*, 4th series, 1908, cxc, 231 for George Harwood on the Liberal tradition of support for nationalism in Greece and Italy; L. T. Hobhouse, *Democracy and Reaction* (London: Fisher Unwin, 1904) pp. 163–4; D. Cannadine, *G. M. Trevelyan: a Life in History* (London: Fontana, 1993) pp. 63–73.

3. R. Shannon, *Gladstone and the Bulgarian Agitation 1876*, 2nd edn (Brighton: Harvester, 1975).

4. R. Robinson and J. Gallagher, *Africa and the Victorians: the Official Mind of Imperialism* (London: Macmillan, 1961) pp. 76–121; A. G. Hopkins, 'The Victorians and Africa: a Reconsideration of the Occupation of Egypt, 1882', *Journal of African History*, 27 (1986) 363–91.

5. For varying interpretations of these events, see A. B. Cooke and J. Vincent, *The Governing Passion: Cabinet Government and Party Politics in Britain, 1885–86* (Brighton: Harvester, 1974); W. C. Lubenow, *Parliamentary Politics and the Home Rule Crisis: the British House of Commons in 1886* (Oxford: Clarendon Press, 1988); T. A. Jenkins, *Gladstone, Whiggery and the Liberal Party, 1874–86* (Oxford: Clarendon Press, 1988).

6. Jenkins, *Gladstone, Whiggery and the Liberal Party*, pp. 230–93.

7. Lady Brassey, 'Mr Gladstone in Norway', *Contemporary Review*, 48 (1885) 494; Gladstone to Hartington, 8 September 1885, quoted in J. L. Hammond,

Gladstone and the Irish Nation (London: Longmans, 1938) pp. 404–5. Gladstone also made some play with colonial analogies, especially Canada, *Hansard*, 3rd series, 1886, ccciv, 1081.

8. D. W. Bebbington, *The Nonconformist Conscience: Chapel and Politics, 1870–1914* (London: George Allen & Unwin, 1982) pp. 84–105; C. Dewey, 'Celtic Agrarian Legislation and the Celtic Revival: Historicist Implications of Gladstone's Irish and Scottish Land Acts, 1870–1886', *Past and Present*, 64 (1974) 30–70.

9. Robbins, *Grey*, p. 26 for the importance of this factor in Sir Edward Grey's decision to reluctantly accept home rule.

10. See Hartington's speech in the Commons to this effect, *Hansard*, 3rd series, 1886, ccciv, 1238–63, especially 1252–6.

11. *Christian World*, 13 May 1886.

12. Add MS 46018, fo. 104, Herbert Gladstone papers, Reid to Herbert Gladstone, 7 January 1886.

13. The Liberal Unionist W. E. H. Lecky in *The Times*, 5 May 1886.

14. Jenkins, *Gladstone, Whiggery and the Liberal Party*, pp. 286–93; W. C. Lubenow, 'Irish Home Rule and the Great Separation in the Liberal Party in 1886: the Dimensions of Parliamentary Liberalism', *Victorian Studies*, 26 (1982–3) 161–80.

15. A. E. Pease, *Elections and Recollections* (London: John Murray, 1932) p. 137.

16. R. R. James, *Rosebery* (London: Phoenix, 1995) pp. 337–40.

17. P. Readman, 'The 1895 General Election and Political Change in Late Victorian Britain', *Historical Journal*, 42 (1999), 467–93.

18. See Add MS 41215, fos 162–4, Herbert Gladstone papers, Gladstone's memorandum, 8 December 1899.

19. D. W. Gutzke, 'Rosebery and Ireland, 1898–1903: a Reappraisal', *Bulletin of the Institute of Historical Research*, 53 (1980) 88–98; P. D. Jacobson, 'Rosebery and Liberal Imperialism, 1899–1903', *Journal of British Studies*, 13 (1973) 83–107.

20. Matthew, *Liberal Imperialists*, pp. 265–86. The phrase 'step by step' seems to have been first used by Haldane as far back as 1896, *The Scotsman*, 30 December 1896.

21. J. A. Spender, *Life of the Right Hon. Sir Henry Campbell-Bannerman, G. C. B.* 2 vols (London: Hodder & Stoughton, 1923) vol. 2, pp. 182–3. Campbell-Bannerman refrained from using the words 'step by step' even though he adopted the substance of the policy.

22. *Liberal Magazine* (March 1902) 98, Campbell-Bannerman to NLF, 19 February 1902.

23. A. K. Russell, *Liberal Landslide: the General Election of 1906*, (Newton Abbot: David and Charles, 1973) pp. 74–6.

24. F. S. L. Lyons, 'The Irish Unionist Party and the Devolution Crisis of 1904–5', *Irish Historical Studies*, 6 (1948) 1–21.

25. Lord Crewe in *The Times*, 3 January 1906.

26. Bodleian Library, Oxford, MS Eng. hist. c369, fos 1–14, MacDonnell papers, 'Outline of Irish constitutional reform', 14 February 1906.

27. *Liberal Magazine* (March 1902) 98.

28. Add MS 41223, fos 160–1, Campbell-Bannerman papers, Morley to Campbell-Bannerman, 30 November 1905.

29. Add MS 41211, fo. 344, Campbell-Bannerman papers, Bryce to Campbell-Bannerman, 8 October 1906.
30. British Library, Add MS 46325, Burns papers, Burns diary, 13 March, 1, 3 May 1907. Burns evidently held MacDonnell, 'the sun-dried bureaucrat', in great contempt.
31. British Library, Add MS 43542, fo. 182, Ripon papers, MacDonnell to Ripon, 24 April 1907 on some of the variations in these figures.
32. Add MS 41239, fo. 250, Campbell-Bannerman papers, Birrell to Campbell-Bannerman, 24 May 1907.
33. S. Peseta, *Before the Revolution: Nationalism, Social Change and Ireland's Catholic Elite, 1879–1922* (Cork: Cork University Press, 1999) pp. 5–27.
34. P. Bew, *Conflict and Conciliation in Ireland, 1890–1910* (Oxford: Clarendon Press, 1987) pp. 145–6, 181–92.
35. See Birrell's defence of his policy in the Commons, *Hansard*, 5th series, 1909, i, 606–27.
36. L. W. McBride, *The Greening of Dublin Castle: the Transformation of Bureaucratic and Judicial Personnel in Ireland, 1892–1922* (Washington DC: Catholic University of America Press, 1991) pp. 124–58.
37. D. Gwynn, *The Life of John Redmond* (London: G. G. Harrap, 1932) pp. 166–9.
38. *The Times*, 11 December 1909.
39. Blewett, *Peers, the Parties and the People*, pp. 317, 326, 124–5, 191–2.
40. *The Times*, 11 February 1910.
41. Asquith papers 23, fos 64–6, Grey to Asquith, 7 February 1910, enclosing memorandum, 31 January 1910.
42. W. S. Blunt, *My Diaries: Being a Personal Narrative of Events, 1888–1914*, 2 vols (London: Martin Secker, 1919–1920) vol. 2, p. 301, Blunt diary, 13 February 1910 for Redmond's belief that the Liberal Imperialist group in the cabinet were not 'really in earnest about Home Rule'.
43. Hazlehurst and Woodland eds, *Liberal Chronicle*, pp. 168–72, Pease diary, 6–20 April 1910.
44. R. Fanning, 'The Irish Policy of Asquith's Government and the Cabinet Crisis of 1910', in A. Cosgrove and D. McCartney eds, *Studies in Irish History: Presented to R. Dudley Edwards* (Dublin: University College, 1979) pp. 279–303.
45. The coalition proposal is reprinted in R. Scally, *The Origins of the Lloyd George Coalition* (Princeton, NJ: Princeton University Press, 1975) pp. 375–86.
46. Gainford papers 39, Pease diary, 6 March 1912, 15 October 1913 for Grey's reluctant attitude to home rule.
47. This process is fully discussed in Jalland, *Liberals and Ireland*, pp. 37–49.
48. The fantastic complexities of this subject are ably dealt with in P. Jalland, 'Irish Home-Rule Finance: a Neglected Dimension of the Irish Question, 1910–14', *Irish Historical Studies*, 23 (1983) 233–53.
49. Cabinet papers 37/105/18, W. S. Churchill, 'Devolution', 1 March 1911.
50. Lloyd George papers C/12/2, Lloyd George, 'Home Rule. Suggestion', 27 February 1911.
51. Asquith papers 106, fos 199–222, 'Government of Ireland Bill', 15 April 1912 was the first draft of the bill to omit Lloyd George's idea.
52. *Hansard*, 5th series, 1912, xxxvi, 1403–4; *The Times*, 20 November 1912.
53. Asquith papers, 106, fos 6–8, 'Memorandum on Clauses of the Home Rule Bill', 29 January 1912.

54. J. E. Kendle, 'The Round Table Movement and "Home Rule All Round"', *Historical Journal*, 11 (1968) 332–53.
55. Asquith papers 12, fo. 198, Grey to Asquith, 26 October 1910.
56. Munro-Ferguson's position is dealt with in Jalland, *Liberals and Ireland*, pp. 96, 101–2, 112, 271. His motives caused some uneasiness among other Scottish MPs who favoured Scottish home rule, eg McCallum Scott papers 1465/4, Scott diary, 22 July 1913. For Liberal ideas on an agreed solution to home rule through federalism in 1913–14 see Loreburn's letter in *The Times*, 11 September 1913, which was savaged by Morley as a policy of those 'Faint-hearts, who want a decent case for cutting HR', Rosebery papers 10048, fo. 42, Morley to Rosebery, 19 September 1913.
57. The following issues are dealt with succinctly in R. J. Finlay, *A Partnership for Good? Scottish Politics and the Union since 1880* (Edinburgh: John Donald, 1997) pp. 12–69.
58. Ibid, pp. 49–51.
59. The Young Scots had been founded in 1900. After a sustained propaganda campaign in 1907–9 Scottish home rule was made an 'object' of the Society and in 1911 it threatened that if a bill on the subject was not forthcoming in the lifetime of the existing parliament it would put up its own candidates, *Young Scots Handbook, 1911–12* (Glasgow, 1912) pp. 5–6. The Young Scots insisted they should not be listed as a 'Liberal organisation' in the *Liberal Year Book* and struggled to remain financially independent of the Liberal party in case it 'should be thought advisable actively to oppose them at any time', National Library of Scotland, Acc. 3721, Roland Muirhead papers 146/1, T. Lochhead to R. Muirhead, 31 January 1912.
60. A criticism that was widely made of the Children's Act, 1908, while legislation that took account of Scottish particularities was received enthusiastically by Scottish Liberals, see J. Stewart, ' "This Injurious Measure": Scotland and the 1906 Education (Provision of Meals) Act', *Scottish Historical Review*, 78 (1999) 76–94.
61. Liberal backbenchers introduced their own bill to amend the Scottish Small Landholders Act in 1914, *Hansard*, 5th series, 1914, lix, 1545–1630. The Temperance Act proved largely ineffective.
62. Muirhead papers 149/11, Muirhead to A. Williams, 16 July 1914.
63. J. F. McCaffrey, 'The Origins of Liberal Unionism in the West of Scotland', *Scottish Historical Review*, 50 (1971) 47–71; D. C. Savage, 'Scottish Politics, 1885–6', *Scottish Historical Review*, 40 (1961) 118–35 for the significant defections to Liberal Unionism over Irish Home Rule in 1886.
64. *The Times*, 7 May 1912.
65. MacCallum Scott papers 1465/5, Scott diary, 1 July 1914.
66. K. Morgan, *Rebirth of a Nation: Wales, 1880–1980* (Oxford: Clarendon Press, 1981) pp. 26–58.
67. J. G. Jones, 'The Litterateur as Politician: Owen M. Edwards M.P.', *Welsh History Review*, 17 (1995) 571–89.
68. J. G. Jones, 'Alfred Thomas's National Institutions (Wales) Bills of 1891–2', *Welsh History Review*, 15 (1990) 218–39.
69. *Hansard*, 4th series, 1906, clxi, 53–4, 58–60 for the Lloyd George-Balfour exchange.

70. Morgan, *Rebirth of a Nation*, pp. 36–7, 81–4, 107–10, 111–12.
71. John announced his campaign in the *Manchester Guardian*, 8 August 1910, but his fellow Welsh Liberal MPs regarded him with some derision, E. W. Davies papers 18/27, H. H. Jones to E. W. Davies, 13 April 1911 on the 'Exhibition he is making at every tinpot meeting he is invited to'.
72. University College of North Wales, Bangor, Library, Minutes of Welsh National Liberal Council, 17 November 1913.
73. *Hansard*, 5th series, 1914, lix, 1235–8.
74. I. Packer, *Lloyd George* (Basingstoke: Macmillan, 1998) pp. 12–13.
75. Vincent ed., *Crawford Papers*, p. 169, Balcarres diary, 19 November 1910.
76. Asquith papers 106, fos 199–222, 'Government of Ireland Bill', 15 April 1912.
77. Asquith papers 6, fos 95–6, Asquith to George V, 7 February 1912.
78. Jalland, *Liberals and Ireland*, pp. 92–102.
79. Notes on these discussions can be found in Asquith papers 38, fos 231–4; 39, fos 3–6.
80. *Hansard*, 5th series, 1914, lix, 906–18.
81. A. T. Q. Stewart, *The Ulster Crisis* (London: Faber & Faber, 1967)
82. Only Agar-Robartes and Sir Clifford Cory voted against the 3rd Reading of the Home Rule bill on 16 January 1913. Sir George Kemp resigned as an MP, partly so that he did not have to support the bill.
83. Dutton ed., *Odyssey of an Edwardian Liberal*, p. 30, Holt diary, 10 April 1914.
84. E. W. Davies papers A/7, Davies diary, 14 July 1914.
85. Jalland, *Liberals and Ireland*, pp. 87–92.
86. L. T. Hobhouse, 'Irish Nationalism and Liberal Principle' in J. H. Morgan ed., *The New Irish Constitution: an Exposition and Some Arguments* (London: Hodder and Stoughton, 1912) pp. 368–9.
87. *Hansard*, 5th series, 1912, xxxix, 785–7.
88. Jalland, *Liberals and Ireland*, pp. 92–102 on the significance of the debate on the Agar-Robartes amendment in making this clear.
89. I. Colvin, *The Life of Lord Carson*, 3 vols (London: Victor Gollancz, 1934) vol. 2, pp. 249–51 for a dramatic description of the differences between northern and southern Irish Unionists.
90. Hobhouse, 'Irish Nationalism' in Morgan ed., *Irish Constitution*, p. 370.
91. Gainford papers 39, Pease diary, 4 March 1914. Asquith papers 7, fos 101–2, Asquith to George V, 5 March 1914 makes it clear that the 'principle' of exclusion was carried without much dissension and the objections were mainly 'financial and administrative'.
92. Foreign Office papers 800/100/307–10, Grey to Asquith, 20 May 1914.
93. *The Times*, 16 March 1914. Also Add MS 46336, Burns diary, 26 March 1914 on the need to establish 'civil supremacy, popular will and democratic control'.
94. Jalland, *Liberals and Ireland*, pp. 207–33.
95. Three Liberal MPs, Neil Primrose, W. F. Roch and Arthur Sherwell, abstained on the vote on the Finance Bill on 7 July 1914 in protest at the failure to arrest Carson, *Daily News*, 8 July 1914.
96. Gainford papers 39, Pease diary, 20 November 1913.
97. Fitzroy, *Memoirs*, vol. 2, p. 541, Fitzroy diary, 17 March 1914.

4 Liberalism and Democracy

1. C. Seymour, *Electoral Reform in England and Wales: the Development and Operation of the Parliamentary Franchise, 1832–85* (New Haven, Ct: Yale University Press, 1915) p. viii.
2. The spread of anti-House of Lords feeling in the nineteenth-century Liberal party has recently been chronicled in A. Taylor, *Lords of Misrule: Hostility to Aristocracy in Late Nineteenth and Early Twentieth-Century Britain* (Basingstoke: Palgrave, 2004) pp. 97–128.
3. Adonis, *Making Aristocracy Work*, p. 20 for these and subsequent figures on Liberal strength in the Lords.
4. National Liberal Federation, *Tenth Annual Report*, 1887, p. 9.
5. H. C. G. Matthew, *Gladstone, 1875–98* (Oxford: Oxford University Press, 1995) pp. 354–5; *Hansard*, 4th series, 1894, xxii, 194–208.
6. Readman, 'The 1895 General Election', 471.
7. Machin, *Politics and the Churches*, pp. 141–2, 222.
8. Packer, *Lloyd George, Liberalism and the Land*, pp. 4–21.
9. Revd W. Tuckwell, *Reminiscences of a Radical Parson* (London: Cassell, 1905) p. 202.
10. House of Lords Record Office, Samuel papers A/4, 'Notebook'.
11. University of Birmingham Library, Joseph Chamberlain papers 5/54/474, Morley to Chamberlain, 7 January 1883, on 'the monopoly of London by three or four Dukes'.
12. See, for instance, W. H. Mallock, 'The House of Lords', *Quarterly Review*, 167 (1888) 217–48.
13. Russell, *Liberal Landslide*, p. 73.
14. Adonis, *Making Aristocracy Work*, pp. 137–44.
15. *The Times*, 21 June 1894 for the NLF resolution. Rosebery outlined some of his ideas in a speech at Glasgow, *The Times*, 15 November 1894. The cabinet's preferences are indicated in Bodleian Library, Oxford, Harcourt papers 412, L. Harcourt journal, 21, 26 November 1894.
16. This membership list and dating is based on the deductions in C. C. Weston, 'The Liberal Leadership and the Lords' Veto, 1907–10', *Historical Journal*, 11 (1968) 508–37; Cabinet papers 37/87/38 for the committee's report. See also, Cabinet papers 37/101/137, Ld Crewe, 'Memorandum on Various Expedients for Adjusting the Relations between the Two Houses of Parliament', 8 March 1907 and Asquith papers 46, fo. 161, Asquith to Crewe, 11 March 1907.
17. Crewe, 'Memorandum'.
18. Matthew, *Liberal Imperialists*, pp. 260–3.
19. Add MS 41208, fos 30–1, Campbell-Bannerman papers, Campbell-Bannerman to Knollys, 25 March 1907.
20. Ibid.
21. The cabinet memorandum expressing Campbell-Bannerman's views is reprinted in Spender, *Life of Campbell-Bannerman*, vol. 2, pp. 351–5.
22. Add MS 41222, fo. 208, Campbell-Bannerman papers, Loreburn to Campbell-Bannerman, 5 June 1907.
23. Spender, *Life of Campbell-Bannerman*, vol. 2, p. 353.

24. *The Times*, 11 December 1909.
25. Blewett, *Peers, the Parties and the People*, p. 320.
26. See Chapter 3.
27. Marquess of Crewe, *Lord Rosebery*, 2 vols (London: John Murray, 1931) vol. 2, pp. 451–4; Robbins, *Grey*, pp. 47, 209.
28. Asquith papers 12, fos 114–15, Harcourt to Asquith, 7 February 1910.
29. Blewett, *Peers, the Parties and the People*, p. 320.
30. Asquith papers 23, fos 63–6, Grey memorandum, 31 January 1910.
31. *The Times*, 6 January 1910 for Lord Lansdowne's, rather vague, endorsement of the idea.
32. Add MS 45922, fos 235–6, H. Gladstone papers, H. Samuel to H. Gladstone, 22 January 1910; Blewett, *Peers, the Parties and the People*, p. 400.
33. Asquith papers 23, fo. 105, Samuel to Asquith, 3 February 1910.
34. Ibid., 23 fos 70–6, Churchill to Asquith, 14 February 1910; Masterman, *Masterman*, p. 158.
35. Asquith papers 23, fos 63–6, Grey memorandum, 31 January 1910; ibid, fos 70–6, Churchill to Asquith, 14 February 1910. Grey suggested a Second Chamber 'based upon the elective principle, with if desired a minority of distinguished life-members'.
36. It is noticeable that at the inter-party conference on the House of Lords in 1917–18 the Liberal delegates favoured a largely elected second chamber, J. D. Fair, *British Interparty Conferences: a Study of the Procedure of Conciliation in British Politics, 1867–1921* (Oxford: Clarendon Press, 1980) pp. 185–6.
37. See Chapter 3.
38. These events have been most recently treated at length in Fair, *Interparty Conferences*, pp. 77–102.
39. See the account of the conference's third sitting in Birmingham University Library, Austen Chamberlain papers AC/10/2/37, 27 June 1910.
40. Asquith papers 23, fo. 141 for Asquith's letter stating the Liberal position (probably dated 3 November 1910).
41. Blewett, *Peers, the Parties and the People*, pp. 165–6.
42. The breakdown of the constitutional conference in November 1910 was followed almost immediately by the decision to call an election and the demand for guarantees from George V, Asquith papers 23, fos 160–1, 'Memorandum on the Royal Prerogative', 14 November 1910.
43. Blewett, *Peers, the Parties and the People*, p. 328 calculates only one Liberal candidate was critical of the idea. 15% of Liberal candidates demanded Lords reform in addition to ending the veto.
44. *The Times*, 18, 24 November 1910.
45. Austen Chamberlain papers AC/10/2/50, 'Notes of Conference', 16th sitting, 13 October 1910.
46. Blewett, *Peers, the Parties and the People*, p. 173 notes the lukewarm reaction of the Tory Press to the proposals.
47. A. V. Dicey, 'The Referendum and its Critics', *Quarterly Review*, 212 (1910); W. E. H. Lecky, *Democracy and Liberty*, 2 vols (London: Longmans, 1896) vol. 1, p. 237.
48. J. A. Hobson, *The Crisis of Liberalism: New Issues of Democracy* (London: P. S. King & Son, 1909) pp. 17–70.

49. See in particular Asquith at Hull, *The Times*, 26 November 1910, and Wolverhampton, *The Times*, 2 December 1910. The nearest he came to an objection to the principle of a referendum was the idea that it would undermine the effective working of the existing system of representative government.
50. *Hansard*, 5th series, 1912, xxxix, 1326.
51. Tanner, *Political Change*, pp. 99–129 unravels some of these intricacies.
52. National Liberal Federation, *Eleventh Annual Meeting, 1888*, pp. 6–9 for the list of policies.
53. M. Barker, *Gladstone and Radicalism: the Reconstruction of Liberal Policy in Britain, 1885–94* (Hassocks: Harvester, 1975) pp. 211–17.
54. Russell, *Liberal Landslide*, p. 73 reveals that in 1906 33% of Liberal candidates mentioned the need to reform the registration system and 29% argued for the abolition of plural voting.
55. *Liberal Magazine*, 18 (1910) 645 listed 29 county seats the Tories had won through plural voting. Unionist agents suggested plural votes had won them 30 seats county seats and eight boroughs. In addition they held all nine University seats, National Archives of Scotland, Steel-Maitland papers GD 193/202/238–40, Memorandum, n.d. [1917].
56. *Hansard*, 5th series, 1912, xl, 2167 for Sir William Anson denouncing the dominance of 'mere numbers'.
57. In 1910 there were an average of 6770 voters in Irish seats and 12664 in English seats (excluding the University seats). To bring the average Irish electorate up to that of England, Irish representation would have to be reduced from 101 seats to 54 seats. Figures calculated from F. Craig, *British Parliamentary Election Results, 1885–1918* (London: Macmillan 1974) pp. 582–3, 588.
58. M. Pugh, *Electoral Reform in War and Peace, 1906–18* (London: Routledge & Kegan Paul, 1978) pp. 29–44.
59. Seymour, *Electoral Reform*, pp. 499–502.
60. Churchill to J. H. Humphries, 8 February 1905, quoted in Pugh, *Electoral Reform*, p. 15.
61. Royal Commission on Systems of Election (1908–10), Cd 5163.
62. Pugh, *Electoral Reform*, pp. 13–14.
63. Gainford papers 112, 'Memorandum of the Cabinet Committee on Franchise and Registration', 1912.
64. M. Pugh, 'The Limits of liberalism: Liberals and Women's Suffrage, 1867–1914' in Biagini ed., *Citizenship and Community*, pp. 45–65.
65. *Hansard*, 3rd series, 1867, clxxxvii, 818. This issue is dealt with deftly in M. Pugh, *The March of the Women: a Revisionist Analysis of the Campaign for Women's Suffrage, 1866–1914* (Oxford: Oxford University Press, 2000) pp. 34–6.
66. Note the analysis of MPs' opinions by the League For Opposing Woman Suffrage, quoted in Pugh, *Electoral Reform*, p. 187.
67. P. Hollis, *Ladies Elect: Women in English Local Government, 1865–1914* (Oxford: Clarendon Press, 1987) pp. 48–9, 251–63.
68. Pugh, 'Liberals and Women's Suffrage', in Biagini ed., *Citizenship and Community*, p. 49.

69. *Hansard*, 5th series, 1912, xxxvi, 654. When one anti-suffrage Liberal MP listed his arguments, the first was 'Different spheres of men and women', MacCallum Scott papers 1465/3, Scott diary, 19 February 1912.

70. *Female Suffrage: a Letter from the Rt Hon. W. E. Gladstone M. P., to Samuel Smith M. P.* (London: John Murray, 1892) for a very full statement of Gladstone's views.

71. *Hansard*, 4th series, 1892, iii, 1510–13.

72. National Liberal Federation, *Annual Report, 1905* (London: Liberal Publication Department, 1906) p. 66.

73. At least according to Lloyd George, *The Times*, 7 December 1908.

74. Pugh, *Electoral Reform*, pp. 35–43.

75. B. Harrison, *Separate Spheres: the Opposition to Women's Suffrage in Britain* (London: Croom Helm, 1978) pp. 165–7.

76. Pugh, *March of the Women*, pp. 143–4.

77. Some Liberals remained suspicious that women would be disproportionately Conservative and subject to clerical influence, but this was an argument from tactics rather than principles, see Cabinet papers 37/108/148, Elibank, 'Effect of registration laws on the Liberal Party', 16 November 1911.

78. Indeed prominent Liberal anti-suffragists were reluctant to publicly associate themselves with anti-suffrage organisations, Harrison, *Separate Spheres*, pp. 165–6.

79. Jenkins, *Asquith*, pp. 28–31 for Asquith's first marriage; Margot Asquith papers d3210, diary 10 July 1914 for Margot impressing her own views on Irish home rule on Redmond. Harrison, *Separate Spheres*, pp. 99–100 on the influence of education, clubland and the classics on the views of some Liberal anti-suffragists.

80. Hollis, *Ladies Elect*, p. 486 calculates there were nearly 2,500 women serving on local authorities by 1914–15.

81. L. Walker, 'Party Political Women: a Comparative Study of Liberal Women and the Primrose League, 1890–1914' in J. Rendall ed., *Equal or Different? Women's Politics, 1800–1914*, (Oxford: Blackwell, 1987) pp. 165–213; C. Hirshfield, 'Fractured Faith: Liberal Party Women and the Suffrage Issue in Britain, 1892–1914', *Gender and History*, 2 (1990) 173–97.

82. *Hansard*, 4th series, 1906, clxiii, 873 for Campbell-Bannerman's vagueness on the whole suffrage issue.

83. *The Times*, 21 May 1908. Asquith was speaking to a deputation of pro-suffrage Liberal MPs.

84. Pugh, *Electoral Reform*, pp. 34–9.

85. Packer ed., *Rowntree Letters*, p. 39, A. S. to M. K. Rowntree, 12 July 1910.

86. Elibank papers 8803, Lloyd George to Elibank, 5 September 1911. See also E. W. Davies papers A/7, Davies diary, 18 November 1911 for the need to avoid enfranchising only 'a certain class of women'.

87. Cabinet papers 37/108/148, Elibank, 'Effect of registration laws on the Liberal Party', 16 November 1911; West Yorkshire Archive Service, Society of Certificated and Associated Liberal Agents, executive committee minutes, 27 January 1912.

88. Pugh, *Electoral Reform*, p. 188.

89. Packer ed., *Rowntree Letters*, p. 72, A. S. to M. K. Rowntree, 23 November 1911 for Arnold Rowntree's approval of these tactics. Ibid, p. 39, A. S. to

M. K. Rowntree, 12 July 1910 for his description of the conciliation bill as 'anti-democratic'.

90. Hirshfield, 'Fractured Faith', 187; the effectiveness of the Election Fighting Fund is much disputed, but it caused serious divisions among Liberal women, Pugh, *March of the Women*, pp. 264–83; U. Masson, ' "Political Conditions in Wales are Quite Different . . ." Party Politics and Votes for Women in Wales, 1912–15', *Women's History Review*, 9 (2000) 369–88.

91. Walker, 'Party Political Women', in Rendall ed., *Equal or Different*, pp. 186–8. The WNLF had under 10% of the membership of the WLF.

92. Hirshfield, 'Fractured Faith', 185–7.

93. C. Roberts, *The Radical Countess; the History of the Life of Rosalind, Countess of Carlisle* (Carlisle: Steel Bros, 1962) pp. 91–102. Apparently, though, it was not true that she had personally destroyed the contents of the wine cellar at Castle Howard, her husband's stately home, D. Henley, *Rosalind Howard, Countess of Carlisle* (London: Hogarth Press, 1958) p. 110.

94. Hollis, *Ladies Elect*, pp. 247–99.

95. P. McHugh, *Prostitution and Victorian Social Reform* (London: Croom Helm, 1980) pp. 163–86 for the role of many Liberal women in campaigning against the Contagious Diseases Acts.

96. This was seen by many in the WLF as a concession to pressure from their organisation, Hirshfield, 'Fractured Faith', 185. The truth was more complex, S. Petrow, *Policing Morals: the Metropolitan Police and the Home Office, 1870–1914* (Oxford: Clarendon Press, 1994) pp. 167–75.

97. Royal Commission on Venereal Diseases (1913–16), Cd. 8189.

5   A Nonconformist Party?

1. T. A. Jenkins, *The Liberal Ascendancy, 1830–86* (Basingstoke: Macmillan, 1994) pp. 14–20.

2. See C. Brown, *The Death of Christian Britain: Understanding Secularization, 1800–2000* (London: Routledge, 2001), for a summary of the debate on this process.

3. P. Clarke, 'Electoral Sociology of Modern Britain', *History*, 57 (1972) 31–55.

4. For the Victorian background, see Bebbington, *Nonconformist Conscience*, pp. 1–17.

5. T. A. McDonald, 'Religion and Voting in an English Borough: Poole in 1859', *Southern History*, 5 (1983) 221–37.

6. Biagini, *Liberty, Retrenchment and Reform*, pp. 198–217; Machin, *Politics and the Churches*, pp. 31–40.

7. Bebbington, *Nonconformist Conscience*, pp. 84–105.

8. National Archives, Education papers 24/116, Cabinet Committee 'Education Bill', 3 January 1906.

9. J. E. B. Munson, 'The Unionist Coalition and Education, 1895–1902', *Historical Journal*, 20 (1977) 607–45 for some of the background to the 1902 Education Act.

10. N. J. Richards, 'Religious Controversy and the School Boards, 1870–1902', *British Journal of Educational Studies*, 18 (1970) 180–96.

11. Exact figures are difficult to determine, but see Machin, *Politics and the Churches*, p. 267.
12. Spender, *Life of Campbell-Bannerman*, vol. 2, p. 64.
13. Russell, *Liberal Landslide*, p. 65.
14. Machin, *Politics and the Churches*, p. 286.
15. Haldane papers 5909, fo. 270, A H. D. Acland to Haldane, 21 October 1912, concluding that the government's record on education was 'wretched' because of the dominance of religious controversies.
16. Matthew, *Liberal Imperialists*, pp. 228–35.
17. W. George, *My Brother and I* (London: Eyre & Spottiswoode, 1958) p. 207, Lloyd George to W. George, 14 December 1905.
18. See for instance the scheme tentatively outlined by Campbell-Bannerman in 1902, Spender, *Life of Campbell-Bannerman*, vol. 2, pp. 76–7, emphasising the need for 'Public control by elected bodies'.
19. Education papers 24/116, Cabinet Committee 'Education Bill', 3 January 1906.
20. Education papers 24/118, A. Birrell, 'Memorandum concerning the Education Bill', 16 February 1906.
21. Add MS 46324, Burns diary, 21 March 1906; Add MS 41213, fos 339–40, Campbell-Bannerman papers, Crewe to Campbell-Bannerman, 28 February 1906.
22. Machin, *Politics and the Churches*, p. 286; Cabinet papers 41/30/66, Campbell-Bannerman to Edward VII, 20 June 1906.
23. Bebbington, *Nonconformist Conscience*, pp. 147–8.
24. Fair, *British Interparty Conferences*, pp. 59–76.
25. The Liberal position is best explained in Lansdowne's memorandum of 18 December 1906 reproduced in Lord Newton, *Lord Lansdowne: a biography* (London: Macmillan & Co., 1929) pp. 356–7.
26. Bebbington, *Nonconformist Conscience*, pp. 139–40.
27. *Christian World*, 6 June 1907.
28. Machin, *Politics and the Churches*, p. 290–2.
29. Bernstein, *Liberalism and Liberal Politics*, pp. 94–5.
30. Blewett, *Peers, the Parties and the People*, p. 326.
31. Cabinet papers 37/117/90, J.A. Pease, 'Note on the Necessity for increased financial aid to Local Education Authorities', 13 December 1913; G. Sherington, *English Education, Social Change and War, 1911–20* (Manchester: Manchester University Press, 1981) pp. 22–38.
32. For Nonconformist pressure, see Education papers 24/630, W. Robertson Nicoll to Asquith, 17 November 1913; Cabinet papers 37/120/79, J. A. Pease, 'Education (Single School Areas) Bill', 30 June 1914 for the result.
33. Packer, *Lloyd George, Liberalism and the Land*, pp. 148–52.
34. Haldane, *Autobiography*, pp. 218–19.
35. Bebbington, *Nonconformist Conscience*, pp. 18–36.
36. A. Simon, 'Church Disestablishment as a Factor in the General Election of 1885', *Historical Journal*, 18 (1975) 791–820.
37. Bebbington, *Nonconformist Conscience*, p. 24.
38. Machin, *Politics and the Churches*, pp. 295–6.
39. Blewett, *Peers, the Parties and the People*, p. 326.
40. J. G. Kellas, 'The Liberal Party and the Scottish Church Disestablishment Crisis', *English Historical Review*, 79 (1964) 31–46.

41. Machin, *Politics and the Churches*, pp. 296–8.
42. Though some local Liberal Associations remained committed to disestablishment this was increasingly rare, South Edinburgh Liberal Association, minutes, 8 September 1913.
43. Morgan, *Rebirth of a Nation*, pp. 40–2.
44. Ibid., pp. 141–2.
45. Add MS 41240, fos 105–6, Campbell-Bannerman papers, Lloyd George to Campbell-Bannerman, 19 October 1907.
46. House of Lords Record Office, Bonar Law papers 31/3/45, Bridgeman to Bonar Law, 28 February 1914 for one Tory MP arguing for the bill's significance even in London.   ·
47. Bonar Law papers 26/2/12, A. Griffith-Boscawen to Bonar Law, 10 April 1912.
48. Earl of Birkenhead, *Halifax: the Life of Lord Halifax* (London: Hamish Hamilton, 1965) pp. 100–1; J. A. Cross, *Sir Samuel Hoare: a Political Biography* (London: Jonathan Cape, 1977) pp. 30–5.
49. Machin, *Politics and the Churches*, p. 301.
50. Rowland, *Last Liberal Governments*, vol. 2, pp. 183–4, 193–4; Elibank papers 8814, A. C. Murray diary, 1 November, 13 December 1912; National Library of Wales, J. H. Lewis papers B26, Lewis diary, 22 May 1912.
51. *Hansard*, 4th series, 1907, clxix, 962.
52. K. Morgan, *Keir Hardie: Radical and Socialist* (London: Weidenfeld & Nicolson, 1975) pp. 9, 64.
53. L. L Shiman, *The Crusade against Drink in Victorian England* (Basingstoke: Macmillan, 1988) pp. 182–8.
54. Bebbington, *Nonconformist Conscience*, pp. 46–50.
55. Henley, *Rosalind Howard*, pp. 127–8.
56. Shiman, *Crusade against Drink*, pp. 99–109.
57. D. W. Gutzke, *Protecting the Pub: Brewers and Publicans against Temperance* (Woodbridge: Boydell & Brewer/Royal Historical Society, 1989) p. 78 for the party division on local option in the 1880s.
58. Readman, '1895 General Election', 471.
59. *Westminster Gazette*, 13 August 1895.
60. Add MS 45992, fos 194–8, Herbert Gladstone papers, Samuel to Gladstone, 14 January 1908.
61. B. S. Rowntree, *Poverty: a Study of Town Life* (London: Macmillan, 1901) p. 142.
62. B. Doyle, 'Temperance and Modernity: the Impact of Local Experience on Rank and File Liberal Attitudes to Alcohol', *Journal of Regional and Local Studies*, 16 (1996) 1–10, for the attitudes of Sir George White, shoe manufacturer and Liberal MP for NW Norfolk, 1900–12, on these lines.
63. Gutzke, *Protecting the Pub*, pp. 122–4 on the role of brewers and publicans in the 1895 election.
64. For instance, Julius Bertram and W. H. Whitbread, two Liberal MPs who were heavily critical of the licensing provisions of the 1909 Budget. Both had to retire as MPs in 1910, Blewett, *Peers, the Parties and the People*, p. 215.
65. Royal Commission on the Licensing Laws (1896–9), C. 9379
66. *Manchester Guardian*, 16 November 1899 for Campbell-Bannerman's formal announcement of the new policy.
67. D. M. Fahey, 'The Politics of Drink: Pressure Groups and the British Liberal Party, 1883–1908', *Social Science*, 54 (1979) 76–85.

68. Add MS 45992, fos 194–8, Herbert Gladstone papers, Samuel to Gladstone, 14 January 1908.
69. Murray, *People's Budget*, pp. 139–43, 154–7, 300–1. In fact, the 1909 budget does not seem to have reduced the number of public houses significantly, though increased spirits duties probably led to less consumption of these items.
70. Bebbington, *Nonconformist Conscience*, pp. 57–8.
71. R. McKibbin, 'Working-Class Gambling in Britain, 1880–1939', *Past and Present*, 82 (1979) 147–78.
72. For an example of a criticism of gambling that was explicitly hostile to working class culture, see S. Churchill, *Betting and Gambling* (London: J. Nisbet, 1893).
73. Ramsay MacDonald, 'Gambling and Citizenship' in B. S. Rowntree ed., *Betting and Gambling: a National Evil* (London: Macmillan, 1905) pp. 117–34.
74. Bebbington, *Nonconformist Conscience*, pp. 51–3. Nonconformist newspaper owners made efforts to exclude gambling odds and tips from their papers, P. Gliddon, 'Politics for Better or Worse: Political Nonconformity, the Gambling Dilemma and the North of England Newspaper Company, 1903–14', *History*, 87 (2002) 227–44.
75. D. Dixon, *From Prohibition to Regulation: Bookmaking, Anti-Gambling and the Law* (Oxford: Clarendon Press, 1991) pp. 114–18, 135–41. Dixon's analysis suggests the 1906 Act was 'not a party issue', ibid., p. 138.
76. *Hansard*, 4th series, 1906, clxii, 1150 for Arnold Lupton on this question.
77. Ibid., 867.
78. F. Mort, 'Purity, Feminism and the State: Sexuality and Moral Politics, 1880–1914' in M. Langan and B. Schwarz, *Crises in the British State, 1880–1930* (London: Hutchinson, 1985) pp. 209–25.
79. Royal Commission on Duties of the Metropolitan Police (1906–8), C. 4156.
80. E. J. Bristow, *Vice and Vigilance: Purity Movements in Britain since 1700* (Dublin: Gill & Macmillan, 1977) pp. 117–18, 165–6.
81. V. Bailey and S. Blackburn, 'The Punishment of Incest Act, 1908: a Case Study of Criminal Law Creation', *Criminal Law Review* (November 1979) 708–18.
82. Petrow, *Policing Morals*, pp. 167–75.
83. *Hansard*, 5th series, 1912, xliii, 735–40.
84. H. Pelling, *Social Geography of British Elections, 1885–1910* (London: Macmillan, 1967) pp. 432–3; D. Bebbington, 'Nonconformity and Electoral Sociology, 1867–1918', *Historical Journal*, 27 (1984) 633–56; M. Kinnear, *The British Voter: an Atlas and Survey since 1885*, 2nd edn (London: Batsford Academic, 1981) pp. 82–3, 125–9.
85. K. Wald, *Crosses on the Ballot: Patterns of British Voter Alignment since 1885* (Princeton, NJ: Princeton University Press, 1983); D. Butler and D. Stokes, *Political Change in Britain: Forces Shaping Electoral Choice* (London: Macmillan, 1969) pp. 133–4.
86. Clarke, *Lancashire and the New Liberalism*, pp. 57–8 for the situation in Warrington; Machin, *Politics and the Churches*, p. 278.
87. Bebbington, *Nonconformist Conscience*, p. 154. The puzzling question of Lloyd George's beliefs is dealt with in G. I. T. Machin, 'Lloyd George and Nonconformity' in J. Loades ed., *The Life and Times of David Lloyd George*

(Bangor: Headstart, 1991) pp. 33–48; religious belief does not seem to have been an important factor in Pease's life, see Hazlehurst and Woodland eds *Liberal Chronicle*, pp. 2–16.

88. Runciman was a supporter of the West London Mission founded by the leading Methodist Hugh Price Hughes and Wood was an active member of the elite King's Weigh House Congregational Chapel, Bebbington, *Nonconformist Conscience*, p. 150; D. A. Hamer, *John Morley: Liberal Intellectual in Politics* (Oxford: Clarendon Press, 1968) pp. 1–32 for Morley and K. Brown, *John Burns* (London: Royal Historical Society, 1977) p. 72 for Burns.

89. C. Binfield, 'Asquith: the Formation of a Prime Minister', *Journal of the United Reformed Church History Society*, 2 (1981) 204–42; Machin, *Politics and the Churches*, p. 274; D. Sommer, *Haldane of Cloan: His Life and Times* (London: George Allen & Unwin, 1960) pp. 42–7; D. Dutton, *Simon: a Political Biography of Sir John Simon* (London: Aurum Press, 1992) pp. 5–6.

90. Binfield, 'Asquith', 230.

91. The Pease, Bright and McLaren clans were all related to each other by marriage and provided no fewer than 11 Liberal MPs in 1885–1914.

92. Blewett, *Peers, the Parties and the People*, p. 344.

93. Bebbington, *Nonconformist Conscience*, pp. 84–105.

94. Note, for instance, the reluctance of Liberals in a Wesleyan-dominated area like Cornwall to support Irish home rule, Pelling, *Social Geography*, pp. 163–7.

95. On this process, see D. Thompson, 'The Emergence of the Nonconformist Social Gospel in England' in K. Robbins ed., *Protestant Evangelicalism: Britain, Ireland, Germany and America c. 1750-c.1950* (Oxford: Blackwell, 1990) pp. 255–80; W. M. King, 'Hugh Price Hughes and the British Social Gospel', *Journal of Religious History*, 13 (June 1984) 66–82; D. Thompson, 'John Clifford's Social Gospel', *Baptist Quarterly*, 31 (1986) 199–217.

96. I. Packer, 'Religion and the New Liberalism: the Rowntree Family, Quakerism and Social Reform', *Journal of British Studies*, 42 (2003) 236–57. Rosebery papers 10053, fos 11–12, Perks to Rosebery, 26 January 1907 for William Robertson Nicoll, editor of the *British Weekly* and ally of Lloyd George, and his support of the new theology.

6 The Economy and Finance

1. G. Dangerfield, *The Strange Death of Liberal England*, 2nd edn (London: Granada, 1970) p. 76 defined the Liberal party as 'an irrational mixture of whig aristocrats, industrialists, dissenters, reformers, trade unionists, quacks and Mr Lloyd George'.

2. S. Newton and D. Porter, *Modernization Frustrated: the Politics of Industrial Decline in Britain since 1900* (London: Unwin Hyman, 1988), pp. 1–30 for a very negative assessment of the Liberal attitude to free trade as a slavish devotion to outmoded ideas and the interests of finance over those of industry.

3. Jenkins, *Liberal Ascendancy*, pp. 46–9, 110–20.

4. A. L. Friedberg, *The Weary Titan: Britain and the Experience of Relative Decline, 1895–1905* (Princeton, NJ: Princeton University Press, 1988) pp. 89–134; Green, *Crisis of Conservatism*, pp., 51–2, 248–53. Green also provides the most

convinsing explanation of why Conservatives embraced tariff reform and remained committed to this policy, despite its unpopularity.

5. Matthew, *Liberal Imperialists*, p. 101. For Storey, see ibid., p. 57 and Blewett, *Peers, the Parties and the People*, p. 438.

6. A. Howe, *Free Trade and Liberal England, 1846–1946* (Oxford: Clarendon Press, 1997) p. 259 on this 'propaganda stroke of genius'.

7. See, for instance, 'A Word to the Women', Liberal Publication Department leaflet 2027, *Pamphlets and Leaflets* 1905.

8. Blewett, *Peers, the Parties and the People*, p. 321.

9. The benefits of the relatively high wage economy were heavily promoted by the investigator of poverty and confectionary manufacturer, Seebohm Rowntree, see *Unemployment: a Social Study* (London: Macmillan, 1911) and *The Problem of Unemployment* (London: Fisher Unwin, 1914). See also the Liberal MP, Chiozza Money, in *British Weekly*, 5 March 1914.

10. J. A. Hobson, 'A Living Wage', *Commonwealth*, 1 (1896) 128–67.

11. Matthew, *Liberal Imperialists*, pp. 228–31 for Haldane's role in particular in promoting technical education; D. C. M. Platt, *Finance, Trade and Politics in British Foreign Policy, 1815–1914* (Oxford: Clarendon Press, 1968) p. 377 for the state and commerce; and Add MS 45988, fos 96–102, Herbert Gladstone papers, J. Brunner to H. Gladstone, 6 May 1904 on transport links.

12. Even in the free trade v. tariff reform election of 1906, 69% of Liberal candidates endorsed reform of the poor law or old age pensions, Russell, *Liberal Landslide*, p. 65.

13. These themes are developed in H. W. Massingham, 'Political Dangers of Protection' in Massingham ed., *Labour and Protection: a Series of Studies* (London: Fisher Unwin, 1903) pp. 1–37.

14. Haldane papers 5906, fo. 46, Haldane to Ashley, 20 September 1903 on the 'unhealthy influence' of protection on national life.

15. Howe, *Free Trade*, pp. 295–302.

16. H. Du Parcq ed., *Life of David Lloyd George*, 4 vols (London: Caxton, 1912–13), vol. 4, p. 636.

17. P. Readman, 'The Liberal Party and Patriotism in Early Twentieth-Century Britain', *Twentieth Century British History*, 12 (2001) 281–8.

18. See Chapter 2.

19. Hobson, *Imperialism*.

20. E. H. H. Green, 'The Political Economy of Empire, 1880–1914' in Porter ed., *Oxford History of the British Empire*, vol. 3, pp. 363–6.

21. Russell, *Liberal Landslide*, p. 65.

22. Blewett, *Peers, the Parties and the People*, p. 317, 326.

23. The flagship of these policies was the Progressive-controlled London County Council in 1889–1907, see S. Pennybacker, *A Vision for London, 1889–1914: Labour, Everyday Life and the LCC Experiment* (London: Routledge, 1995). For a similar situation in York, Packer, 'Religion and the New Liberalism', 254–5.

24. G. Alderman, *The Railway Interest* (Leicester: Leicester University Press, 1973), p. 195.

25. The impact of rising unemployment on the government's popularity is discussed in Blewett, *Peers, the Parties and the People*, pp. 50–1.

26. K. D. Brown, *Labour and Unemployment, 1900–14* (Newton Abbot: David & Charles, 1971) pp. 68–85.

27. Emy, *Liberals, Radicals and Social Politics*, pp. 152–3.
28. The discussion was instigated by Herbert Gladstone, see Add MS 45988, fo. 129, Herbert Gladstone papers, Campbell-Bannerman to Gladstone, 23 November 1904, agreeing to informal sub-committees to examine unemployment and other issues; Campbell-Bannerman's position was outlined in his speech at Limehouse, *The Times*, 21 December 1904.
29. Add MS 41214, fos 258–60, Campbell-Bannerman papers, Fowler to Campbell-Bannerman, 26 December 1904.
30. Add MS 41210, fos 241–2, Campbell-Bannerman papers, Asquith to Campbell-Bannerman, 1 January 1905.
31. In general terms, the Liberals supported the 1905 Unemployed Workmen's Act, Add MS 41238, fos 8–11, Campbell-Bannerman papers, Sydney Buxton to Campbell-Bannerman, 16 January 1905.
32. Royal Commission on Canals and Inland Navigation of the United Kingdom (1906–9), C. 4979.
33. Emy, *Liberals, Radicals and Social Politics*, pp. 153, 176. The increase in the grant in 1908 was only agreed after the cabinet overruled Burns, the President of the Local Government Board, Cabinet papers 41/31/68, Asquith to Edward VII, 20 October 1908.
34. Brown, *Labour and Unemployment*, pp. 89–92.
35. *Hansard*, 4th series, 1908, clxxxvi, 86.
36. Ibid, 4th series, 1908, clxxxvi, 10–19.
37. J. A. Hobson, 'The Right to Labour', *Nation*, 8 February 1908.
38. Churchill had been thinking along these lines since early 1908, Asquith papers 11, fos 10–15, Churchill to Asquith, 14 March 1908. However, his proposals did not reach the cabinet until the end of the year, Cabinet papers 37/96/159, 'Unemployment insurance: labour exchanges', 30 November 1908.
39. Asquith papers 22, fo. 142, 'Memorandum on Taxation of Petrol used by Motor Cars', 24 March 1909; J. Harris, *Unemployment and Politics: a Study in English Social Policy, 1886–1914* (Oxford: Oxford University Press, 1972) pp. 340–6.
40. Churchill ed., *Churchill*, vol. 2, companion, part 2, pp. 895–8, Churchill to Lloyd George, 20 June 1909.
41. For Gladstone's financial strategy, see H. C. G. Matthew, *Gladstone, 1809–74* (Oxford: Oxford University Press, 1988) pp. 109–28.
42. Friedberg, *Weary Titan*, pp. 89–134.
43. Green, *Crisis of Conservatism*, pp. 248–53.
44. Friedberg, *Weary Titan*, p. 131.
45. Russell, *Liberal Landslide*, p. 65.
46. Matthew, *Gladstone*, p. 122.
47. Bodleian Library, Sir William Harcourt papers 122, fos 21–7, Memorial to Sir William Harcourt, 12 January 1894.
48. Sir William Harcourt papers 70, Harcourt to A. Milner, 10 March 1894.
49. *Hansard*, 4th series, 1894, xxiii, 469–509 for Harcourt's 1894 budget.
50. Harcourt had rejected the practicability of distinguishing between earned and unearned income for the purposes of income tax, Sir William Harcourt papers 69, fos 79–93, A. Milner, 'Note on differential income tax'. But the combination of a graduated death duty and abatements for small income tax payers achieved this ideal by a more circuitous route.

51. *Hansard*, 4th series, 1902, cix, 371–89.
52. Parliamentary Papers 1906 ix, Report from the Select Committee on Income Tax.
53. National Archives, Treasury papers T/171/3, Papers on Income Tax Reform, 26 March 1907.
54. Murray, *People's Budget*, pp. 44–5, 97.
55. *Hansard*, 5th series, 1909, iv, 472–548.
56. Cabinet papers 37/98, L. Harcourt, 'Income Super-Tax', 25 March 1909, on raising supertax in steps from the lowest threshold; Asquith papers 22, fo. 99, 'Finance Bill. Draft Clauses', 8 April 1909 on reducing estate duty at the lowest levels.
57. See the assessment in Murray, *People's Budget*, pp. 169–70.
58. Ibid., pp. 180–3.
59. For instance, *Westminster Gazette*, 25 October 1909 on the budget as 'a question of equity and good policy between various classes of the population'.
60. Blewett, *Peers, the Parties and the People*, p. 323. This argument was used by 60% of Liberal candidates.
61. Du Parcq ed., *Lloyd George*, vol. 4, p. 679 on Britain's position among the nations as 'probably the richest in the world, if not the richest the world has ever seen'.
62. *Hansard*, 5th series, 1909, iv, 548.
63. Blewett, *Peers, the Parties and the People*, p. 323.
64. This idea dates back to Hobson's *The Evolution of Modern Capitalism* (London: W. Scott, 1894). J. M. Robertson, Liberal MP for Tyneside 1906–18 had developed a similar concept in *The Fallacy of Saving* (London: Swan Sonnenschein, 1892).
65. For instance, George Harwood, *Hansard*, 5th series, 1909, xii, 1734–5.
66. Searle, 'Edwardian Liberal Party' on Lloyd George's admiration of business in this era.
67. An approach pioneered, once again, by Hobson in *The Social Problem: Life and Work* (London: J. Nisbet, 1902) pp. 8–16.
68. *Westminster Gazette*, 30 April 1909.
69. See, for instance, J. A. Hobson, 'The Taxation of Monopolies', *Independent Review*, 9 (1906) 20–33. The principle could be traced back to J. S. Mill. See the *Nation*, 27 April 1907, 27 July 1912 for fairly typical examples of arguments about taxation based on this idea.
70. National Archives, Inland Revenue papers 73/2, Lloyd George to Sir R. Chalmers, 5 September 1908, Chalmers to Lloyd George, 3 December 1908.
71. This complex process is explained in Murray, *People's Budget*, pp. 149–71.
72. Ibid., pp. 209–35; Du Parcq ed., *Lloyd George*, vol. 4, pp. 678–96 for the Limehouse and Newcastle speeches.
73. *Nation*, 21 June 1913 pointed out land was the most easily identifiable form of unearned increment and the simplest to tax.
74. Du Parcq ed. *Lloyd George*, vol. 4, pp. 682–3.
75. For the origins of the land taxation issue, see Packer, *Lloyd George, Liberalism and the Land*, pp. 28–30.
76. Ibid., pp. 54–7.
77. Murray, *People's Budget*, pp. 154–7, 168.
78. See Chapter 5.

79. *Hansard*, 5th series, 1909, iv, 773.
80. Murray, *People's Budget*, pp. 288–9.
81. A. Offer, 'Empire and Social Reform: British Overseas Investment and Domestic Politics, 1908–1914', *Historical Journal*, 26 (1983) 119–38; Bernstein, *Liberalism and Liberal Politics*, p. 100.
82. Murray, *People's Budget*, p. 168.
83. *Hansard*, 5th series, 1909, iv, 501–2.
84. Murray, *People's Budget*, pp. 293–5.
85. Ibid., pp. 148–71, 180–3; Blewett, *Peers, the Parties and the People*, pp. 215–18.
86. Rowland, *Last Liberal Governments*, vol. 2, pp. 27–35.
87. For instance, Lloyd George at Birmingham, 10 June 1911, Du Parcq ed., *Lloyd George*, vol. 4, pp. 776–91.
88. Murray, *People's Budget*, p. 293.
89. *Hansard*, 5th series, 1914, lxii, 56–94.
90. Lloyd George at Ipswich, *Daily Chronicle*, 23 May 1914.
91. Inland Revenue papers, 73/2, J. Wedgwood, 'Memorandum on the taxation of land values', n.d. [1909].
92. Packer, 'Liberal Cave and the 1914 Budget'.

7 Social Reform and Labour Relations

1. For some important summaries and contributions to this issue, see A. Sykes, *The Rise and Fall of British Liberalism, 1776–1988* (Harlow: Longman, 1997) pp. 153–76; Clarke, *Liberals and Social Democrats*; Freeden, *New Liberalism*; Bernstein, *Liberalism and Liberal Politics*; Emy, *Liberals, Radicals and Social Politics*; Searle, *Liberal Party*, pp. 84–104; Collini, *Liberalism and Sociology*; B. B. Gilbert, *The Evolution of National Insurance in Great Britain* (London: Michael Joseph, 1966); Harris, *Unemployment and Politics*; J. R. Hay, *The Origins of the Liberal Welfare Reforms, 1906–1914* (Basingstoke: Macmillan, 1975).
2. For important contributions to this debate, see Clarke, *Lancashire and the New Liberalism*; McKibbin, *Evolution of the Labour Party*; Tanner, *Political Change*.
3. This theory and its decline are well described in J. Harris, *Private Lives, Public Spirit: Britain, 1870–1914* (Oxford: Oxford University Press, 1993) pp. 180–219.
4. Clarke, *Liberals and Social Democrats*; Collini, *Liberalism and Sociology*; Freeden, *New Liberalism*.
5. L. T. Hobhouse, *Liberalism*, (London: Williams and Norgate, 1911) p. 85.
6. Ibid., p. 91.
7. Ibid., p. 146.
8. Keele University Library, Josiah Wedgwood papers, L. T. Hobhouse to J. Wedgwood, 5 December 1912.
9. Hobson, *Crisis of Liberalism*, p. 97.
10. Hobhouse, *Liberalism*, p. 158.
11. Ibid, p. 164.
12. The term New Liberalism was being widely used by the second half of the 1890s, Emy, *Liberals, Radicals and Social Politics*, p. 68.
13. Masterman, *Masterman*, pp. 26–46. Five Liberal MPs elected in 1906–14, four of whom at least reached the ranks of parliamentary private secretary, had

been residents of Toynbee Hall, J. A. R. Pimlott, *Toynbee Hall: Fifty Years of Social Progress, 1884–1934* (London: J. M. Dent & Sons, 1935) pp. 283–99.

14. E. W. Davies papers A/6, Davies diary, 31 October 1906.
15. Emy, *Liberals, Radicals and Social Politics*, pp. 185–7, 279.
16. Rosebery papers, 10171, fos 188–91, Rosebery to Allard, 21 November 1907.
17. D. Powell, 'The Liberal Ministries and Labour, 1892–1895', *History*, 68 (1983) 408–26.
18. P. T. Marsh, *Joseph Chamberlain: Entrepreneur in Politics* (New Haven, Ct: Yale University Press, 1994) pp. 326–31, 337–41, 349–61.
19. In 1895, 52% of Unionist election addresses mentioned pensions, making it the third most popular issue after home rule and disestablishment, Readman, '1895 General Election', 475.
20. Russell, *Liberal Landslide*, p. 71.
21. Jenkins, *Asquith*, pp. 165–7; J. Macnicol, *The Politics of Retirement in Britain, 1878–1948* (Cambridge: Cambridge University Press, 1998) pp. 155–7. The consistency of the cabinet's commitment to pensions from 1906 onwards is emphasised in Hay, *Liberal Welfare Reforms*, pp. 46–7.
22. Cabinet papers 37/92/54, 'Old Age Pensions, Report of the Cabinet Committee', April 1908.
23. *Hansard*, 4th series, 1908, clxxxviii, 471–5.
24. Murray, *People's Budget*, pp. 124–7.
25. P. Thane, 'The Working Class and State "Welfare" in Britain, 1880–1914', *Historical Journal*, 27 (1984) 877–900.
26. Green, *Crisis of Conservatism*, pp. 253–6; the official Tory position was that in the future a more generous, but contributory, pensions scheme should be introduced, Sir A. Chamberlain, *Politics from Inside: An Epistolary Chronicle, 1906–1914* (London: Cassell, 1936) p. 118, A. to M. E. Chamberlain, 4 June 1908.
27. *Hansard*, 4th series, 1908, cxc, 604.
28. Ibid., 584.
29. Blewett, *Peers, the Parties and the People*, p. 317.
30. Emy, *Liberals, Radicals and Social Politics*, pp. 148–9.
31. P. Thane, *The Foundations of the Welfare State* (Harlow: Longman, 1982) pp. 69, 75–6.
32. S. Blackburn, 'Ideology and Social Policy: the Origins of the Trade Boards Act', *Historical Journal*, 34 (1991) 43–64.
33. This case was made very strongly in B. and S. Webb, *Industrial Democracy*, 2 vols (London: Longman, 1897) vol. 2, pp. 748–74. *Nation*, 25 April 1914 for the concept of 'parasitic' industries.
34. Cabinet papers 37/98/42, W. Churchill, 'Trade boards bill', 12 March 1909.
35. Emy, *Liberals, Radicals and Social Politics*, pp. 55–8.
36. Russell, *Liberal Landslide*, p. 65.
37. R. Gregory, *The Miners and British Politics, 1906–1914* (London: Oxford University Press, 1968) pp. 8–13.
38. The issue is dealt with perceptively in Bernstein, *Liberalism and Liberal Politics*, pp. 101–4.
39. Gilbert, *National Insurance*, remains the best analysis of the legislation and its origins.

40. Lloyd George had made it clear when introducing old age pensions in 1908 that this was only a start in tackling poverty, *Hansard*, 4th series, 1908, cxc, 585.

41. See Chapter 6. Lloyd George seems to have been deeply impressed by what he saw of the German system of national insurance, *Daily News*, 27 August 1908.

42. Brown, *Labour and Unemployment*, pp. 141–63.

43. For instance in Lloyd George's budget speech of 29 April 1909, *Hansard*, 5th series, 1909, iv, 482–7.

44. *Hansard*, 5th series, 1911, xxvi, 757.

45. Green, *Crisis of Conservatism*, pp. 288–90.

46. Elibank papers 8814, A. C. Murray diary, 6 January 1912 for Lloyd George's hopes about national insurance.

47. Riddell, *More Pages*, p. 54, Riddell diary, 27 April 1912.

48. See Chapter 6.

49. E. H. Phelps Brown, *The Growth of British Industrial Relations: a Study from the Standpoint of 1906–14* (London: Macmillan, 1965) pp. 325–8.

50. E. W. Davies papers A/7, Davies diary, 12 March 1912.

51. *Hansard*, 5th series, 1912, xxxv, 1732.

52. Ibid., xxxv, 2185.

53. Bernstein, *Liberalism and Liberal Politics*, pp. 136–7. The cabinet was badly divided on whether to insert specific figures for the miners' minimum wage, see David ed., *Inside Asquith's Cabinet*, pp. 112–13, Hobhouse diary, 27 March 1912. But nobody opposed the need for some sort of intervention.

54. Riddell, *More Pages*, pp. 47–9, Riddell diary, 24 March 1912.

55. *Daily News*, 13 May 1912.

56. Packer, *Lloyd George, Liberalism and the Land*, pp. 16–17.

57. Ibid., pp. 7–9.

58. A. Warren, 'Gladstone, Land and Social Reconstruction in Ireland, 1881–1887', *Parliamentary History*, 2 (1983) 153–73; E. A. Cameron, *Land for the People?: The British Government and the Scottish Highlands, c. 1880–1925* (East Linton: Tuckwell Press, 1996).

59. Jenkins, *Gladstone, Whiggery and the Liberal Party*, pp. 198–229; D. Brooks ed., *The Destruction of Lord Rosebery: from the Diary of Sir Edward Hamilton* (London: Historians Press, 1986) pp. 104–5.

60. A. Adonis, 'Aristocracy, Agriculture and Liberalism: the Politics, Finances and Estates of the third Lord Carrington', *Historical Journal*, 31 (1988) 871–97.

61. Add MS 45922, fos 235–6, Herbert Gladstone papers, H. Samuel to H. Gladstone, 22 January 1910.

62. A. Briggs, *Social Thought and Social Action: a Study of the Work of Seebohm Rowntree, 1871–1954* (London: Longmans, 1961) pp. 64–7.

63. Land Enquiry Committee, *The Land*, 2 vols (London: Hodder & Stoughton, 1913) vol. 1.

64. Hobhouse noted of the cabinet's discussions, 'no one took much objection to any particular point' and 'it was much more that we debated details than that we differed on principles', Gainford papers 90, C. Hobhouse to J. Pease, 22 October 1913. For Liberal attitudes to the campaign, see Packer, *Lloyd George, Liberalism and the Land*, pp. 126–32.

65. Barker, *Gladstone and Radicalism*, p. 257 on Liberal performance in the boroughs in 1885.

66. Lloyd George papers C/2/1/9, Heath to Lloyd George, 17 August 1912.
67. Ibid., C/15/1/14, Memorial on Land and Taxation Reform, 18 May 1911, signed by 133 Liberal MPs.
68. J. Wedgwood, *Memoirs of a Fighting Life* (London: Hutchinson, 1940) p. 67.
69. Murray, *People's Budget*, pp. 296–8.
70. Elibank papers 8814, A.C. Murray diary, 21 November 1912.
71. Land Enquiry Committee, *The Land*, vol. 2.
72. Joseph Rowntree Foundation, B. S. Rowntree papers, 6(a), B. S. Rowntree to J. Rowntree, 30 February 1914.
73. Lloyd George papers C/1/1/18, E. Montagu to Lloyd George, 12 June 1914.
74. Biagini, *Liberalism, Retrenchment and Reform* convincingly describes why Gladstonian Liberalism was so appealing to many members of the working class.
75. J. Shepherd, 'Labour and Parliament: the Lib-Labs as the First Working-Class MPs, 1885–1906' in Biagini and Reid eds, *Currents of Radicalism*, pp. 187–213.
76. J. Shepherd, 'James Bryce and the Recruitment of Working-Class Magistrates in Lancashire, 1892–1894', *Bulletin of the Institute of Historical Research*, 52 (1979) 155–69; Searle, *Corruption in British Politics*, pp. 227–9.
77. Tanner, *Political Change and the Labour Party*, for the unending complexities of Liberal-Labour relations in this period.
78. F. Bealey, 'Negotiations between the Liberal Party and the Labour Representation Committee before the General Election of 1906', *Bulletin of the Institute of Historical Research*, 29 (1956) 261–74; R. McKibbin, 'James Ramsay MacDonald and the Problem of the Independence of the Labour Party, 1910–1914', *Journal of Modern History*, 42 (1970) 216–35.
79. Bernstein, *Liberalism and Liberal Politics*, pp. 64–77.
80. See for instance Elibank papers 8814, A. C. Murray diary, 27 August 1911 on the effects of the railway union's strike on the working class in Lancashire.
81. N. McCord, 'Taff Vale Revisited', *History*, 78 (1993) 243–60 for a lucid discussion of some of the very complex issues involved.
82. Russell, *Liberal Landslide*, p. 65.
83. As the Liberal attorney-general, Sir John Walton, put it in 1906, immunity from prosecution would 'give a sort of benefit of clergy to Trade Unions', *Hansard*, 4th series, 1906, cliv, 1307.
84. Asquith papers 92, fo. 9, Haldane, 'Trade Disputes Memorandum', April 1905.
85. J. Thompson, 'The Genesis of the 1906 Trade Disputes Act: Liberalism, Trade Unions and the Law', *Twentieth Century British History*, 9 (1998) 175–200.
86. *Hansard*, 4th series, 1906, clv, 51–4.
87. Ibid., 52.
88. Bernstein, *Liberalism and Liberal Politics*, pp. 130–4.
89. Phelps Brown, *Industrial Relations*, pp. 338–43.
90. For instance, Add MS 46038, fos 52–5, Herbert Gladstone papers, J. Henry to H. Gladstone, 26 August 1911, giving the views of West Leeds Liberals on the railway strike.
91. Alderman, *Railway Interest*, pp. 208–12.
92. Emy, *Liberals, Radicals and Social Politics*, pp. 257–62.

93. J. Morgan, *Conflict and Order: the Police and Labour Disputes in England and Wales, 1900–39* (Oxford: Clarendon Press, 1987) pp. 43–4.
94. A. M. O'Brien, 'Churchill and the Tonypandy Riots', *Welsh History Review*, 17 (1994) 67–99.
95. I. C. Fletcher, ' "Prosecutions . . . are always risky business": Labor, Liberals and the 1912 "Don't Shoot" Prosecutions', *Albion*, 28 (1996) 251–78.
96. Cabinet papers 37/110/62, Memorandum by S. Buxton, 13 April 1912.
97. Runciman papers 63, Crawshaw to Runciman, 17 January 1912.

8 Epilogue: A Liberal War?

1. 'Personally I know no better amusement than commanding a squadron on a good horse' reflected the Tory ex-cabinet minister, George Wyndham, J. W. Mackail and G. Wyndham, *Life and Letters of George Wyndham*, 2 vols (London: Hutchinson, 1925) vol. 2, p. 509, G. Wyndham to mother, 13 June 1905. In contrast, Asquith's response to the declaration of war was to reflect 'We are on the eve of horrible things', Brock and Brock eds, *Asquith Letters*, p. 151, Asquith to V. Stanley, 4 August 1914.
2. In January 1915 139 Tory MPs were serving in the armed forces, but only 41 Liberals. This reflected the much higher percentage of Conservatives who had prior military service or membership of the Territorial forces, C. Hazlehurst, *Politicians at War, July 1914 to May 1915: a Prologue to the Triumph of Lloyd George* (London: Jonathan Cape, 1971) p. 128; Ramsden, *Age of Balfour and Baldwin*, p. 98.
3. See Chapter 2.
4. This is one of the themes of T. Wilson, *The Downfall of the Liberal Party, 1914–35*, 2nd edn (Fontana, 1968) pp. 23–50.
5. Williams, *Defending the Empire*, pp. 197–8.
6. Robbins, *Grey*, pp. 260–3.
7. Wilson ed., *Scott Diaries*, p. 91, Scott diary, 27 July 1914.
8. Brock and Brock eds, *Asquith Letters*, p. 140, Asquith to V. Stanley, 1 August 1914.
9. Grey of Fallodon, *Twenty-Five Years, 1892–1916*, 2 vols (London: Hodder & Stoughton, 1925) vol. 1, pp. 314–22.
10. Gainford papers 39, Pease diary, 27 July 1914.
11. Brock and Brock eds, *Asquith Letters*, p. 140, Asquith to V. Stanley, 1 August 1914.
12. Hazlehurst, *Politicians at War*, pp. 60–5.
13. J. A. Spender and C. Asquith, *Life of Herbert Henry Asquith, Lord Oxford and Asquith*, 2 vols (London: Hutchinson, 1932) vol. 2, p. 81, Asquith to George V, 30 July 1914.
14. Ibid., 'Sir E. Grey should be authorised to inform the German and French Ambassadors that at this stage we were unable to pledge ourselves in advance, either under all conditions to stand aside, or in any conditions to join in.'
15. Brock and Brock eds, *Asquith Letters*, p. 146, Asquith to V. Stanley, 2 August 1914; Gainford papers 39, Pease diary, 2 August 1914.
16. Burns announced his resignation at the morning cabinet of 2 August and Morley on the morning of 3 August, Gainford papers 39, Pease diary, 2,

3 August 1914. Trevelyan's resignation was dismissed by Asquith as 'happily, *il n'y a pas d'homme necessaire*', Brock and Brock eds, *Asquith Letters*, p. 150, Asquith to V. Stanley, 4 August 1914.

17. Morley was 75 and had been in the cabinet as long ago as 1886; Burns was only 55, but his political career was in eclipse, Brown, *John Burns*, pp. 166–72. Neither declared their motivation to the cabinet or made a resignation statement in parliament, but both were hostile to 'entangling' continental commitments, Add MS 46337, Burns diary, 23 September 1915; Oxford and Asquith, *Memories and Reflections, 1852–1927*, 2 vols (London: Cassell, 1928) vol. 2, pp. 10–14, Morley to Asquith, 4 August 1914.

18. Brock and Brock eds, *Asquith Letters*, p. 150, Asquith to V. Stanley, 4 August 1914.

19. Harcourt to F. G. Thomas, 5 August 1914, quoted in Hazlehurst, *Politicians at War*, p. 114.

20. Grey of Fallodon, *Twenty-Five Years*, vol. 2, pp. 294–309 reprints Grey's speech.

21. Dutton ed., *Odyssey of an Edwardian Liberal*, p. 33, Holt diary, 2, 9 August 1914.

22. *Hansard*, 5th series, 1914, lxv, 2079.

23. Ibid., 4th series, 1907, clxxii, 1665 (Randal Cremer); 5th series, 1909, ii, 970 (Arnold Lupton).

24. B. Hollingsworth, 'The Society of Friends of Russian Freedom: English Liberals and Russian Socialists, 1890–1917', *Oxford Slavonic Papers*, 3 (1970) 45–64. For the views of two Liberal cabinet ministers who were far from hostile to Germany's culture and institutions before 1914, see Hamer, *John Morley*, pp. 360–9; and K. Morgan, 'Lloyd George and Germany', *Historical Journal*, 39 (1996) 755–66.

25. Wilson ed., *Scott Diaries*, pp. 98, Scott diary, 4 August 1914.

26. R. D. Holt referred to the loss of one ship to U-boat action as 'sheer brutal murder intended to terrorise the people of this country', Dutton ed., *Odyssey of an Edwardian Liberal*, p. 38, Holt diary, 4 April 1915.

27. K. G. Robbins, 'Lord Bryce and the First World War', *Historical Journal*, 10 (1967) 255–77.

28. Gainford papers 39, Pease diary, 1 March 1915.

29. MacCallum Scott papers 1465/5, Scott diary, 3 August 1914

30. See Oxford and Asquith, *Memories and Reflections*, vol. 2, pp. 38–9.

31. K. G. Robbins, *The Abolition of War: the 'Peace Movement' in Britain, 1914–1919* (Cardiff: University of Wales Press, 1976) p. 53.

32. FO 800/84, Grey papers Minute by Asquith, 23 September 1914.

33. Brock and Brock eds, *Asquith Letters*, p. 501, Asquith to V. Stanley, 23 March 1915; David ed., *Inside Asquith's Cabinet*, pp. 227–8, Hobhouse diary, 9 March 1915.

34. Cabinet papers 41/35/54, Asquith to George V, 20 October 1914.

35. Brock and Brock eds, *Asquith Letters*, pp. 477, 509–10, Asquith to V. Stanley, 13, 25 March 1915.

36. Bodleian Library, Oxford, Denman papers, 4(3), Minute Book, 6 August 1914. The maximum attendance at any meeting was 20 MPs, on 25 August 1914.

37. Ibid., 10 August 1914. Regular meetings stopped after only 4 MPs attended on 16 September and the last gathering was on 23 February 1915.

38. Packer ed., *Rowntree Letters*, p. 156, A. R. to M. K. Rowntree, 4 August 1914.

39. Jones, *Arthur Ponsonby*, pp. 90–122.

40. Packer ed., *Rowntree Letters*, pp. 18–19.
41. R. E. Dowse, 'The Entry of the Liberals into the Labour Party, 1910–20', *Yorkshire Bulletin of Economic and Social Research*, 13 (1961) 78–87; A. J. A. Morris, *C. P. Trevelyan: Portrait of a Radical* (Belfast: Blackstaff, 1977) pp. 128–30; Jones, *Arthur Ponsonby*, pp. 95–6, 113.
42. See Chapter 2.
43. These points are excellently summarised in G. R. Searle, *A New England?: Peace and War, 1886–1918* (Oxford: Clarendon Press, 2004) pp. 492–3.
44. For McKenna's defence of the navy's role in 1911, see Chapter 2; for Runciman and Harcourt's views, Runciman papers 63, Runciman to Harcourt, 24 August 1911.
45. D. French, *British Economic and Strategic Planning, 1905–15* (London: George Allen & Unwin, 1982) pp. 51–73.
46. Readman, 'Conservative Party', 142–5, the most reliable classification of Liberal MPs' views in the 1900 election, lists Runciman as a Liberal Imperialist; Harcourt shared his father, Sir William's, antipathy to Liberal Imperialism, A. G. Gardiner, *The Life of Sir William Harcourt*, 2 vols (London: Constable, 1923) vol. 2, pp. 524–5; McKenna had been Sir Charles Dilke's protégée, McKenna, *Reginald McKenna*, pp. 12–14 and Dilke had been studiously neutral between Liberal factions over the Boer war, R. Jenkins, *Sir Charles Dilke: a Victorian Tragedy*, 2nd edn (London: Macmillan, 1996) pp. 399–400.
47. Murray, *People's Budget*, pp. 72–3, 149; for Runciman's views see also M. Pugh, 'Yorkshire and the New Liberalism', *Journal of Modern History*, 50 (1978) D1139–55.
48. See Chapters 6–7.
49. French, *British Planning*, pp. 34–5.
50. Grey to Bertie, 1 August 1914, quoted in Hazlehurst, *Politicians at War*, p. 87.
51. Brock and Brock eds, *Asquith Letters*, pp. 157–8, Asquith to V. Stanley, 5, 6 August 1914.
52. Gainford papers 39, Pease diary, 28 August 1914.
53. For the sudden expansion of the state's role in early August 1914, see French, *British Planning*, pp. 88–95.
54. Ibid., pp. 152, 112, 113–18, 104.
55. Brock and Brock eds, *Asquith Letters*, p. 157, Asquith to V. Stanley, 5 August 1914.
56. Ibid., p. 158, Asquith to V. Stanley, 6 August 1914; Grey of Fallodon, *Twenty-Five Years*, vol. 2, pp. 68–9.
57. See French, *British Planning*, pp. 132, 99, 162–3.
58. Cabinet papers 37/124/40, Lloyd George, 'Some further considerations on the conduct of the war', 22 February 1915.
59. For instance, Dutton ed., *Odyssey of an Edwardian Liberal*, p. 37, Holt diary, 26 January 1915.
60. French, *British Planning*, p. 110.
61. Brock and Brock eds, *Asquith Letters*, p. 198, Asquith to V. Stanley, 26 August 1914; Grey of Fallodon, *Twenty-Five Years*, pp. 69–70.
62. David ed., *Inside Asquith's Cabinet*, pp. 184–5, Hobhouse diary, 25 August 1914; Gainford papers 39, Pease diary, 25 August 1914.
63. Adams and Poirier, *Conscription Controversy*, pp. 69–70.
64. Hazlehurst, *Politicians at War*, pp. 265–6.

65. French, *British Planning*, pp. 75–6.
66. C. Andrew, *Secret Service: the Making of the British Intelligence Community* (London: Heinemann, 1985) pp. 60–1, 63–4. However, the pre-war MI5 was scarcely an intimidating organisation, as its entire staff amounted to the Director, four assistants and seven clerks, ibid., p. 73.
67. As Churchill said when arguing for conscription, 'Germany if victorious would annex us politically, and if defeated would depart with her system of militarism into limbo', David ed., *Inside Asquith's Cabinet*, Hobhouse diary, 25 August 1914.
68. For the government's relaxed approach to domestic subversion in the early years of the war, see Andrew, *Secret Service*, pp. 192–3.
69. As, for instance, displayed in the Liberals' opposition to the 1905 Aliens Act and their tolerant attitude to its operation, J. A. Garrard, *The English and Immigration, 1880–1910* (London: Oxford University Press, 1971) pp. 85–153.
70. D. French, 'Spy-Fever in Britain, 1900–15', *Historical Journal*, 21 (1978) 355–70.
71. Add MS 49703, fo. 116, Balfour papers, Hankey to Balfour, 8 December 1914.
72. C. Clifford, *The Asquiths* (London: John Murray, 2002) p. 230.
73. Brock and Brock eds, *Asquith Letters*, pp. 292–3 deals with this issue judiciously. However, Margot Asquith was reported to be 'very strung up altogether' by reports of the Asquiths' pro-Germanism, including the allegation that she had played tennis with German prisoners of war, Lady Cynthia Asquith, *Diaries, 1915–18* (London: Hutchinson, 1968) p. 35, C. Asquith diary, 1 June 1915.
74. A meeting between Carson and Redmond on 5 August 1914 was a complete failure, Gainford papers 39, Pease diary 6 August 1914.
75. Brock and Brock eds, *Asquith Letters*, pp. 187–8, Asquith to V. Stanley, 22 August 1914.
76. Ibid, p. 163, Asquith to V. Stanley, 10 August 1914.
77. Points made forcefully in Lloyd George papers C6/10/10, Runciman to Illingworth, 19 August 1914.
78. Brock and Brock eds, *Asquith Letters*, pp. 198, 228, Asquith to V. Stanley, 26 August, 9 September 1914.
79. Morgan, *Rebirth of a Nation*, pp. 171–2.
80. *The Times*, 21 September 1914.
81. Gainford papers 39, Pease diary, 28, 30 October 1914; A. J. P. Taylor ed. *Lloyd George: a Diary by Frances Stevenson* (London: Hutchinson, 1971) pp. 7–9, F. Stevenson diary, 30 October, 2 November 1914.
82. P. Bew, *Ideology and the Irish Question: Ulster Unionism and Irish Nationalism, 1912–1916* (Oxford: Clarendon Press, 1994) pp. 135–7.
83. *Hansard*, 5th series, 1914, lxvi, 201–18.
84. *The Times*, 1 March 1915; the speech is best read in the context of Cabinet papers 37/124/40, Lloyd George, 'Some further considerations on the conduct of the war', 22 February 1915.
85. This case is argued convincingly in J. Turner, 'State Purchase of the Liquor Trade in the First World War', *Historical Journal*, 23 (1980) 589–615.
86. P. Williamson ed., *The Modernisation of Conservative Politics: The Diaries of William Bridgeman, 1904–35* (London: Historian's Press, 1987) p. 86, Bridgeman diary, June 1915.
87. Brock and Brock eds, *Asquith Letters*, p. 536, Asquith to V. Stanley, 8 April 1915.
88. Austen Chamberlain papers 13/3/39, Bonar Law to A. Chamberlain, 2 April 1915.

89. Brock and Brock eds, *Asquith Letters*, p. 525, Asquith to V. Stanley, 31 March 1915.
90. Ibid., pp. 552–3, 563, 567, Asquith to V. Stanley, 19, 22, 23 April 1915.
91. *Hansard*, 5th series, 1914, lxxi 864–96.
92. Brock and Brock eds, *Asquith Letters*, p. 582, Asquith to V. Stanley, 3 May 1915.
93. Add MS 49693, fos 192–3, Balfour papers, Long to Balfour, 27 January 1915.
94. Williamson ed, *Conservative Politics*, pp. 83–4, Bridgeman diary, May 1915.
95. McKenna was vilified because as Home Secretary he had not done more to intern enemy aliens; Haldane because of his well-known sympathies with German culture, Sommer, *Haldane of Cloan*, pp. 317–22. It was perhaps unfortunate that Haldane had called his St Bernard 'Kaiser', ibid., p. 384.
96. There is a huge amount of historical writing on these events, see in particular M. Pugh, 'Asquith, Bonar Law and the First Coalition', *Historical Journal*, 17 (1974) 813–36.
97. One contemporary account of these events is Austen Chamberlain papers, 2/2/25, Memorandum, 17 May 1915.
98. *Daily News*, 20 May 1915.
99. This view is summarised in Hazlehurst, *Politicians at War*, p. 264.
100. R. J. Q. Adams, *Arms and the Wizard: Lloyd George and the Ministry of Munitions, 1915–1916* (London: Cassell, 1978) pp. 16–27.
101. Austen Chamberlain papers 2/2/25, Memorandum, 17 May 1915.
102. Note the letter from Bonar Law to Asquith, 17 May 1915, reproduced in Oxford and Asquith, *Memories and Reflections*, vol. 2, p. 96.
103. R. J. Q. Adams, *Bonar Law* (London: John Murray, 1999) pp. 186–7.
104. Oxford and Asquith, *Memories and Reflections*, vol. 2, pp. 95–6, Asquith to cabinet, 17 May 1915.
105. Ibid.
106. A. F. Cooper, *British Agricultural Policy, 1912–36: a Study in Conservative Politics* (Manchester: Manchester University Press, 1989) pp. 28–37.
107. Asquith noted 'Winston, who has got on all his war-paint, is longing for a sea-fight in the early hours of to-morrow morning, resulting in the sinking of the *Goeben*. The whole thing fills me with sadness.', Brock and Brock eds, *Asquith Letters*, pp. 150–1, Asquith to V. Stanley, 4 August 1914.
108. G. Riddell, *Lord Riddell's War Diary, 1914–1918* (London: Ivor Nicholson & Watson, 1933), p. 12, Riddell diary, 9 August 1914.

Bibliography

Primary sources

Allard, W. papers (University of Birmingham Library).
Asquith, H. H. papers (Bodleian Library, Oxford).
Asquith, Margot papers (Bodleian Library, Oxford).
Balfour, A. papers (British Library).
Burns, J. papers (British Library).
Cabinet papers (National Archives).
Campbell-Bannerman, Sir H. papers (British Library).
Chamberlain, Austen papers (University of Birmingham Library).
Chamberlain, Joseph papers (University of Birmingham Library).
Chester Liberal Party (Cheshire and Chester Archives).
Cobden papers (West Sussex Record Office).
Davies, E. W. papers (National Library of Wales).
Denman, R. papers (Bodleian Library, Oxford).
Dickinson, W. H. papers (Gloucestershire Record Office).
Dumbartonshire Liberal Association (National Library of Scotland).
Edinburgh, South Liberal Association (National Library of Scotland).
Education papers (National Archives).
Elibank papers (National Library of Scotland).
Foreign Office papers (National Archives).
Gainford papers (Nuffield College Library, Oxford).
Gladstone, Herbert papers (British Library).
Grey, Sir E. papers (National Archives).
Haldane, R. papers (National Library of Scotland).
Harcourt, Sir W. and L. papers (Bodleian Library, Oxford).
Hill, Sir Francis papers (Lincolnshire Archives).
Inland Revenue papers (National Archives).
Kinross Liberal Association (National Library of Scotland).
Law, A. Bonar papers (House of Lords Record Office).
Leeds Liberal Federation (West Yorkshire Archive Service).
Lewis, J. H. papers (National Library of Wales).
Lincolnshire Liberal Association (Lincolnshire Archives).
Lloyd George, D. papers (House of Lords Record Office)
MacDonnell, Sir A papers (Bodleian Library, Oxford).
McKenna, R. papers (Churchill College Library, Cambridge).
Muirhead, Roland papers (National Library of Scotland).
Ponsonby, A. papers (Bodleian Library, Oxford).
Portsmouth, Earl of papers (Hampshire Record Office).
Ripon, Marquess of papers (British Library).
Rosebery, Earl of papers (National Library of Scotland).
Rowntree, B. S. papers (Joseph Rowntree Foundation).
Runciman, W. papers (University of Newcastle Library).

Samuel, H. papers (House of Lords Record Office).
Sandars, J. papers (Bodleian Library, Oxford).
Society of Certificated and Associated Liberal Agents papers (West Yorkshire Archive Service).
Spender, J. A. papers (British Library).
Steel-Maitland, Sir A. papers (National Archives of Scotland).
Treasury papers (National Archives).
Wedgwood, J. papers (Keele University Library).
Welsh National Liberal Council papers (University College of North Wales, Bangor, Library).
Yorkshire Liberal Federation (West Yorkshire Archive Service).

Primary printed sources

Parliamentary Debates (Commons and Lords) 4th and 5th series
Royal Commission on the Licensing Laws (1896–9), C. 9379.
Royal Commission on Duties of the Metropolitan Police (1906–8), C. 4156.
Royal Commission on Canals and Inland Navigation of the United Kingdom (1906–9), C. 4979.
Royal Commission on Systems of Election (1908–10), Cd. 5613.
Royal Commission on Venereal Diseases (1913–16), Cd. 8189.

Newspapers

Brixton Free Press
Christian World
Daily News
Land Values
Liberal Agent
Liberal Magazine
Manchester Guardian
Nation (formerly *The Speaker*)
Quarterly Review
The Scotsman
The Times
Westminster Gazette

Unpublished thesis

Hancock, J. W., 'The Anatomy of the British Liberal Party, 1908–18: a Study of its Character and Disintegration' (University of Cambridge PhD, 1992).

Printed books and articles

Adams, R. J. Q., *Arms and the Wizard: Lloyd George and the Ministry of Munitions, 1915–1916* (London: Cassell, 1978).

——, *Bonar Law* (London: John Murray, 1999).

—— and Poirier, P., *The Conscription Controversy in Great Britain, 1900–18* (London: Macmillan, 1987).

Adonis, A., 'Aristocracy, Agriculture and Liberalism: the Politics, Finances and Estates of the Third Lord Carrington', *Historical Journal*, 31 (1988) 871–97.

——, *Making Aristocracy Work: the Peerage and the Political System in Britain, 1884–1914* (Oxford: Clarendon Press, 1993).

al-Sayyid-Marsot, A. L., 'The British Occupation of Egypt from 1882' in A. Porter ed., *The Oxford History of the British Empire*, 5 vols (Oxford: Oxford University Press, 1999) vol. 3, pp. 651–64.

Alderman, G., *The Railway Interest* (Leicester: Leicester University Press, 1973).

Andrew, C., *Secret Service: the Making of the British Intelligence Community* (London: Heinemann, 1985).

Asquith, Cynthia, Lady, *Diaries, 1915–18* (London: Hutchinson, 1968).

Bailey, V., and Blackburn, S., 'The Punishment of Incest Act, 1908: a Case Study of Criminal Law Creation', *Criminal Law Review* (November 1979) 708–18.

Baker, E. B., and Noel-Baker, P. J., *J. Allen Baker* (London: Swarthmore Press, 1927).

Barclay, T., Sir, *Thirty Years: Anglo-French Reminiscences, 1876–1906* (London: Constable, 1914).

Barker, M., *Gladstone and Radicalism: the Reconstruction of Liberal Policy in Britain, 1885–94* (Hassocks: Harvester, 1975).

Bateman, J., *The Great Landowners of Great Britain and Ireland* (Leicester: Leicester University Press, 1971).

Bealey, F., 'Negotiations between the Liberal Party and the Labour Representation Committee before the General Election of 1906', *Bulletin of the Institute of Historical Research*, 29 (1956) 261–74.

Bebbington, D. W., *The Nonconformist Conscience: Chapel and Politics, 1870–1914* (London: George Allen & Unwin, 1982).

——, 'Nonconformity and Electoral Sociology, 1867–1918', *Historical Journal* 27 (1984), 633–56.

Bernstein, G., *Liberalism and Liberal Politics in Edwardian England* (London: Allen & Unwin, 1986).

Berrington, H., 'Partisanship and Dissidence in the Nineteenth-Century House of Commons', *Parliamentary Affairs*, 21 (1968) 338–74.

Bew, P., *Conflict and Conciliation in Ireland, 1890–1910* (Oxford: Clarendon Press, 1987).

——, *Ideology and the Irish Question: Ulster Unionism and Irish Nationalism, 1912–1916* (Oxford: Clarendon Press, 1994).

Biagini, E., *Liberty, Retrenchment and Reform: Popular Liberalism in the Age of Gladstone, 1860–80* (Cambridge: Cambridge University Press, 1992).

Binfield, C., 'Asquith: the Formation of a Prime Minister', *Journal of the United Reformed Church History Society*, 2 (1981) 204–42.

Birkenhead, Earl of, *Halifax: the Life of Lord Halifax* (London: Hamish Hamilton, 1965).

Birrell, A., *Things Past Redress* (London: Faber and Faber, 1937).

Blackburn, S., 'Ideology and Social Policy: the Origins of the Trade Boards Act', *Historical Journal*, 34 (1991) 43–64.

Blewett, N., *The Peers, the Parties and the People: the British General Elections of 1910* (London: Macmillan, 1972).

Blunt, W. S., *My Diaries: Being a Personal Narrative of Events, 1888–1914*, 2 vols (London: Martin Secker, 1919–1920).

Bond, B., *The Victorian Army and the Staff College, 1854–1918* (London: Eyre Methuen, 1972).

Brett, M. V., and Esher, Viscount (eds), *Journals and Letters of Reginald, Viscount Esher*, 4 vols (London: Ivor Nicholson & Watson, 1938).

Briggs, A., *Social Thought and Social Action: a Study of the Work of Seebohm Rowntree, 1871–1954* (London: Longmans, 1961).

Bristow, E. J., *Vice and Vigilance: Purity Movements in Britain since 1700* (Dublin: Gill & Macmillan, 1977).

Brock, M., and Brock, E. (eds), *H. H. Asquith: Letters to Venetia Stanley* (Oxford: Oxford University Press, 1985)

Brooks, D. (ed.), *The Destruction of Lord Rosebery: from the Diary of Sir Edward Hamilton* (London: Historians Press, 1986).

Brown, C., *The Death of Christian Britain: Understanding Secularization, 1800–2000* (London: Routledge, 2001).

Brown, K., *Labour and Unemployment, 1900–14* (Newton Abbot: David & Charles, 1971).

——, *John Burns* (London: Royal Historical Society, 1977).

Butler, D., and Stokes, D., *Political Change in Britain: Forces Shaping Electoral Choice* (London: Macmillan, 1969).

——, and Sloman, A. (eds), *British Political Facts, 1900–79* (London: Macmillan, 1980).

Cameron, E. A., *Land for the People? The British Government and the Scottish Highlands, c. 1880–1925* (East Linton: Tuckwell Press, 1996).

Cannadine, D., *The Decline and Fall of the British Aristocracy* (New Haven, Ct: Yale University Press, 1990).

——, *G. M. Trevelyan: a Life in History* (London: Fontana, 1993).

Cassar, G. H., *Asquith as War Leader* (London: Hambledon Press, 1994).

Chamberlain, Sir A., *Down the Years* (London: Cassell, 1935).

——, *Politics from Inside: an Epistolary Chronicle, 1906–1914* (London: Cassell, 1936).

Churchill, R. and Gilbert, M., *Winston S. Churchill*, 8 vols (London: Heinemann, 1966–88).

Churchill, S., *Betting and Gambling* (London: J. Nisbet, 1893).

Clarke, P., *Lancashire and the New Liberalism* (Cambridge: Cambridge University Press, 1971).

——, 'Electoral Sociology of Modern Britain', *History*, 57 (1972) 31–55.

——, *Liberals and Social Democrats* (Cambridge: Cambridge University Press, 1978).

Clifford, C., *The Asquiths* (London: John Murray, 2002).

Cline, C., *E. D. Morel, 1873–1924: the Strategies of Protest* (Belfast: Blackstaff Press, 1980).

Cobden Club, *The Burden of Armaments: a Plea for Retrenchment* (London: Fisher Unwin, 1905).

Collini, S., *Liberalism and Sociology: L. T. Hobhouse and Political Argument in England, 1880–1914* (Cambridge: Cambridge University Press, 1979).

Colvin, I. and Majoribanks, E., *The Life of Lord Carson*, 3 vols (London: Victor Gollancz, 1932–6).

Cooke, A. B., and Vincent, J., *The Governing Passion: Cabinet Government and Party Politics in Britain, 1885–86* (Brighton: Harvester, 1974).

Cooper, A. F., *British Agricultural Policy, 1912–36: a Study in Conservative Politics* (Manchester: Manchester University Press, 1989).

Craig, F., *British Parliamentary Election Results, 1885–1918* (London: Macmillan, 1974).

Crewe, Marquess of, *Lord Rosebery*, 2 vols (London: John Murray, 1931).

Cross, J. A., *Sir Samuel Hoare: a Political Biography* (London: Jonathan Cape, 1977).

Dangerfield, G., *The Strange Death of Liberal England*, 2nd edn (London: Granada, 1970).

Das, M. N., *India under Morley and Minto* (London: George Allen & Unwin, 1964).

David, E. (ed.), *Inside Asquith's Cabinet: from the Diaries of Charles Hobhouse* (London: John Murray, 1977).

Dewey, C., 'Celtic Agrarian Legislation and the Celtic Revival: Historicist Implications of Gladstone's Irish and Scottish Land Acts, 1870–1886', *Past and Present*, 64 (1974) 30–70.

Diamond, M., 'Political Heroes of the Victorian Music Hall', *History Today*, 40 (January 1990) 33–9.

Dixon, D., *From Prohibition to Regulation: Bookmaking, Anti-Gambling and the Law* (Oxford: Clarendon Press, 1991).

Dowse, R. E., 'The Entry of the Liberals into the Labour Party, 1910–20', *Yorkshire Bulletin of Economic and Social Research*, 13 (1961) 78–87.

Doyle, B., 'Temperance and Modernity: the Impact of Local Experience on Rank and File Liberal Attitudes to Alcohol', *Journal of Regional and Local Studies*, 16 (1996) 1–10.

Du Parcq, H. (ed.), *Life of David Lloyd George*, 4 vols (London: Caxton, 1912–13).

Dutton, D., *Simon: a Political Biography of Sir John Simon* (London: Aurum Press, 1992).

—— (ed.), *Odyssey of an Edwardian Liberal: the Political Diary of Richard Durning Holt* (Gloucester: Alan Sutton, 1989).

Emy, H. V., *Liberals, Radicals and Social Politics, 1892–1914* (Cambridge: Cambridge University Press, 1973).

Fahey, D. M., 'The Politics of Drink: Pressure Groups and the British Liberal Party, 1883–1908', *Social Science*, 54 (1979) 76–85.

Fair, J. D., *British Interparty Conferences: a Study of the Procedure of Conciliation in British Politics, 1867–1921* (Oxford: Clarendon Press, 1980).

Fanning, R., 'The Irish Policy of Asquith's Government and the Cabinet Crisis of 1910', in A. Cosgrove and D. McCartney eds, *Studies in Irish History: Presented to R. Dudley Edwards* (Dublin: University College, 1979) pp. 279–303.

Fforde, M., *Conservatism and Collectivism, 1886–1914* (Edinburgh: Edinburgh University Press, 1990).

Finlay, R. J., *A Partnership for Good? Scottish Politics and the Union since 1880* (Edinburgh: John Donald, 1997).

Fitzroy, A., Sir, *Memoirs*, 2 vols (London: Hutchinson & Co., 1925).

Fletcher, I. C., ' "Prosecutions . . . are always risky business": Labor, Liberals and the 1912 "Don't Shoot" Prosecutions', *Albion*, 28 (1996) 251–78.

Freeden, M., *The New Liberalism: An Ideology of Social Reform* (Oxford: Clarendon Press, 1978).

French, D., 'Spy-Fever in Britain, 1900–15', *Historical Journal*, 21 (1978) 355–70.

——, *British Economic and Strategic Planning, 1905–15* (London: George Allen & Unwin, 1982).

Friedberg, A. L., *The Weary Titan: Britain and the Experience of Relative Decline, 1895–1905* (Princeton, NJ: Princeton University Press, 1988).

Gardiner, A. G., *Prophets, Priests and Kings*, 2nd edn (London: J. M. Dent, 1914).
——, *The Life of Sir William Harcourt*, 2 vols (London: Constable, 1923).
Garrard, J. A., *The English and Immigration, 1880–1910* (London: Oxford University Press, 1971).
George, W., *My Brother and I* (London: Eyre & Spottiswoode, 1958).
Gilbert, B. B., *The Evolution of National Insurance in Great Britain* (London: Michael Joseph, 1966).
——, 'David Lloyd George and the Great Marconi Scandal', *Historical Research*, 62 (1989) 295–317.
Gladstone, W. E., *Female Suffrage: a Letter from the Rt Hon. W. E. Gladstone M. P., to Samuel Smith M. P.* (London: John Murray, 1892).
Gliddon, P., 'Politics for Better or Worse: Political Nonconformity, the Gambling Dilemma and the North of England Newspaper Company, 1903–14', *History*, 87 (2002) 227–44.
Gordon, D. C., *The Dominion Partnership in Imperial Defence, 1870–1914* (Baltimore: Johns Hopkins Press, 1965).
Gordon, P. (ed.), *The Red Earl: the Papers of the Fifth Earl Spencer, 1835–1910*, 2 vols (Northampton: Northamptonshire Record Society, 1981–6).
Green, E. H. H., *The Crisis of Conservatism: the Politics, Economics and Ideology of the British Conservative Party, 1880–1914* (London: Routledge, 1995).
——, 'The Political Economy of Empire, 1880–1914' in A. Porter ed., *The Oxford History of the British Empire*, 5 vols (Oxford: Oxford University Press, 1999), vol. 3, pp. 346–68.
——, *Ideologies of Conservatism: Conservative Political Ideas in the Twentieth Century* (Oxford: Oxford University Press, 2002).
Gregory, R., *The Miners and British Politics, 1906–14* (London: Oxford University Press, 1968).
Grey of Fallodon, Viscount, *Twenty-Five Years, 1892–1916*, 2 vols (London: Hodder & Stoughton, 1925).
Gutzke, D. W., 'Rosebery and Ireland, 1898–1903: a Reappraisal', *Bulletin of the Institute of Historical Research*, 53 (1980) 88–98.
——, *Protecting the Pub: Brewers and Publicans against Temperance* (Woodbridge: Royal Historical Society/Boydell & Brewer, 1989).
Gwynn, D., *The Life of John Redmond* (London: G. G. Harrap, 1932).
Haldane, R., *Autobiography* (London: Hodder & Stoughton, 1929).
Hamer, D. A., *John Morley: Liberal Intellectual in Politics* (Oxford: Clarendon Press, 1968).
——, *Liberal Politics in the Age of Gladstone and Rosebery: a Study in Leadership and Policy* (Oxford: Clarendon Press, 1972).
Hammond, J. L., *Gladstone and the Irish Nation* (London: Longmans, 1938).
Harris, J., *Unemployment and Politics: a Study in English Social Policy, 1886–1914* (Oxford: Oxford University Press, 1972).
——, *Private Lives, Public Spirit: Britain, 1870–1914* (Oxford: Oxford University Press, 1993).
Harrison, B., *Separate Spheres: the Opposition to Women's Suffrage in Britain* (London: Croom Helm, 1978).
Hawkins, A., and Powell, J. (eds), *The Journal of John Wodehouse, First Earl of Kimberley for 1862–1902* (Cambridge: Cambridge University Press/Royal Historical Society, 1997).

Hay, J. R., *The Origins of the Liberal Welfare Reforms, 1906–1914* (Basingstoke: Macmillan, 1975).

Hazlehurst, C., 'Asquith as Prime Minister, 1908–16', *English Historical Review*, 85 (1970) 502–31.

——, *Politicians at War, July 1914 to May 1915: a Prologue to the Triumph of Lloyd George* (London: Jonathan Cape, 1971).

——, and Woodland, C. (eds), *A Liberal Chronicle: Journals and Papers of J. A. Pease, 1st Lord Gainford, 1908–10* (London: Historians Press, 1994).

Henley, D., *Rosalind Howard, Countess of Carlisle* (London: Hogarth Press, 1958).

Hind, R. J., *Henry Labouchere and the Empire, 1880–1905* (London: Athlone Press, 1972).

Hirshfield, C., 'Fractured Faith: Liberal Party Women and the Suffrage Issue in Britain, 1892–1914', *Gender and History*, 2 (1990) 173–97.

Hobhouse, L. T., *Democracy and Reaction* (London: Fisher Unwin, 1904).

——, *Liberalism* (London: Williams & Norgate, 1911).

——, 'Irish Nationalism and Liberal Principle' in J. H. Morgan ed., *The New Irish Constitution: an Exposition and Some Arguments* (London: Hodder and Stoughton, 1912).

Hobson, J. A., *The Evolution of Modern Capitalism* (London: W. Scott, 1894).

——, 'A Living Wage', *Commonwealth*, 1 (1896) 128–67.

——, *The Psychology of Jingoism* (London: G. Richards, 1901).

——, *Imperialism: a Study* (London: J. Nisbet, 1902).

——, *The Social Problem: Life and Work* (London: J. Nisbet, 1902).

——, 'The Taxation of Monopolies', *Independent Review*, 9 (1906) 20–33.

——, *The Crisis of Liberalism: New Issues of Democracy* (London: P. S. King & Son, 1909).

Hollingsworth, B., 'The Society of Friends of Russian Freedom: English Liberals and Russian Socialists, 1890–1917', *Oxford Slavonic Papers*, 3 (1970) 45–64.

Hollis, P., *Ladies Elect: Women in English Local Government, 1865–1914* (Oxford: Clarendon Press, 1987).

Hopkins, A. G.,'The Victorians and Africa: a Reconsideration of the Occupation of Egypt, 1882', *Journal of African History*, 27 (1986) 363–91.

Hosking, G., and King, A., 'Radicals and Whigs in the British Liberal Party, 1906–14' in W. Aydelotte ed., *The History of Parliamentary Behaviour* (Princeton, NJ: Princeton University Press, 1977), pp. 136–58.

Howe, A., *Free Trade and Liberal England, 1846–1946* (Oxford: Clarendon Press, 1997).

Hyam, R., *Elgin and Churchill at the Colonial Office, 1905–8* (London: Macmillan, 1968).

——, 'The Colonial Office mind, 1900–14', *Journal of Imperial and Commonwealth History*, 8 (1979) 30–55.

Jacobson, P. D., 'Rosebery and Liberal Imperialism, 1899–1903', *Journal of British Studies*, 13 (1973) 83–107.

Jalland, P., *The Liberals and Ireland: the Ulster Question in British Politics to 1914* (Hassocks: Harvester Press, 1980).

——, 'Irish Home-Rule Finance: a Neglected Dimension of the Irish Question, 1910–14', *Irish Historical Studies*, 23 (1983) 233–53.

James, R. R., *Rosebery* (London: Phoenix, 1995).

Jenkins, R., *Asquith* (London: Collins, 1964).

——, *Sir Charles Dilke: a Victorian Tragedy*, 2nd edn (London: Macmillan, 1996).

Jenkins, T. A., *Gladstone, Whiggery and the Liberal Party, 1874–86* (Oxford: Clarendon Press, 1988).

——, *The Liberal Ascendancy, 1830–86* (Basingstoke: Macmillan, 1994).

Jolly, W. P., *Lord Leverhulme: a Biography* (London: Constable, 1976).

Jones, J. G., 'Alfred Thomas's National Institutions (Wales) Bills of 1891–2', *Welsh History Review*, 15 (1990) 218–39.

——, 'The Litterateur as Politician: Owen M. Edwards M. P.', *Welsh History Review*, 17 (1995) 571–89.

Jones, R. A., *Arthur Ponsonby: the Politics of Life* (Bromley: Christopher Helm, 1989).

Jordan, G. H. S.,'Pensions not Dreadnoughts: the Radicals and Naval Retrenchment' in A. J. A. Morris ed., *Edwardian Radicalism, 1900–1914* (London: Routledge & Kegan Paul, 1974) pp. 162–79.

Kaminsky, A. P., *The India Office, 1880–1910* (London: Mansell, 1986).

Kellas, J. G., 'The Liberal Party and the Scottish Church Disestablishment Crisis' *English Historical Review*, 79 (1964) 31–46.

Kendle, J. E., *The Colonial and Imperial Conferences, 1887–1911* (London: Longmans, 1967).

——, 'The Round Table Movement and "Home Rule All Round"', *Historical Journal*, 11 (1968) 332–53.

Kent, M., 'Constantinople and Asiatic Turkey, 1905–14' in F. H. Hinsley ed., *British Foreign Policy under Sir Edward Grey* (Cambridge: Cambridge University Press, 1977), pp.148–64.

King, W. M., 'Hugh Price Hughes and the British Social Gospel', *Journal of Religious History,* 13 (June 1984), 66–82.

Kinnear, M., *The British Voter: an Atlas and Survey since 1885*, 2nd edn (London: Batsford Academic, 1981).

Koss, S., *John Morley at the India Office, 1905–10* (New Haven, Ct: Yale University Prees, 1969).

——, *Sir John Brunner: Radical Plutocrat, 1842–1919* (Cambridge: Cambridge University Press, 1970).

——, *Fleet Street Radical: A. G. Gardiner and the Daily News* (London: Allen Lane, 1973).

Land Enquiry Committee, *The Land*, 2 vols (London: Hodder & Stoughton, 1913–14).

Langhorne, R. T. B., 'Anglo-German Negotiations concerning the Future of the Portuguese Colonies 1911–14, *Historical Journal*, 16 (1973) 361–87.

Lecky, W. E. H., *Democracy and Liberty*, 2 vols (London: Longmans, 1896).

Lee, A. J., *The Origins of the Popular Press in England, 1855–1914* (London: Croom Helm, 1976).

Liberal Publication Department, 'A Word to the Women', leaflet 2027, *Pamphlets and Leaflets*, 1905.

——, *Liberal Year Book, 1914*

Lloyd, T., 'The Whip as Paymaster: Herbert Gladstone and Party Organization', *English Historical Review*, 89 (1974) 785–813.

Lloyd George, D., *War Memoirs*, 2nd edn, 2 vols (London: Odhams, 1938).

Low, S., *The Governance of England*, 2nd edn (London: Fisher Unwin, 1914).

Lubenow, W. C., 'Irish Home Rule and the Great Separation in the Liberal Party in 1886: the Dimensions of Parliamentary Liberalism', *Victorian Studies*, 26 (1982–3) 161–80.

——, *Parliamentary Politics and the Home Rule Crisis: the British House of Commons in 1886* (Oxford: Clarendon Press, 1988).

Lynch, P., *The Liberal Party in Rural England, 1885–1910: Radicalism and Community* (Oxford: Clarendon Press, 2003).

Lyons, F. S. L., 'The Irish Unionist Party and the Devolution Crisis of 1904–5', *Irish Historical Studies*, 6 (1948) 1–21.

MacDonald, R., 'Gambling and Citizenship' in B. S. Rowntree ed., *Betting and Gambling: a National Evil* (London: Macmillan, 1905) pp. 117–34.

Machin, G. I. T., *Politics and the Churches in Great Britain, 1869 to 1921* (Oxford: Clarendon Press, 1987).

——, 'Lloyd George and Nonconformity' in J. Loades ed., *The Life and Times of David Lloyd George* (Bangor: Headstart, 1991) pp. 33–48.

Mackail, J. W., and Wyndham, G., *Life and Letters of George Wyndham*, 2 vols (London: Hutchinson, 1925).

Macnicol, J., *The Politics of Retirement in Britain, 1878–1948* (Cambridge: Cambridge University Press, 1998).

Mallock, W. H., 'The House of Lords', *Quarterly Review*, 167 (1888) 217–48.

Marsh, P. T., *Joseph Chamberlain: Entrepreneur in Politics* (New Haven, Ct: Yale University Press, 1994).

Martel, G., *Imperial Diplomacy: Rosebery and the Failure of Foreign Policy* (London: Mansell, 1986).

Massingham, H. W., 'Political Dangers of Protection' in H. W. Massingham ed., *Labour and Protection: a Series of Studies* (London: Fisher Unwin, 1903) pp. 1–37.

Masson, U., ' "Political Conditions in Wales are Quite Different..." Party Politics and Votes for Women in Wales, 1912–15', *Women's History Review*, 9 (2000) 369–88.

Masterman, L., *C. F. G. Masterman: a Biography* (London: Frank Cass, 1968).

Matthew, H. C. G., *The Liberal Imperialists: the Ideas and Politics of a Post-Gladstonian Elite* (London: Oxford University Press, 1973).

——, *Gladstone, 1809–74* (Oxford: Oxford University Press, 1988).

——, *Gladstone, 1875–98* (Oxford: Clarendon Press, 1995).

McBride, L. W., *The Greening of Dublin Castle: the Transformation of Bureaucratic and Judicial Personnel in Ireland, 1892–1922* (Washington, DC: Catholic University of America Press, 1991).

McCaffrey, J. F., 'The Origins of Liberal Unionism in the West of Scotland', *Scottish Historical Review*, 50 (1971) 47–71.

McCord, N., 'Taff Vale Revisited', *History*, 78(1993) 243–60.

McDonald, T. A., 'Religion and Voting in an English Borough: Poole in 1859', *Southern History*, 5 (1983) 221–37.

McHugh, P., *Prostitution and Victorian Social Reform* (London: Croom Helm, 1980).

McKenna, S., *Reginald McKenna, 1863–1943: a Memoir* (London: Eyre & Spottiswoode, 1948).

McKibbin, R., 'James Ramsay MacDonald and the Problem of the Independence of the Labour Party, 1910–1914', *Journal of Modern History*, 42 (1970) 216–35.

——, *The Evolution of the Labour Party, 1910–24* (Oxford: Clarendon Press, 1974).

——, 'Working-Class Gambling in Britain, 1880–1939', *Past and Present*, 82 (1979), 147–78.

McLean, D., 'English Radicals, Russia, and the Fate of Persia 1907–13', *English Historical Review*, 93 (1978) 338–52.

Miller, J. B. D., *Norman Angell and the Futility of War* (Basingstoke: Macmillan, 1986).

Minto, Mary, Countess of, *India, Minto and Morley, 1905–1910* (London: Macmillan, 1934).

Monger, G., *The End of Isolation: British Foreign Policy, 1900–1907* (London: Nelson, 1963).

Moore, R. J., 'The Twilight of the Whigs and the Reform of the Indian Councils, 1886–1892', *Historical Journal*, 10 (1967) 400–14.

Morgan, J., *Conflict and Order: the Police and Labour Disputes in England and Wales, 1900–39* (Oxford: Clarendon Press,1987).

Morgan, K.,'Cardiganshire Politics: the Liberal Ascendancy, 1885–1923', *Ceredigion*, 5 (1967), 311–45.

——, *Keir Hardie: Radical and Socialist* (London: Weidenfeld & Nicolson, 1975).

——, *Rebirth of a Nation: Wales, 1880–1980* (Oxford: Clarendon Press, 1981).

——, 'Lloyd George and Germany', *Historical Journal*, 39 (1996) 755–66.

Morley, Lord, *Recollections*, 2 vols (London: Macmillan, 1917).

Morris, A. J. A., *Radicalism against War, 1906–14* (London: Longman, 1972).

——, *C. P. Trevelyan: Portrait of a Radical* (Belfast: Blackstaff, 1977).

Mort, F., 'Purity, Feminism and the State: Sexuality and Moral Politics, 1880–1914' in M. Langan and B. Schwarz eds, *Crises in the British State, 1880–1930* (London: Hutchinson, 1985) pp. 209–25.

Munson, J. E. B., 'The Unionist Coalition and Education, 1895–1902', *Historical Journal*, 20 (1977) 607–45.

Murray, B. K., *The People's Budget 1909/10: Lloyd George and Liberal Politics* (Oxford: Clarendon Press, 1980).

National Liberal Federation, *Eleventh Annual Meeting, 1888*.

——, *Annual Report, 1905* (London: Liberal Publication Department, 1906).

Newman, R. K., 'India and the Anglo-Chinese Opium Agreements, 1907–14', *Modern Asian Studies*, 23 (1989) 525–60.

Newton, Lord, *Lord Lansdowne: a Biography* (London: Macmillan & Co., 1929).

Newton, S., and Porter, D., *Modernization Frustrated: the Politics of Industrial Decline in Britain since 1900* (London: Unwin Hyman, 1988).

O'Brien, A. M., 'Churchill and the Tonypandy Riots', *Welsh History Review*, 17 (1994) 67–99.

O'Brien, P. P., 'The Titan Refreshed: Imperial Overstretch and the British Navy before the First World War', *Past and Present*, 172 (2001) 146–69.

Offer, A., 'Empire and Social Reform: British Overseas Investment and Domestic Politics, 1908–1914', *Historical Journal*, 26 (1983) 119–38.

Osborne, J. B., 'Wilfred G. Thesiger, Sir Edward Grey and the British Campaign to Reform the Congo, 1905–9', *Journal of Imperial and Commonwealth History*, 27 (1999), 59–80.

Ostrogorski, M., *Democracy and the Organisation of Political Parties*, 2 vols (London: Macmillan, 1902).

Oxford and Asquith, Earl of, *Memories and Reflections, 1852–1927*, 2 vols (London: Cassell, 1928).

Packer, I., 'The Liberal Cave and the 1914 Budget', *English Historical Review*, 111 (1996) 620–35.

——, *Lloyd George* (Basingstoke: Macmillan, 1998).

——, *Lloyd George, Liberalism and the Land: The Land Issue and Party Politics in England, 1906–1914* (Woodbridge: Royal Historical Society/Boydell and Brewer, 2001).

—— (ed.), *The Letters of Arnold Stephenson Rowntree to Mary Katherine Rowntree, 1910–18* (Cambridge: Cambridge University Press/Royal Historical Society, 2002).

——, 'Religion and the New Liberalism: the Rowntree Family, Quakerism and Social Reform', *Journal of British Studies*, 42 (2003) 236–57.

Parry, J., *The Rise and Fall of Liberal Government in Victorian Britain* (New Haven, Ct.: Yale University Press, 1993).

Pease, A. E., *Elections and Recollections* (London: John Murray, 1932).

Pelling, H., *Social Geography of British Elections, 1885–1910* (London: Macmillan, 1967).

Pennybacker, S., *A Vision for London, 1889–1914: Labour, Everyday Life and the LCC Experiment* (London: Routledge, 1995).

Peseta, S., *Before the Revolution: Nationalism, Social Change and Ireland's Catholic Elite, 1879–1922* (Cork: Cork University Press, 1999).

Petrow, S., *Policing Morals: the Metropolitan Police and the Home Office, 1870–1914* (Oxford: Clarendon Press, 1994).

Phelps Brown, E. H., *The Growth of British Industrial Relations: a Study from the Standpoint of 1906–14* (London: Macmillan, 1965).

Pimlott, J. A. R., *Toynbee Hall: Fifty Years of Social Progress, 1884–1934* (London: J. M. Dent & Sons, 1935).

Pinto-Duschinsky, M., *British Political Finance, 1830–1980* (Washington, DC: American Enterprise Institute for Public Policy Research, 1981).

Platt, D. C. M., *Finance, Trade and Politics in British Foreign Policy, 1815–1914* (Oxford: Clarendon Press, 1968).

Port, M. H., ' "The Best Club in the World"? The House of Commons, c. 1860–1915', *Parliamentary History*, 21 (2002) 166–99.

Porter, B., *Critics of Empire: British Radical Attitudes to Colonialism in Africa, 1895–1914* (London: Macmillan, 1968).

Powell, D., 'The Liberal Ministries and Labour, 1892–1895', *History*, 68 (1983) 408–26.

Pugh, M., 'Asquith, Bonar Law and the First Coalition', *Historical Journal*, 17 (1974) 813–36.

——, *Electoral Reform in War and Peace, 1906–18* (London: Routledge & Kegan Paul, 1978).

——, 'Yorkshire and the New Liberalism', *Journal of Modern History*, 50 (1978) D1139–55.

——, 'The Limits of liberalism: Liberals and Women's Suffrage, 1867–1914' in E. Biagini ed., *Citizenship and Community: Liberals, Radicals and Collective Identities in the British Isles, 1865–1931* (Cambridge: Cambridge University Press, 1996) pp. 45–65.

——, *The March of the Women: a Revisionist Analysis of the Campaign for Women's Suffrage, 1866–1914* (Oxford: Oxford University Press, 2000).

Ramsden, J., *The Age of Balfour and Baldwin, 1902–40* (London: Longman, 1978).

Readman, P., 'The 1895 General Election and Political Change in Late Victorian Britain', *Historical Journal*, 42 (1999) 467–93.

——, 'The Conservative Party, Patriotism, and British Politics: the Case of the General Election of 1900', *Journal of British Studies*, 40 (2001) 107–45.

——, 'The Liberal Party and Patriotism in Early Twentieth-Century Britain', *Twentieth Century British History*, 12 (2001) 269–302.

Richards, N. J., 'Religious Controversy and the School Boards, 1870–1902', *British Journal of Educational Studies*, 18 (1970) 180–96.

Riddell, G., *Lord Riddell's War Diary, 1914–1918* (London: Ivor Nicholson & Watson, 1933).
——, *More Pages from my Diary, 1908–14* (London: Country Life Ltd, 1934).
Ridley, J., 'The Unionist Opposition and the House of Lords, 1906–10', *Parliamentary History*, 11 (1992) 235–53.
Robbins, K. G., 'Lord Bryce and the First World War', *Historical Journal*, 10 (1967) 255–77.
——, *Sir Edward Grey: a Biography of Lord Grey of Fallodon* (London: Cassell, 1971).
——, *The Abolition of War: the 'Peace Movement' in Britain, 1914–1919* (Cardiff: University of Wales Press, 1976).
Roberts, C., *The Radical Countess; the History of the Life of Rosalind, Countess of Carlisle* (Carlisle: Steel Bros, 1962).
Robertson, J. M., *The Fallacy of Saving* (London: Swan Sonnenschein, 1892).
Robinson, R., and Gallagher, J., *Africa and the Victorians: the Official Mind of Imperialism* (London: Macmillan, 1961).
Rowland, P., *The Last Liberal Governments*, 2 vols (London: Barrie & Jenkins, Barrie & Cresset, 1968–71).
Rowntree, B. S., *Poverty: a Study of Town Life* (London: Macmillan, 1901).
——, *Unemployment: a Social Study* (London: Macmillan, 1911).
——, *The Problem of Unemployment* (London: Fisher Unwin, 1914).
Rush, M., *The Role of the Member of Parliament since 1868: from Gentlemen to Players* (Oxford: Oxford University Press, 2001).
Russell, A. K., *Liberal Landslide: The General Election of 1906* (Newton Abbot: David and Charles, 1973).
Savage, D. C., 'Scottish Politics, 1885–6', *Scottish Historical Review*, 40 (1961) 118–35.
Scally, R., *The Origins of the Lloyd George Coalition* (Princeton, NJ: Princeton University Press, 1975).
Searle, G., 'The Edwardian Liberal Party and Business', *English Historical Review*, 98 (1983) 28–60.
——, *Corruption in British Politics, 1895–1930* (Oxford: Clarendon Press, 1987).
——, *The Liberal Party: Triumph and Distintegration, 1886–1929*, 2nd edn (Basingstoke: Palgrave, 2001).
——, *A New England? Peace and War, 1886–1918* (Oxford: Clarendon Press, 2004).
Seymour, C., *Electoral Reform in England and Wales: the Development and Operation of the Parliamentary Franchise, 1832–85* (New Haven, Ct: Yale University Press, 1915).
Shannon, R., *Gladstone and the Bulgarian Agitation 1876*, 2nd edn (Brighton: Harvester, 1975).
Shepherd, J., 'James Bryce and the Recruitment of Working-Class Magistrates in Lancashire, 1892–1894', *Bulletin of the Institute of Historical Research*, 52 (1979) 155–69.
——, 'Labour and Parliament: the Lib-Labs as the First Working-Class MPs, 1885–1906' in E. Biagini and A. Reid eds, *Currents of Radicalism: Popular Radicalism, Organised Labour and Party Politics in Britain, 1850–1914* (Cambridge: Cambridge University Press, 1991), pp. 187–213.
Sherington, G., *English Education, Social Change and War, 1911–20* (Manchester: Manchester University Press, 1981).
Shiman, L. L., *Crusade against Drink in Victorian England* (Basingstoke: Macmillan, 1988).

Simon, A., 'Church Disestablishment as a Factor in the General Election of 1885', *Historical Journal*, 18 (1975) 791–820.

Sommer, D., *Haldane of Cloan: His Life and Times* (London: George Allen & Unwin, 1960).

Spender, J. A., *Life of the Right Hon. Sir Henry Campbell-Bannerman, G. C. B*, 2 vols (London: Hodder & Stoughton, 1923).

——, and Asquith C., *Life of Herbert Henry Asquith, Lord Oxford and Asquith*, 2 vols (London: Hutchinson, 1932).

Spiers, E. M., *Haldane: an Army Reformer* (Edinburgh: Edinburgh University Press, 1980).

Stansky, P., *Ambitions and Strategies: the Struggle for the Leadership of the Liberal Party in the 1890s* (Oxford: Clarendon Press, 1964).

Steiner, Z., *The Foreign Office and Foreign Policy, 1898–1914* (Cambridge: Cambridge University Press, 1969).

Stewart, A. T. Q., *The Ulster Crisis* (London: Faber & Faber, 1967).

Stewart, J., ' "This Injurious Measure": Scotland and the 1906 Education (Provision of Meals) Act, *Scottish Historical Review*, 78 (1999) 76–94.

Sykes, A., *Tariff Reform in British Politics, 1903–13* (Oxford: Clarendon Press, 1979).

——, *The Rise and Fall of British Liberalism, 1776–1988* (Harlow: Longman, 1997).

Tanner, D., *Political Change and the Labour Party, 1900–1918* (Cambridge: Cambridge University Press, 1990).

——, 'Ideological Debate in Edwardian Labour Politics: Radicalism, Revisionism and Socialism' in E. Biagini and A. J. Reid eds, *Currents of Radicalism: Popular Radicalism, Organised Labour and Party Politics in Britain, 1850–1914* (Cambridge: Cambridge University Press, 1991) pp. 271–93.

Taylor, A., *Lords of Misrule: Hostility to Aristocracy in Late Nineteenth and Early Twentieth Century Britain* (Basingstoke: Palgrave, 2004).

Taylor, A. J. P. (ed.), *Lloyd George: a Diary by Frances Stevenson* (London: Hutchinson, 1971).

Taylor, H. A., *Robert Donald* (London: Stanley Paul & Co., 1934).

Thane, P., *The Foundations of the Welfare State* (Harlow: Longman, 1982).

——, 'The Working Class and State "Welfare" in Britain, 1880–1914', *Historical Journal*, 27 (1984) 877–900.

Thompson, D., 'John Clifford's Social Gospel', *Baptist Quarterly*, 31 (1986) 199–217.

——, 'The Emergence of the Nonconformist Social Gospel in England' in K. Robbins ed., *Protestant Evangelicalism: Britain, Ireland, Germany and America c. 1750–c.1950* (Oxford: Blackwell, 1990) pp. 255–80.

Thompson, J., 'The Genesis of the 1906 Trade Disputes and the Law', *Twentieth Century British History*, 9 (1998) 175–200.

Trebilcock, C., 'Radicalism and the Armaments Trust' in A. J. A. Morris ed., *Edwardian Radicalism, 1900–1914* (London: Routledge & Kegan Paul, 1974), pp. 180–202.

Trentmann, F., 'The Strange Death of Free Trade: the Erosion of "Liberal Consensus" in Great Britain, c. 1903–32' in E. Biagini ed., *Citizenship and Community: Liberals, Radicals and Collective Identities in the British Isles, 1865–1931* (Cambridge: Cambridge University Press, 1996) pp. 219–50.

Tuckwell, W., Revd., *Reminiscences of a Radical Parson* (London: Cassell, 1905).

Turner, J., 'State Purchase of the Liquor Trade in the First World War', *Historical Journal*, 23 (1980) 589–615.

Vincent, J. (ed.), *The Crawford Papers: the Journals and Letters of David Lindsay, Twenty-seventh Earl of Crawford and Tenth Earl of Balcarres, 1871–1940* (Manchester: Manchester University Press, 1984).

Wald, K., *Crosses on the Ballot: Patterns of British Voter Alignment since 1885* (Princeton, NJ: Princeton University Press, 1983).

Walker, L., 'Party Political Women: a Comparative Study of Liberal Women and the Primrose League, 1890–1914' in J. Rendall ed., *Equal or Different? Women's Politics, 1800–1914*, (Oxford: Blackwell, 1987) pp. 165–213.

Warren, A., 'Gladstone, Land and Social Reconstruction in Ireland, 1881–1887', *Parliamentary History*, 2 (1983) 153–73.

Wasti, S. R., *Lord Minto and the Indian Nationalist Movement, 1905–1910* (Oxford: Oxford University Press, 1964).

Webb, B., and Webb, S., *Industrial Democracy*, 2 vols (London: Longman, 1897).

Wedgwood, J., *Memoirs of a Fighting Life* (London: Hutchinson, 1940).

Weinroth, H., 'Left-Wing Opposition to Naval Armaments in Britain before 1914', *Journal of Contemporary History*, 6 (1971) 93–120.

——, 'Norman Angell and The Great Illusion: an Episode in Pre-1914 Pacifism', *Historical Journal*, 17 (1974) 551–74.

Weston, C. C., 'The Liberal Leadership and the Lords' Veto, 1907–10', *Historical Journal*, 11 (1968) 508–37.

Williams, B., 'Great Britain and Russia, 1905 to the 1907 Convention' in F. H. Hinsley ed., *British Foreign Policy under Sir Edward Grey* (Cambridge: Cambridge University Press, 1977), pp. 133–47.

Williams, R., *Defending the Empire: the Conservative Party and British Defence Policy, 1899–1915* (New Haven, Ct: Yale University Press, 1991).

Williamson, P. (ed.), *The Modernisation of Conservative Politics: the Diaries and Letters of William Bridgeman, 1904–1935* (London: Historians' Press, 1987).

Williamson, S. R., *The Politics of Grand Strategy: Britain and France Prepare for War, 1904–14* (Cambridge, Mass: Harvard University Press, 1969).

Wilson, J., *CB: a Life of Sir Henry Campbell-Bannerman* (London: Purnell Book Services, 1973).

Wilson, K. M., 'The Making and Putative Implementation of a British Foreign Policy of Gesture, December 1905 to August 1914: the Anglo-French Entente Revisited', *Canadian Journal of History*, 31 (1996) 228–55.

Wilson, R. E., *Two Hundred Precious Metal Years: a History of the Sheffield Smelting Co. Ltd, 1760–1960* (London: Ernest Benn, 1960).

Wilson, T., *The Downfall of the Liberal Party, 1914–35*, 2nd edn (Fontana, 1968).

——, (ed.), *The Political Diaries of C. P. Scott, 1911–28* (London: Collins, 1970).

Wolpert, S. A., *Morley and India, 1906–1910* (Berkeley, Calif.: University of California Press, 1967).

Young, D., *Member for Mexico: a Biography of Weetman Pearson, first Viscount Cowdray* (London, Cassell, 1966).

Young Scots Handbook, 1911–12 (Glasgow, 1912).

Index